Alpha

Studies in Early Christianity

ΙΝΑ ΕΠΙΓΝΩΣ ΠΕΡΙ ΩΝ ΚΑΤΗΧΗΘΗΣ ΛΟΓΩΝ ΤΗΝ ΑΣΦΑΛΕΙΑΝ

Volume 1

Warring States Project

UNIVERSITY OF MASSACHUSETTS AT AMHERST

2017

Alpha

ISSN 2331-270X (print)
ISSN 2331-2718 (online)

Volume 1

ISBN 978-1-936166-41-1 (print)
ISBN 978-1-936166-51-0 (E-book)

Preface

Alpha provides a home and venue for studies of text growth and interaction in the early Christian writings, with attention also to contemporary religious developments, and to Homer and the Hebrew Scriptures as parallel cases of text formation over time. With our sister journal Warring States Papers, which is responsible for classical China (and which exchanges articles of mutual interest with *Alpha*), we seek to demonstrate the applicability of standard philological methods to all fields of humanistic inquiry. What are those methods?

As William L Holladay said in his 1986 Jeremiah commentary, "The first question . . . is the integrity of the passage: is it one unit or more?" We recognize strata, interpolations, and any other signs of text growth that internal evidence may suggest. We remember (with Tischendorf) that, of related passages, the one which is more readily seen as giving rise to the other is likely to be the earlier, and (with Ranke) we prefer the earlier evidence, while being aware that all texts have their own agendas. We apply the test of coherence to individual results, and that of historical plausibility to the gradually emerging large picture.

Proceeding thus has led us to regard several Gospels (not only John) as stratified, and to view the genuine Pauline Epistles as having been improved by Paul's editors. So clarified, the texts attest a humanly intelligible Paul, free of the additions by which he was made less divisive for a future Christian readership, and reveal in the Gospel record a pre-Pauline Christianity which we call Alpha: a Christianity based not on the Resurrection or any other theory of Jesus' death, but on his teachings during his life. This early Christianity, at first little more than a Messianic Jewish sect, continued alongside the later Pauline or Beta Christianity down to the time of Pliny and beyond. Though it has long been institutionally extinct, it still survives in a sort of tacit form, in the practical day-to-day living of many Christians.

Each *Alpha* volume begins with articles of general and methodological interest, and then runs chronologically: early witnesses, the immediate post-Apostolic generation, and later developments including Gnostic tendencies and post-Temple Judaism.

At present, there can be said to be an "Alpha Christianity" community, and papers in this first volume are mostly the work of the founding figures. It is not required that *Alpha* authors agree among themselves, but the editors select what seem to them the best current solutions, and combine them in a Working Chronology at the end of the volume. It will be updated annually. Dates of articles are those of original presentation; most papers have been revised by their authors for their appearance here.

This Volume focuses on what we find to be the key pre-Pauline texts: the earliest layer of Mark, the Epistle of Jacob, and the core of the Didache. The non-Markan material in Matthew and Luke receives special attention; we see no need to conjecture an outside source for it, and find instead a two-way relation between the two Gospels. We also discover a division within Acts, and an unsuspected second Sermon in Luke. We compare Mandaean and Gospel tradition echoes of the John the Baptist movement and begin a consideration of the non-Synoptic portions of the Gospel of Thomas.

Conventions for *Alpha* include the following:

Dates. As a convention which works well in languages other than English, we use a leading zero in place of BC(E). 65 BC becomes 065, while AD 14 is simply 14. The "03rd century" (which can be abbreviated as 03c) is the 3rd BC; "3rd" is the 3rd AD. The advantages of this leading zero over a minus sign are that it allows unambiguous hyphenation of dates which cross the century line (Horace, 065-08; Augustus, 063-14). It also avoids a conflict with astronomers, whose "-65" is *not* the "-65" of historians.

Abbreviations for books of the Bible are mostly standard, though we distinguish Phm (Philemon) and Php (Philippians). For the Epistle of James, we use Ja, which suggests the correct Jacob (as in the OT) and the Anglicized James (in English Bibles in the NT). Jesus, it is now known, was a Jew, and so, presumably, were his brothers (and, as we suspect in connection with that Epistle, the brother of Levi of Alphaeus).

Greek Text. For the NT, we follow the latest edition of the United Bible Societies (UBS) text and the corresponding Nestle-Aland (NA) edition, but are inclined to accept the minority opinion of Bruce Metzger on several points. There has been a drift away from the decisions of Westcott and Hort (1881), including the recent readmission to the text of such stories as "The Woman Taken in Adultery," a tendency from which we prefer to hold ourselves apart. In citing manuscripts, we resist the temptation to abbreviate Vaticanus as V, but use S for Sinaiticus. Papyri are cited with a capital P. Among translations, we suggest the ASV, which preserves Mark's historical presents, but no one version is required of our contributors.

References. Short citations (in the form Surname **Keyword**) are expanded in the Works Cited list at the end of each article. To save space, often cited standard works are not normally included in those lists. For them, and for journals cited by acronym, see the reference lists at the end of the volume. Also at the end of the volume are indexes to subjects and to passages discussed, along with the above-mentioned Working Chronology of texts and events.

Original Venues of these articles include meetings of the Society of Biblical Literature, the Project's own conferences, and several E-lists. Some articles are repeated here from Warring States Papers; they are indicated by a formula such as

Alpha v1 (2017) < Warring States Papers v1 (2010)

at the bottom of the first page.

Contributions from interested scholars are welcome. Our formal Call for Papers will be found at http://www.umass.edu/wsp/publications/alpha/call.html. Except for first serial and database rights, our contributors retain full ownership of their material, and do not require our permission for its further use in any form.

We conclude with the hope that publication of these studies will bring them more effectively to the attention of potentially interested readers, both in the NT field proper and in the wider historical community. We hope they may also serve to suggest that, whether at the level of general methodology or at the more specific substantive level, humanity, and the study of humanity, are ultimately one.

The Editors

Contents

Continued on Next Page

Later Texts and Tendencies

End Matter

Language, Ambience, and Methodology

Adjectival φαῦλος in James 3:16

Keith L Yoder

University of Massachusetts at Amherst

Corpus Paulinum (27 Aug 2013)

Might there be a word play on "Paul" in the final phrase of James 3:16?

πᾶν φαῦλον πρᾶγμα "every evil thing"

πᾶν Παῦλον πρᾶγμα "every Paulish thing"

If the name Παῦλος "Paul" appeared within close textual context of Ja 3:16, a word play would be apparent. Obviously, that is not the case. But if Ja 2:14-26 is reacting against a text or reputed teachings of Paul,[1] then "Paul" would be in the echo chamber of James' performance arena.

Phonetics. In this alliterative phrase, the initial "ph" sound of φαῦλον in the written text could naturally be attracted to the "p" sound of the initial consonant of the preceding and following words. Further, the first syllables of all three words contain the same "ah" vowel sound (using the historical Koine pronunciation), which might further encourage attraction to an initial "p" sound for the middle word. See the last three words of Ja 1:2, πειρασμοῖς περιπέσητε ποικίλοις ("you fall into various trials") for an alliterative triplet using initial "p," as well as other consonance or assonance features. James uses many rhythmic and alliterative doublets and triplets. Dibelius (p37) mentions, among others including the above, these examples:

Ja 1:1,2. χαίρειν ‖ χαράν   grace . . . joy
Ja 1:25. παρακύψας ‖ παραμείνας   having looked . . . having remained
Ja 3:6. φλογίζουσα ‖ φλογιζομένη   setting on fire . . . being set on fire
Ja 3:7. δαμάζεται ‖ δεδάμασται   is tamed . . . has been tamed

---

[1]For such a proposal, see Hengel **Anti-Pauline**.

To which may be added:

Ja 1:12f. πειρασμόν ‖ πειρζόμενος ‖ πειράζομαι
                                     testing . . . being tested . . . I am tested
Ja 1:24. ἀπελήλυθεν ‖ ἐπελάθετο   went away . . . forgot
Ja 3:8. δαμάσαι ‖ δύναται   to tame . . . is able

Usage. φαῦλος is used 5 other times in the Greek NT: 2 Cor 5:10. Rom 9:11 (both "evil," in contrast to ἀγαθὸν "good"), Tit 2:8 ("[having nothing] evil [to say of us]"), Jn 3:20 ("evil things"), Jn 5:29 ("evil things," in contrast to ἀγαθὰ "good things"). None of these is in a noun phrase with πρᾶγμα "practices," though both John instances coordinate φαῦλος with a form of the cognate verb πράσσω "practice, do." There are no other Greek NT or Septuagint combinations of φαῦλος and πρᾶγμα. φαῦλος occurs 10 times in the Septuagint (5 in Proverbs, 3 in Job, and 1 each in Maccabees and Sirach), mostly in the milder sense "worthless."

Classical usage is milder still; instances of φαῦλον πρᾶγμα are usually translated as "trifling matter/affair," "light task," unimportant business" (Aristophanes Lysistrata line 14, Isocrates Evangoras 59, Plato Republic 2:374e, Plato Phaedo 95e, Plato Symposium 213c, Xenophon Anabasis 6:6).

Comment
Glenn Holland, 2013

I wonder if your argument is bolstered by the Latin equivalent *paulus* "small," which might occur to any audience members familiar with Latin. We might expect that at least some would hear the phrase as "every Paulish thing," whether the author intended them to or not, and the effect on the audience is ultimately more important than authorial intention. This is one reason why the Jesus movement and later the Church acknowledged the role of the Spirit in its work and message.

Works Cited

E Bruce Brooks. The Epistle of Jacob. Alpha v1 (2017) 58-70
Martin Dibelius. The Epistle of James. 11ed ed (rev Greeven) 1964; tr Fortress 1976
Martin Hengel. The Letter of James as Anti-Pauline Polemic. 1987; in Meeks et al ed,
    The Writings of St Paul, 2ed Norton (2007) 242-253

Antiochus' Persecution in Josephus' *War*

Chris Seeman
Walsh University

SBL/EGL (17 March 2017)

The persecution of the Jews by Antiochus Epiphanes marks a watershed in Jewish history. The targeting of cult and culture by a Hellenistic ruler crystalized an ethos of resistance that manifested itself in martyrdom and rebellion. Foreshadowed by the Book of Daniel and commemorated in the Maccabean literature, the Antiochene persecution offered fertile ground for Jewish historiography.

Given its pivotal significance for Jewish history, it's unsurprising that Flavius Josephus showcased it in his *Jewish Antiquities*. What is surprising is that he chose to begin his *Jewish War* with the same event. To be sure, backstories are important for establishing context, but this fails to explain why Josephus felt compelled to reach back nearly two centuries to explain what happened in 66 CE. He might as easily have begun with Herod the Great, to whose reign he devotes most of Book 1 of the *War*. In his prologue, Josephus offers this justification:

> To speak of ancient things in the case of the Jews, in fact – **who** some of these were, **how** they up and fled from the Egyptians, **what sort** of country they encountered while they were wandering, **how many** places they seized in sequence, and **how** they found themselves displaced – I consider to be untimely now and in any case redundant, seeing that many Jews before me have recounted the deeds of our ancestors with precision, and **certain Greeks** have recast those things into their native speech without veering much from the truth. So just where both the historical writers of this group and our **own prophets** finished, from there I shall establish the beginning of my account. (*War* 1:17-18).

On the face of it, this sounds reasonable, but a closer inspection of Josephus' Maccabean narrative reveals clear dependence on 1 Maccabees, thereby undercutting his pretense of filling an historiographical gap. Josephus' rhetorical claim to begin at the beginning, then, is insufficient to account for the presence of the Antiochene persecution in his narrative. A brief review of the narrative itself is in order.

> **Factional strife** arose among the leaders of the Jews at the time when Antiochus surnamed Epiphanes had a quarrel with Ptolemy VI concerning all of Syria. Their ambition was control of the government because each person of rank could not bear being subject to his peers. Onias, one of the high priests, gained the upper hand and drove the descendants of Tobias out of the city. The latter fled to Antiochus and pleaded with him to invade Judea, using them as guides The king, who had long had similar plans, was (easily) persuaded. Having marched out with a very sizable army, he himself took the city by storm and did away with a large number of Ptolemy's supporters.

> In addition, he gave the soldiers license to collect spoils without restraint, whereas he himself not only plundered the Temple but also interrupted the continuity of the daily sacrifices for three years and six months. The high priest Onias, however, fled to Ptolemy and received from him a place in the district of Heliopolis where he founded a small town that resembled Jerusalem, with a similar temple. (*War* 1:31-33)

It is hardly coincidental that the first word of Josephus' narrative proper (stasis, factional strife) is the leitmotif of the whole work. The dynamic with which Josephus opens his history foreshadows the circumstances that will determine Jerusalem's fate.

Josephus continues:

> For Antiochus, however, neither the unhoped-for conquest of the city nor the looting with so much slaughter was sufficient. So, lacking control over his passions and remembering what he had suffered during the siege, he tried to force the Jews both to keep their infants uncircumcised and to sacrifice swine on the altar, thus **abolishing ancestral customs**. All disobeyed these dispositions, and those who were most esteemed were slain. (*War* 1:34-35)

While Josephus' description of the persecution is unremarkable, the idiom he employs to sum up the event – abolishing ancestral customs – is a charged expression in *War*. In fact, most of Josephus' use of the verb καταλύω pertains only to political or military disruption. Only at the center (Book 4) and the ends (Books 1 and 7) of the work is the verb applied to the overthrow of the laws. It would seem then that (as many scholars have observed) Josephus deliberately chose to begin the *War* with the chronologically remote Antiochene persecution because it allowed him to highlight factional strife, constitutional overthrow, and Jerusalem besieged – all fundamental themes of his work – at the very outset.

To borrow an expression from Steve Mason, the Antiochene persecution serves as a "signpost of symmetry," not only at the macro level of the whole *War*, but also within Book 1 where the event itself takes place. Book 1 is framed at the other end by the story of Jewish opposition to Herod the Great's ornamental eagle on the Temple facade. What is noteworthy is how the resistance expresses itself. Scholars of the ancestral laws incite some "daring" youths to tear down the eagle:

> They mentioned to their acquaintances that now was perhaps the most appropriate time to avenge God and tear down the artifact put up in violation of their ancestral laws, for it was unlawful for the Temple to contain either images or busts or a work representing some living creature. Even so, the king had set up a golden eagle above the great gate. It was this creature which the learned men at that time exhorted [the youths] to knock down, arguing that **it was a noble deed to die for one's ancestral law**. (*War* 1:649-650)

In contrast to the *Antiquities*, which features multiple instances of the "Herod as violator of ancestral custom" trope, the golden eagle incident at the close of Book 1 is the only such instance in the *War*. Its placement, coupled with the Antiochene persecution, seems deliberate on Josephus' part.

Another important Antiochus appears in Book 7. Josephus introduces him early:

> It happened about this time that the remnant of Jews at Antioch were incriminated and in danger of extermination, the Antiochene community having been greatly incited against them in consequence not only of the false accueations now laid to their charge, but also of certain incidents which had taken place not long before. (*War* 7:41-42)

> The Jewish race, densely interspersed among the populations of every part of the world, is particularly numerous in Syria, where intermingling is due to the proximity of the two countries. But it was at Antioch that they especially congregated, partly owing to the greatness of the city, but mainly because the successors of King Antiochus had enabled them to live there in security. For although Antiochus surnamed Epiphanes sacked Jerusalem and plundered the Temple his successors on the throne restored to the Jews of Antioch all such votive offerings as were made of brass, to be laid up in their synagogue, and moreover granted them citizen rights on equality with the Greeks. Continuing to receive similar treatment from later monarchs, the Jewish colony grew in number, and their richly designed and costly offerings formed a splendid ornament to the Temple. Moreover, they were constantly attracting to their religious ceremonies multitudes of Greeks, and these they had in some measure incorporated with themselves. (*War* 7:43-45)

Josephus continues:

> Now just at the time when war had been declared and Vespasian had recently landed in Syria, and when hatred of the Jews was everywhere at its height . . .

Note how Josephus chronologically displaces this backstory, which refers to the outbreak of the First Revolt narrated back in Book 2 of the *War*, to the beginning of this post-war survey in Book 7. This four-year time lag is transparently designed to set the events he is about to narrate parallel to the Antiochene persecution in Book 1:

> . . . a certain Antiochus, one of their own number and highly respected for the sake of his father, who was chief magistrate of the Jews in Antioch, entered the theater during an assembly of the people and denounced his own father and the other Jews, accusing them of a design to burn the whole city to the ground in one night; he also delivered up some foreign Jews as accomplices to the plot. On hearing this the people, in uncontrollable fury, ordered the men who had been delivered up to be instantly consigned to the flames, and all were forthwith burnt to death in the theater. They then rushed for the Jewish masses, believing the salvation of their native place to be dependent on their prompt chastisement. Antiochus further inflamed their fury, for, thinking to furnish proof of his conversion and of his detestation of Jewish customs by sacrificing after the manner of the Greeks, he recommended that the rest should be compelled to do the same, as the conspirators would thus be exposed by their refusal. The test being applied to the Antiochenes, a few submitted, and the recalcitrants were massacred.

. . . Antiochus, having next procured the aid of troops from the Roman general, domineered with severity over his Jewish fellow-citizens, not permitting them to repose on the seventh day, but **compelling** them to do everything exactly as on other days, and so strictly did he enforce this, that not only at Antioch was the weekly day of rest **abolished**, but the example having been started there spread for a short time to the other cities as well. (*War* 7:46-53)

Conclusion

Josephus' decision to include the Antiochene persecution in his narrative serves at least three purposes:

(1) It introduces a cluster of motifs that figure prominently in his account of the First Revolt: civil strive as a precipitant of national calamity, threats to Jerusalem and its shrine, and the overthrow of the ancestral laws. All these themes reach their crescendo in Book 4, the center of his seven-voume history.

(2) The Antiochene persecution showcases the archetypical response to sacrilege: a daring drive to avenge God and country. The Maccabees, in this capacity, prepare Josephus' audience to comprehend the psychology of the vandals who dare to tear down Herod's golden eagle from the Temple facade at the end of Herod's reign, thus providing framing elements for Book 1

(3) The pre-war persecution of the Jews by Antiochus Epiphanes parallels the post-war persecution of the Antiochene Jewish community by one of their own. The juxtaposition of these stories, I suggest, invites reflection on the part of the reader/hearer. When Titus visits Antioch following the destruction of Jerusalem, and the Judeophobic Antiochenes petition him to expel the Jews or at least strip them of their citizenship, the victorious general declines, leaving the community untouched. The Romans, suggests Josephus – or at any rate the Flavians – are not like Antiochus Epiphanes, in spite of their sharing with him the opprobrium of having ravaged Jerusalem.

Another moral the Antiochene persecutions deliver is that the Jews' deadliest enemies are not – or need not be – Greeks or Romans; the enemy may be within (a major theme of Josephus' retelling of the tragedy of the First Revolt).

Josephus' point is not naively propagandistic. As a Jewish aristocrat writing for his educated Roman counterparts, Josephus' goal is to build a bridge of empathy. Jews and Romans alike can appreciate the sort of political debacles that can lead to the madness of an Antiochus, whether that Antiochus be a Macedonian monarch or a Jewish magistrate.

Works Cited

Steve Mason. A History of the Jewish War. Cambridge 2016

Four Gospel Trajectories

E Bruce Brooks

University of Massachusetts at Amherst

Synoptic-L (14 June 2006)

One kind of evidence for sequence in time is plausible developments: trajectories. I here identify four trajectories in the New Testament Gospels, Matthew, Mark, Luke, and John, and find that they imply the sequence Mk > Mt > Lk > Jn.

1. The Divinization Trajectory. Jesus in **Mark** is a man. He first makes contact with God at his Baptism (Mk 1:10, "Straightway . . . he saw the heavens rent asunder, and the Spirit as a dove descending upon him"). His divine power is drained in use (Mk 5:30, "perceiving . . . that the power from him had gone forth"), renewed by prayer (Mk 9:29, "This kind [of demon] can come out by nothing, save by prayer"), and lost at his Crucifixion (Mk 15:34, "My God, my God, why hast thou forsaken me?"). **Matthew** gives Jesus a divine birth (Mt 1:18, "Mary . . . was found with child of the Holy Spirit"), thus making him godlike from the beginning. **Luke** tops this by giving his cousin John the Baptist also a divine birth (Lk 1:36f, the angel to Mary: "And behold, Elizabeth thy kinswoman . . . hath conceived a son in her old age"), and by having John acknowledge Jesus prenatally (Lk 1:41, "When Elizabeth heard the salutation of Mary, the babe leaped in her womb"). In **John**, Jesus exists from the beginning of the universe (Jn 1:1, "In the beginning was the Word;" 1:14, "And the Word became flesh, and dwelt among us"). Founders are often aggrandized by their followers, and nothing could be more natural than this increasing divinization of Jesus, and the associated reluctance to ascribe to him any human feelings or shortcomings.[1] The implied order is Mk > Mt > Lk > Jn.

2. The Mary Trajectory. Mary is rejected by Jesus in **Mark** (Mk 3:33f, "Who are my mother and brothers?"). In **Matthew**, Mary is favored by God to be Jesus' mother (Mt 1:20f, the angel to Joseph: "Do not fear to take Mary your wife, for that which is conceived in her is of the Holy Spirit"). In **Luke** Mary reacts fully and eloquently to the news that she is to be so favored (Lk 1:46f, the Magnificat). Luke adds a childhood narrative of Jesus in the Temple, where Mary speaks to Jesus (Lk 2:41-51). In **John**, for reasons above noted, there is no birth scene, but Mary is part of Jesus' ministry. She persuades him to perform his first miracle at Cana (Jn 2:3f, Mary to the servants: "Whatsoever he saith unto you, do it"), and at the end is touchingly commended by him, from the very cross, to the care of a disciple (Jn 19:26f, "Jesus . . . saith unto his mother, Woman, behold thy son. Then saith he to the disciple, Behold thy mother"). It is emotionally unlikely that the later Jesus tradition increasingly *disdained* Mary. The implied order is Mk > Mt > Lk > Jn.

---

[1]For a long list of instances where Matthew shows greater respect for Jesus in passages parallel to Mark, see the commentary of Willoughby C Allen (3ed Clark 1912) xxxi-xxxiii.

3. The Baptism Trajectory. In **Mark**, Jesus is simply baptized by John (Mk 1:9). In **Matthew**, John protests that Jesus should baptize *him*, and is persuaded to proceed only in order "to fulfil all righteousness" (Mt 3:15). In **Luke**, the baptism is mentioned but not described (Lk 3:21b). As in Mark and Matthew, Luke's verb is the passive "was baptized," but John is not specified as the *agent* of the verb. In **John**, the baptism is not even reported; only the detail of the Spirit as a dove resting on Jesus (Jn 1:32f). Jesus' baptism may have been offensive as implying that John was Jesus' spiritual superior, or that Jesus had sins to be forgiven. The gradual attenuation of the baptism in the Gospel accounts is compatible with the divinization trajectory noticed above, and with the theological idea that Jesus' death had the power to atone for others' sins because Jesus was himself without sin. The implied order is Mk > Mt > Lk > Jn.

4. The Jerusalem Trajectory. In all the Gospels, Galilee is Jesus' home country; his first preaching is done there. Jerusalem figures in the Jesus story in different ways. In **Mark**, Jesus visits many Galilean towns, and goes to Jerusalem only to be crucified. The disciples return to Galilee, and though the ending of Mark is missing in our text, it is predicted (Mk 14:28, 16:7) that Jesus will appear to them there. In **Matthew**, some of Jesus' preaching is done on his journey to Jerusalem, and three Galilean towns, Chorazin, Bethsaida, and Capernaum, are cursed as unbelieving (Mt 11:21-24); the risen Jesus first appears in Jerusalem, to the Women at the Tomb (Mt 28:9-10), though there is also a later Galilean appearance, of the kind that was predicted if not displayed in Mark (Mt 28:16f). In **Luke**, the risen Jesus not only appears on the road from Jerusalem, but orders the disciples to *remain* in Jerusalem (Lk 24:15f); there is no Galilee appearance. **John**, like Luke, limits the appearances of the risen Jesus to Jerusalem;[2] he has Jesus visit Jerusalem repeatedly before that, and often preach there. The Jerusalem shift in the Jesus story is thus furthest advanced in John.

A Galilee-to-Jerusalem shift in the history of Christianity is attested by Paul, who never mentions Galilee, and who visits Jerusalem (not Galilee) to meet with Peter, and incidentally one Jacob whom he thinks of as the brother of Jesus (Gal 1:18). It seems that the Gospels increasingly project that later administrative shift back into Jesus' lifetime, so the least Jerusalemized Gospel will probably also be the earliest Gospel. The implied order is Mk > Mt > Lk > Jn.

Conclusion. More examples might be given, but these show how the winds are blowing. All the winds blow in the same direction. They amount to three trends: (1) increasing respect for Jesus and his family, (2) reduction in the prominence given to John's baptism of Jesus; and (3) an administrative shift of the later Jesus movement from Galilee to Jerusalem. It is these trends (the first predictable on general grounds) that differences in the Gospels seem to reflect. Complications there surely are, some due to growth processes in one or more Gospel, but the overall pattern is clear.

Such developments are strong evidence for the Historical Jesus. Enthusiasm (as for Mary) proves nothing, but embarrassment (as concerning John) is quite another matter. If there was no baptism, why do the Gospels increasingly minimize its importance? And if John baptized him, then there probably was a Jesus there to be baptized.

---

[2]Save for the inconsistent, and clearly later appended, final chapter, Jn 21.

Evidence for Interpolation in Paul

William O Walker Jr

Trinity University

(August 2001)

EDITORS' NOTE: Pages 15-90 of **Interpolations in the Pauline Letters** (Sheffield 2001) are here greatly condensed and slightly revised, with the permission of the author, to make them more directly available to our readers.

Definition. A *gloss* is an explanatory note or comment, generally written in the margin or between the lines of a manuscript by a reader, scribe, or the author of the document. A later scribe might copy a gloss into the document, assuming that it was meant to be part of it. Unlike a gloss, an *interpolation* is foreign material inserted deliberately and directly into the text.

A Priori Probability of Interpolations. That interpolations were introduced into many Classical writings cannot be questioned. Ancient critics believed that Homer had suffered interpolation, and that it was possible for critics to recover something like the original text.[1] Zenodotus, the first head of the library in Alexandria (03c), relied on four principles of criticism: Interpolations could be detected (1) if they broke the continuity of the poem, (2) if they lacked poetic art or were unsuitable to the characters of gods and men, (3) if they contained errors about ancient events, (4) if they differed from the usual style of the poet.[2] Maurer has asserted that 'the fact [of interpolations in Homer] is notorious,'[3] and Bolling has identified numerous interpolations in the texts of the Iliad and the Odyssey.[4] Interpolations have also been detected in the works of Hippocrates, Aristophanes, Euripides, and Thucydides.[5] Of direct relevance to the question of interpolations in the Pauline letters is the almost certain presence of interpolations in precisely the genre of ancient literature most closely akin to those letters: the letters of philosophers (eg Plato, Aristotle, Epicurus, and Seneca), and particularly those 'letters of exhortation in which teachers seek to guide and mold the character of disciples.'[6] The Epicurean correspondence, for example, 'has been heavily edited by Epicurus' followers who amplified the master's teachings and adapted them to later situations.'[7] This provides a close parallel to the letters of Paul, which can also be seen as 'letters of exhortation in which [a teacher] seek[s] to guide and mold the character of disciples.'

---

[1]Grant **Letter** 17.

[2]Grant **Marcion** 211; cf Pfeiffer **History** 108-113.

[3]Maurer **Thucydides** 181.

[4]Bolling **External**.

[5]Grant **Heresy** 21-22 and 61-66; Maurer **Thucydides**.

[6]Stowers **Greek** 292.

[7]Stowers **Greek** 292.

Beyond this, there is evidence that early Christians introduced interpolations into Jewish writings. It is widely agreed, for example, that material was added to the Greek text of Josephus to create non-Christian testimony to the messiahship and resurrection of Jesus.[8] Similarly, Celsus charged that Christians had added interpolations to the Sibylline Oracles to provide pagan support for the truth of the Christian religion.[9] Other Jewish texts in which Christian interpolations have been identified are the Hellenistic Synagogal Prayers, the Testaments of the Twelve Patriarchs, the Martyrdom and Ascension of Isaiah, and 4 Ezra.[10]

The presence of interpolations in other ancient literature would lead us to expect, on a priori grounds, that the Pauline letters may contain non-Pauline interpolations.

The Lack of Manuscript Evidence. Apart from two passages,[11] every proposed interpolation in the Pauline letters appears in all extant manuscripts of the letters. This raises the crucial question: Might a passage appear in all surviving manuscripts and yet be a non-Pauline interpolation? I suggest that the absence of direct manuscript evidence for interpolation should be seen precisely as the *absence* of evidence. Barrett reminds us that 'the evidence of the [extant manuscripts] can tell us nothing about the state of the Pauline . . . literature before its publication' (presumably late in the 1st century).[12] Further, the evidence of the manuscripts provides no clear information regarding the state of the Pauline literature prior to the date of the oldest surviving manuscript of the letters – that is, near the end of the 2nd century. Koester notes that 'critics of classical texts know that the first century of their transmission is the period in which the most serious corruptions occur,' and that 'the Gospels [and the same could be said of the Pauline letters], from the very beginning, were not archival materials but used texts.' This 'is the worst thing that could happen to any textual tradition,' because 'a text not protected by canonical status, but used in liturgy, apologetics, homiletics, and instruction of catechumens is most likely to be copied frequently and is thus subject to frequent modifications and alterations.'[13]

It would thus appear that the period between the composition of Paul's letters (mid 1st century) and the date of the earliest extant manuscript (late 2nd century at best) was precisely the time when the letters would have been most susceptible to alteration, including interpolation.[14] Indeed, the circumstances provided ample motivation and opportunity for the introduction of interpolations. All of this, in my judgement, makes it reasonable to assume that interpolations are likely to have been introduced into the Pauline letters prior to the date of the earliest surviving manuscripts.

It remains to ask: Precisely how shall such interpolations be recognized?

---

[8]Josephus Antiquities 18/3:3; see Feldman **Josephus** 990f, Sanford **Propaganda** 127-145.

[9]Grant **Heresy** 24; see also Collins **Sibylline** 2-6.

[10]Charlesworth **Christian** 28.

[11]Rom 16:25-27 and 1 Cor 14:34-35 occur at different places in different manuscripts.

[12]Barrett **First** 14.

[13]Koester **Text** 19f.

[14]See further Walker **Unexamined**.

External Evidence for Interpolation

1. Absence from Witnesses. The most obvious type of evidence for interpolation would be the absence of a passage from ancient manuscripts, versions, or lectionaries. Such evidence exists for one Pauline passage. The doxology of Rom 16:25-27 appears in all the "best" manuscripts, but there is evidence for an early version of Romans without it. It was apparently not in the texts used by Marcion (2c), Priscillian (4c), or Jerome 4/5c); Gamble has argued that 'this patristic testimony is buttressed by . . . the complete omission of the doxology' in the original Old Latin.[15]

2. Presence in Different Locations. Besides being absent from some witnesses, Rom 16:25-27 is located after Rom 15 in the oldest extant manuscript, P46 (late 2c or early 3c); after Rom 16 in most of the "best" witnesses, including Sinaiticus (4c), Vaticanus (4c), Ephraemi Rescriptus (5c), and Bezae (6c); after Rom 14 in several witnesses; after *both* Rom 14 and 16 in a few including Alexandrinus (5c); and after both Rom 14 and 15 in one 14c manuscript. Such uncertainty about the appropriate location of the passage suggests that it may be a later addition.[16]

3. Lack of Citation in an Early Writer who might reasonably be expected to have mentioned it. 1 Cor 14:34-35 is cited by no Apostolic Father, and indeed by no early ecclesiastical writer prior to Tertullian (160-240).[17]

Internal Evidence for Interpolation

4. Interruption. A passage which seems to interrupt its context, so that the context becomes continuous when the passage is removed, is likely to be an interpolation. Of 1 Cor 14:34-35, Fee observes that 'one can make much better sense of the structure of Paul's argument without these intruding sentences,' which have little, if anything, to do with the subject matter of the surrounding material. In short, 1 Cor 14:34-35 is a self-contained unit that interrupts the context in which it appears, and its removal leaves a complete and coherent discussion of spiritual gifts in 1 Cor 12 and 14.[18]

5. Repetition From Context. Another phenomenon suggesting that a seemingly interruptive passage may be an interpolation is the repetition – near the end of that passage or in the verse directly following – of a significant word or phrase from the verse preceding. This might represent an attempt to improve the transition between the passage and its context. In 1 Cor 12:31a, for example, Paul encourages his readers to be 'zealous for the greater gifts.' This is repeated in 14:1b-c with the substitution of 'the spiritual gifts' for 'the greater gifts' and the addition of 'that you may prophesy.'

---

[15]Gamble **Textual** 25-26; see the entire discussion on p24-29.

[16]The most extreme example of presence in different locations is the story of the Woman Taken in Adultery, which is absent from the best texts of John, but occurs in 12th century and later manuscripts after John 7:52, or John 7:36, or John 4:44, or even Luke 21:38.

[17]Payne **Fuldensis** 247-248.

[18]Fee **First** 701f. [For the interpolated nature of 1 Cor 13, see Walker **Interpolations** 147f. Further examples of obvious interruption are Mark 14:28 and Mark 16:7, the second of which refers back to the first. Both feature a remark which is ignored by the persons in the following passage, who instead respond to a remark made in the *preceding* passage – The Editors].

With the elimination of 12:31b-14:1a as a non-Pauline interpolation, it would become necessary to remove either 12:31a or (more likely) 14:1b, which may have been added to provide a smoother transition between 12:31b-14:1a and its context.

6. Linguistic Evidence. With due allowance for the effect of subject matter on vocabulary, unusual vocabulary or grammatical forms in a passage may suggest that it is an interpolation. At several points, the vocabulary of 1 Cor 14:34-35 appears not to be characteristically Pauline.[19] (1) The verb ὑποτάσσω 'be subject' appears often in the authentic Pauline letters, but in all except three cases it refers to submission either to God, Christ, God's law, God's righteousness, or to 'futility' (Rom 8:20). Apart from 1 Cor 14:34, it refers to submission to humans at only three places, one of which (Rom 13:1, 5; governing authorities) is regarded by some as a non-Pauline interpolation. The others are 1 Cor 14:32 (prophets) and 1 Cor 16:16 (Christian leaders). In the pseudo-Pauline Colossians, Ephesians, and Titus, however, it almost *always* has in mind submission to other human beings.[20] (2) The verb ἐπεροτάω 'to ask' appears elsewhere in the undisputed letters only at Rom 10:20, in a quotation from Isaiah; otherwise it is found in the New Testament only in the Gospels. (3) The adjective αἰσχρός 'shameful' is found in the undisputed letters only at 1 Cor 11:16, which is part of another suspected non-Pauline interpolation; otherwise, it is found in the New Testament only in the pseudo-Pauline Eph 5:12 and Tit 1:11.

7. Content Evidence for the distinctiveness of a passage is the counterpart of linguistic evidence. The content of 1 Cor 14:34-35 contradicts its immediate context in 1 Cor 14, where women are among those who speak in church (note the 'all' in verses 5, 18, 23, 24, 31 and 'each' in v 26), and its wider context in 11:3-16, where it is assumed without reproof that women pray and prophesy in the assembly.[21] 1 Cor 14:34-35 also contradicts the egalitarianism of Gal 3:27-28 (in Christ 'there is neither male nor female, for you are all one in Christ Jesus'). Also, the phrase "just as the law says" in 1 Cor 14:34 appears not to be characteristically Pauline. As Collins notes, 'Paul generally expresses a somewhat negative view of the law' (cf 1 Cor 15:56).[22]

8. Situational Evidence. The case for distinctiveness is stronger when the language or content of a passage is not merely different from its context, but can be related to specific outside material, or to a later situation. Thus, 1 Cor 14:34-35 resembles the pseudo-Pauline 1 Tim 2:11-12. Both use the verb ἐπιτρέπειν to enjoin silence on the part of women; both require that women be 'submissive' (using the same root, ὑποτάσσειν in 1 Cor 14:34-35 and ὑποταγή in 1 Tim 2:11), presumably to men, an idea that also occurs elsewhere in the pseudo-Pauline writings.[23]

---

[19]There is a danger of circularity, in that the definition of "Pauline" is tentative until all interpolations have been identified. It is also to be expected that interpolators in Paul, as in any other text, may attempt with more or less success to imitate the style and content of that text.

[20]To other Christians, women to men, slaves to masters, and subjects to rulers. The only exception is Eph 5:24, which speaks of the church being in submission to Christ.

[21]Fee **First** 702.

[22]Collins **First** 515.

[23]Col 3:18, Eph 5:24, Tit 2:5; cf 1 Pet 3:1, 5 (all using the verb ὑποτάσσειν).

Apart from 1 Cor 14:34-35 (and perhaps 1 Cor 11:3-16, which is also regarded by some as an interpolation), there is nothing in the undisputed letters to suggest that the activity of women in the church was a problem for Paul. Clearly, however, such activity *was* later seen as problematic. This makes 1 Cor 14:34-35 anachronistic, and suggests that it was not composed until after the time of Paul.

9. Motivational Evidence for 1 Cor 14:34-35 is closely related to the situational evidence. After the time of Paul, when the status and role of women in the Church apparently came to be regarded as problematic, it may have appeared desirable to have the Apostle say something to address the problem. Hence the addition of a passage such as 1 Cor 14:34-35 to an authentic letter.

10. Location. Why was an interpolated passage inserted precisely where it is? The position of 1 Cor 14:34-35 is appropriate in several ways. (1) 1 Cor 14 as a whole deals with 'speaking' in church, which is also the theme of 14:34-35. (2) v28 speaks of 'keeping silent' in church, a notion picked up in v34. (3) v32 speaks of 'being subject,' an idea that reappears at v34 (with the same verb, ὑποτάσσεσθαι). (4) v33 includes the phrase 'in all of the churches,' and this reappears almost verbatim in v34 ('in the churches'). In short, it may simply have been the common themes of speech, silence, and submission, together with the setting of public worship in the churches, that led to the insertion of 14:34-35 at its present location in 1 Corinthians.

Comment
The Editors (2017)

The above paper is an example of criticism of a text from internal evidence: signs *in the text itself* that something has been inserted, at an early date, into the original.

Time was when textual criticism was recognized as having two components: (1) the lower, in which scribal corruptions were removed by comparison of manuscript variants, and (2) the higher, in which the formation process leading to the final state of the original text (including authorial or editorial adjustments prior to publication) was detected by evidence internal to the text. Those practicing the higher criticism now often hear "You have no evidence," or encounter the idea that when scribal errors are eliminated, what remains is "the author's holograph." What manuscript criticism actually reaches is the archetype **A**, the version from which the other manuscripts are descended. But this archetype may be centuries later than the author.[24] Given a first beginning **F**, much may thus lie between the point when a text is given out to be copied for a wider public (**P**), and the date of the oldest reconstructible archetype (**A**):

F . . Author(s), Proprietor(s), Editor(s) . . **P** . . . .Scribe(s). . . **A** . More Scribe(s) . . .
    ⇐ Formation Process ⇒   ‖   ⇐ Corruption Process ⇒

If scribal changes between **P** and **A** are to be detected, it must be by the methods of the higher criticism. So also *authorial or editorial* changes during the formation process, between **F** and **P**, which by definition elude manuscript criticism.

---

[24]West **Textual** 9, "Most classical authors come to us in parchment or paper manuscripts which are seldom earlier than the ninth century, and often as late as the sixteenth."

Authority Texts, by their nature, are especially liable to be adjusted or extended so as to remain relevant to changing conditions. Culturally central texts like the Iliad tend to evolve to suit that culture's changing idea of itself.[25] Advocacy texts like the Confucian Analects or the Gwǎndž statecraft tracts steadily grow by adding new tracts, including new commentaries on the older tracts, over the course of centuries. Religious texts are especially liable to such change, and the four Gospels show it in progress.[26] The Pauline texts, which are the doctrinal foundation for much of later Christianity, are *for that reason*, not merely because they are exhortational in an Epicurean sense, intrinsically likely to have undergone editorial improvements and adjustments.

Works Cited

C K Barrett. A Commentary on the First Epistle to the Corinthians. Harper 1957

George Melville Bolling. The External Evidence for Interpolation in Homer. Oxford 1925

E Bruce Brooks. Four Gospel Trajectories. Alpha v1 (2017) 11-12

E Bruce Brooks. The Reader in the Text. Alpha v1 (2017) 23-27

E Bruce Brooks and A Taeko Brooks. The Original Analects. Columbia 1998

James H Charlesworth. Christian and Jewish Self-Definition; in Sanders et al (ed), Jewish and Christian Self-Definition v2, Fortress (1981) 27-55

John J Collins. Sybilline Oracles. ABD (1992) 6/2-6

Raymond F Collins. First Corinthians. Liturgical 1999

William G Doty. Letters in Primitive Christianity. Fortress 1973

Gordon D Fee. The First Epistle to the Corinthians. Eerdmans 1987

Louis Feldman. Josephus. ABD (1992) 3/981-998

Harry Gamble Jr. Textual History of the Letter to the Romans. Eerdmans 1977

Robert M Grant. Heresy and Criticism. Westminster 1993

Robert M Grant. The Letter and the Spirit. Macmillan 1957

Robert M Grant. Marcion and the Critical Method; in Richardson et al ed, From Jesus to Paul, Wilfred Laurier (1984) 207-215

Helmut Koester. The Text of the Synoptic Gospels in the Second Century; in Petersen (ed), Gospel Traditions in the Second Century, Notre Dame (1989) 19-37

Karl Maurer. Interpolation in Thucydides. Brill 1995

Philip B Payne. Fuldensis. NTS v41 (1995) 240-262

Rudolf Pfeiffer. History of Classical Scholarship from the Beginnings to the End of the Hellenistic Age. Oxford 1968

W Allyn Rickett. The Guanzi. Princeton 1985 (rev C & T, 2001), 1998

Eva Matthews Sanford. Propaganda and Censorship in the Transmission of Josephus. TPAPA v66 (1935) 127-145

Stanley K Stowers. Greek and Latin Letters. ABD (1992) 4/290-293

William O Walker Jr. Interpolations in the Pauline Letters. Sheffield 2001

William O Walker Jr. An Unexamined Presupposition in Studies of the Synoptic Problem. Religion in Life v48 (1979) 41-5

M L West. Textual Criticism and Editorial Technique. Teubner 1973

[25][See Brooks **Reader** 12-13 – The Editors]

[26][See Brooks **Four** – The Editors].

Departure From Expectation

E Bruce Brooks
University of Massachusetts at Amherst
WSWG Note 56rev (10 Feb 1996)

We expect one thing, but we get another. There were 10 students in your class last year; this year, 15. There were 112 incidents of car theft last year, but this year, 121. Is this significant? Such questions come up all the time. They have a simple solution.

Normal Expectation

If occurrences diverge randomly from an expected value, the pattern of those departures is given by the normal distribution, whose curve looks like this:

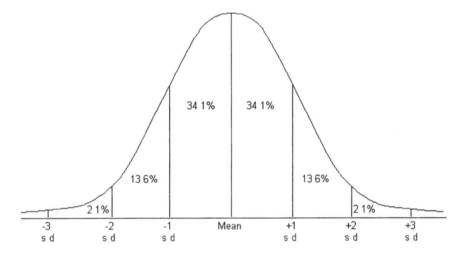

Not so scary. All it means is that if things are varying randomly around a norm, 68·2% of all occurrences will fall within ±1 standard deviations (sd), and 95·4% within ±2 sd. If the matter is important, we want instead a 99% assurance that a given departure from expectation is meaningful, not random. That level is defined by ±2·54 sd.

For a given pair of E (expected) and A (actual) numbers, how do we figure the sd? The usual approximation formula[1] is:

$$(A - E) / \sqrt{E}$$

Which is simple enough. But to make it self-interpreting, so that the formula will give 1·00 when the 99% level of assurance is reached, we multiply by 0·39.[2]

---

[1]For the basic formula, see Paul G Hoel **Elementary Statistics** (2ed Wiley 1966) 103-106.

[2]Multiplying by 0·39 is the same as dividing by 2·54, the number of standard deviations.

Alpha v1 (2017)

The absolute value of (A – E) needs to be used in calculating, and any minus sign should be appended to the final result[3]. A further factor with human data is that once something unusual occurs, it is likely to repeat (a rare word in a text, a copycat crime). To compensate for this, we take the square root of the result. The final formula is:

$$S = \sqrt{\ [(0\cdot39)(A-E)\ /\ \sqrt{E}\ ]}$$

This can be done in seconds on a hand calculator, as long as it has a square root key.

Practical Applications

1. Your class had 10 students last year; the expectation (E) is for 10 this year too. You actually (A) had 15. The significance (S) of this works out to

$$\sqrt{[(0\cdot39)(15-10)\ /\ \sqrt{10}]} = \sqrt{(0\cdot39)(5)}\ /\ (3\cdot16) = \sqrt{0\cdot61} = +0\cdot78,\ \textbf{not significant}$$

2. Over the 242 years covered by the Lǔ chronicle Chūn/Chyōu (CC), there are 524 military events, or 2·17 per average year. For the 18-year reign of Lǔ Hwán-gūng, we thus expect 39·06 military events; instead there are actually 16. The significance is:

$$\sqrt{[(0\cdot39)(16-39\cdot06)\ /\ \sqrt{39\cdot06}]} = \sqrt{(0\cdot39)(-23\cdot06)}\ /\ (6\cdot25) = \sqrt{-1\cdot44} = -1\cdot20,\ \textbf{significant}$$

3. The average number of CC diplomatic events is 2·73 per year; for Hwán-gūng we expect 49·14 and actually get 58. The significance of this is:

$$\sqrt{[(0\cdot39)(58-49\cdot14)\ /\ \sqrt{49\cdot14}]} = \sqrt{(0\cdot39)(8\cdot86)}\ /\ (7\cdot01) = \sqrt{0\cdot49} = +0\cdot70,\ \textbf{not}\ \text{significant}$$

but this plus the preceding result suggests that the dip in military events may have had something to do with diplomatic efforts by Hwán-gūng, who went often to other states.

4. ευσεβεια "religion" occurs 15× in the New Testament (138,019 words), never in Paul, but 10× (A) in the post-Pauline Pastoral Epistles (9,488 words, so E = 1·03).

$$\sqrt{[(0\cdot39)(10-1\cdot03)\ /\ \sqrt{1\cdot03}]} = \sqrt{(0\cdot39)(8\cdot97)}\ /\ (1\cdot01) = \sqrt{3\cdot46} = +1\cdot86,\ \textbf{significant}$$

This reflects the conventionalizing of Christian belief in the years after Paul.

5. The following are the actual crime statistics for a certain city in 1994 and 1995,[4] and their calculated significance:

	1994 (E)	1995 (A)	S	Interpretation
Murder	0	1	+0·62	not significant
Sexual Assault	55	47	–0·65	not significant
Assault/Battery	295	308	+0·54	not significant
Breaking/Entering	91	109	+0·86	**not yet** significant
Car Theft	112	121	+0·58	not significant
Vandalism	571	520	–0·91	**not yet** significant

Some of this should be watched by an alert Chief, though there is no present need to shift staff from one category to another. But there is an interesting social undercurrent: profitless crimes (vandalism) are down; profitable crimes (breaking/entering) are up.

S, as here presented, is for situations adequately described by one A and one E. Any real-life Chief would of course be tracking crimes over more than one year.

---

[3]A more elaborate way to say this is to multiply the final result by (A - E) / | A - E |.

[4]From the Daily Hampshire Gazette, 21 Feb 1996. As a matter of retrospective compassion, I do not here discuss the paper's own interpretation of these events.

The Reader in the Text

E Bruce Brooks

University of Massachusetts at Amherst

WSWG Note 285 (8 Mar 2004)

I here call attention to a device found in many literary traditions, a variant of prolepsis (the anticipation of an opponent's argument) in which the opponent is a reader envisioned by the author, or a character actually present inside the text, who complains of something new and is silenced, or prefers something else and is satisfied. Such passages may signal the presence of late material, and thus (as in these examples) may help to reveal compositional strata in that text.

Iliad 2:53-444

High on the list of Iliadic military idiocies[1] is Agamemnon's response to a dream of victory over Troy, a dream sent by Zeus to mislead him, but ostensibly favorable. He calls the Greeks together in 2:50, but presently he proposes to the chiefs:

73 First, I with words will make trial of them, as is fitting,
74 Ordering them to flee in their many-benched ships together –
75 Do ye take care, from this side and that, to restrain them with words

Given the rush for the ships which ensues, nothing less "fitting" could be imagined.[2] I suggest that the phrase ἣ θέμις ἐστί "as is fitting" is meant to excuse this nonsense: to lull the sensible reader (or hearer) over the absurdity of the suggestion.

Themis θέμις in the Iliad usually means social entitlement. Some instances (with Smith's translations) are: 9:33 "as is my *privilege*," 9:276 "in the *manner* of men and women," 23:44 "it is noway *right*," 24:652 "as they *have a right* to." The privilege of Diomedes to speak in assembly, in 9:33, is based on his status as a chief and thus as a counselor; he is one who is socially entitled to be heard. Themis in Iliad 2:73 lacks this social or customary dimension, and thus seems to be anomalous in this group.

Evidence of Interpolation. The *natural* thing for Agamemnon to do, if he believes the dream, would be to gather the Greeks and march on Troy. Was this the original plot? Or, to put the question in a form in which philology can deal with it: Is there a point in Iliad 2 from which the story *actually takes* that course? There is: at 2:445f. The preceding lines, 2:442-444, are nearly identical with the 2:50-52 assembly call. After the episode of the flight to the ships, the tale goes back to its starting point, and at 2:442 it calls the assembly all over again. When the material between 2:52 and 2:445 is removed, the two assembly calls can be merged as one. For the standard reason that the text is more coherent without it, 2:53-2:444 looks like an interpolation.

[1] For a defense, with citation of previous literature, see Cook **Test**.
[2] For the perplexities of the commentators, see eg Jevons (1886) 307, Knox (1989).

Without that passage, Iliad 2:50-452 would read this way:

50~442   Straightway to the heralds clear-voiced, he gave his instruction
51=443   to summon unto the battle the flowing-haired men of Achaia.
52=444   These did indeed issue summons, and those did assemble right quickly.
445   And those who surrounded Atrides, the nurtured of Zeus, the princes,
446   hastened to marshal the host; among them, blue-eyed Athena,
447   wearing the aegis so precious, free from all age and immortal,
448   wherefrom a hundred of tassels, all of them gold, were suspended,
449   cunningly woven, a hundred of oxen the value of each,
450   and with this, dazzling the eye, she sped through the host of Achaians,
451   urging them onward; great strength did she inspire in each one,
452   a heart to make war without ceasing, and still to do battle.

Implications for the Text. If 2:442-445f has a satisfactory narrative flow, and no one has ever said it does not, then so does 2:50-52 *plus* 445f. The largely comical material between the two assembly calls (featuring garrulous Nestor, rude Thersites, and repentant Agamemnon) would be suspect simply on grounds of inconsistent tone.[3]

The story line in the Iliad sometimes pauses for comic relief (the Wounding of Aphrodite, 5:311-430) or civic affirmation (the Shield of Achilles, 18:483-608). Perhaps it was once more compact and was later extended for audiences more leisured, more civilian, than those for whose sensibilities the tale was first crafted?

Mahâ-Parinibbâna Sutta 5:41-44

The Buddha has been traveling from village to village with his disciples; at 5:1, he has reached Kusinârâ. He is ill; his followers know he will soon die. Disciple Ânanda mourns (5:32-35). But he also finds the time to object, not to Buddha's death as such, but to the fact that it is taking place in a mere jerkwater town of no repute. Then:

> 5:41. When he had thus spoken, the venerable Ânanda said to the Blessed One, "Let not the Blessed One die in this little wattle-and-daub town in the midst of the jungle, in this branch township. For, Lord, there are other great cities, such as Campâ, Râjagaha, Sâvatthi, Sâketa, Kosambi, and Benâres. Let the Blessed One die in one of them. There, there are many wealthy nobles and Brahmans and heads of houses, believers in the Tathâgata, who will pay due honor to the remains of the Tathâgata." [42] "Say not so, Ânanda! Say not so, Ânanda, that this is but a small wattle-and-daub town in the midst of the jungle, a branch township. Long ago, Ânanda, there was a king, by name Mahâ-Sudassana, a King of Kings, a righteous man who ruled in righteousness, Lord of the Four Quarters of the Earth, conqueror, the protector of his people, possessor of the seven Royal Treasures. This Kusinârâ, Ânanda, was the royal city of King Mahâ-Sudassana, under the name of Kusâvatî, and on the east and on the west it was twelve leagues in length, and on the north and on the south it was seven leagues in breadth."

---

[3]The secondarity of this passage is noted by West **Making** 101 "If 49 were immediately followed by 442 (=50), the narrative would run on perfectly smoothly (cf Fick 4, Erhardt 17). I take this to have been [the poet's] original version."

[43]"That royal city Kusâvatî, Ânanda, was mighty, and prosperous, and full of people, crowded with men, and provided with all things for food. Just, Ânanda, as the royal city of the gods, Âlakamandâ by name, is mighty, prosperous, and full of people, crowded with the gods and provided with all kinds of food, so, Ânanda, was the royal city Kusâvatî mighty and prosperous, full of food, crowded with men, and provided with all kinds of food. [44] Both by day and by night, Ânanda, the royal city Kusâvatî resounded with the ten cries, that is to say: the noise of elephants, and the noise of horses and the noise of chariots; the sounds of the drum, of the tabor, and of the lute; the sound of singing and the sounds of the cymbal and of the gong; and lastly, with the cry, Eat, drink, and be merry!"

With that reassurance, the text resumes its previous business, and Ânanda is sent to notify the Mallas of Kusinârâ of the Buddha's impending demise. The Kusâvatî passage lifts the tale out of its humble setting, making it grander and so more agreeable to a devout but disappointed posterity, whose interests Ânanda briefly represents.

Evidence of Interpolation. The interruptive quality of the passage is obvious, as is the change in the role of Ânanda in that passage. Its independence as a narrative unit is shown by the fact that it recurs as the beginning of the Mahâ-Sudassana Sutta, which describes the royal city Kusâvatî and the world conquests of its King Sudassana, ending with the death of the King (modeled on the death of the Buddha from MPnS). Finally (MSdS 2:37), the Buddha reveals that he himself was that King, that he had previously died and been buried there six times, that the King's death was the seventh, and that his coming death would be the eighth and last. This whole Sutta may be seen as a further development of the already legendary and elaborative MPnS 5:41-44.[4]

Implications for the Text. May not the intermittently humble Mahâ-Parinibbâna Sutta have been at first a relatively realistic narrative of the last days of the Buddha, subsequently modified to be more suitable to the sensibilities of a later, more devout, more pilgrimage oriented, and above all, a richer and more urban, posterity?

---

[4]That passage has interest in other directions too: it seems to have influenced the rewriting of the first death scene of Confucius (LY 7:35, c0450) as LY 9:12 (c0405). In the latter, Confucius is dying in humble status, and his followers, led by Dž-lù, thinking this inappropriate for so great a man, masquerade as the retinue of a nobleman to create what for them was a more suitable setting. If so, then the interpolated MPnS 5:41-44 must somewhat predate c0405; the core MPnS narrative must be earlier than the interpolation; and the death of Buddha, which it is the central task of the MPnS to describe, must be earlier still. The effect of this is to put the Buddha's death in the early 05c, which is where at least one older tradition also located it.

Rhys Davids ends his Introduction to the MPnS by suggesting that the Buddha's death must be redated from that traditional c0485 to c0420/0400, since the transmission series of Theras from Asoka (mid 03c) back to Upâli will account for "only about 150 years." This assumes that Upâli and monastic Buddhism itself date from the time of the Buddha, but that assumption is against all economic probability. The likely stages are: (1) In MPnS, Buddha and his followers are itinerant. (2) The Prâtimokṣa (Pâli, Pâtimokkha), a confessional for monks living separately and assembling twice a month, defines a period of *semi*-monastic Buddhism, which must intervene. (3) Full monastic Buddhism *does* begin with Upâli, but it requires wealthy patrons, and can arise only at a later, more prosperous stage of Ganga urbanization: the time of Asoka..

Analects 13:3

The Analects supposedly reflects Confucius. To those used to the tone of the late 04c part of the work (LY 12-15), the jv̀ng-míng 正名 "rectification of names" theory which is urged in LY 13:3 is startling, since to the educated reader, the idea itself, and the chain argument form in which it is expounded, do not suggest Confucius, but rather the 03rd century philosopher Sýwndž 荀子, who has a whole chapter (SZ 22) on that subject. We are surprised. In Analects 13:3, the disciple Dž-lù is surprised too. "Confucius" proceeds to berate him for that surprise, in these terms:

> "Dž-lù said, If the Ruler of Wèi were waiting for the Master to be in charge of his government, what would the Master do first? The Master said, It would certainly be to rectify names, would it not? Dž-lù said, The Master is off the track. What is all this about rectifying? The Master said, Boorish indeed is Yóu! The gentleman, with respect to what he does not understand, should maintain an abashed silence. If names are not rectified, speech will not be representative. If speech is not representative, things will not get done . . ."

No mere emollient Iliad 2:73 adverb here: this is heavy stuff. But in its different way, it too recognizes (in the person of a disciple) and silences (by haranguing that disciple) the doubts of readers who might otherwise be inclined to find its novelty anomalous.

Evidence of Interpolation. LY 13:3 interrupts a pattern of paired sayings in that chapter (13:1/2 and 13:4/5). There is no place for the LY 13:3 saying in that pattern. It is then structurally intrusive, and for that reason also, probably of later date.

Implications for the Text. Other Sýwndzian moments occur in the next layer of the text (LY 16-20; 03c); by contrast, these passages do not seem to be interpolated.[5] May not they and the interpolated LY 13:3 together imply contact with a rival 03c Confucianism which could not be named without anachronism, but was too important to be altogether ignored by the proprietors of the Analects, the leaders of the waning but still active 03rd century Confucian School of Lǔ?

Mark 4:10-20 and 4:34

In much of the Gospel of Mark, Jesus heals, and calls to repentance. The Kingdom is coming. Crowds gather and listen. We listen too. Suddenly, we overhear this astonishing remark of Jesus (incorporating the "cursing oracle" of Isaiah 6:9-10):

> 4:10. And when he was alone, those who were about him with the Twelve asked him concerning the parables, [11] and he said to them, "To you has been given the secret of the Kingdom of God, but for those outside, everything is in parables, [12] so that they may indeed see but not perceive, and may indeed hear but not understand; lest they should turn again, and be forgiven. [13] And he said to them, Do you not understand this parable? How then do you expect to understand all the parables?"

An explanation of the Parable of the Sower then follows, in 4:14-20.

---

[5]See the comments in Brooks **Analects** to LY 17:2a/b, 17:3, 17:8a, and 17:9 (where the Analects either opposes Sýwndž or sides with his enemies, the Mencians), and all of LY 19.

A bit further on (4:34), we are told that "he did not speak to them save in parables, but privately, to his own disciples, he explained everything." Jesus' preaching, seemingly successful, has become, not merely ineffectual, but *intentionally* ineffectual. What has happened?

Evidence of Interpolation. In 4:21-32, with no narrative retransition, Jesus again addresses the multitude. Mk 4:1-9 plus 21-32 would make a plausible, if veiled, public sermon. That sermon is interrupted by the change of setting in 4:10-20, from the crowd to a private conversation and back to the crowd again in 4:21 Quite apart from the difference of content, this unexplained double change of scene independently suggests that the dark 4:10-20 (and the related and equally dark 4:34) are interpolated.

Implications for the Text. The suggestion is that Jesus' meaning will be revealed *only later,* and only to a few; and that Jesus' original hearers, even his disciples, fail to understand him. Wrede called the message of such passages the Messianic Secret.[6] They seem to rebuke expectations about Jesus which are implied elsewhere in Mark. May they not be an attempt to impose a post-Crucifixion meaning on teachings which some readers remembered as having been the teachings of Jesus during his lifetime?

Conclusion

Readers within texts, whether presented as mindfulness on a hero's part or as actual characters in the story, may sometimes represent a text arguing with its early elements on behalf of its late elements. In an evolving text, such devices can serve to maintain audience contact: satisfying any disturbed readers. In rhetorically intense instances, such as the last two given above, the point at issue may merely be more consequential: the art of ruling men; the salvation of humankind.

Works Cited

E Bruce Brooks. Mark's Parables of the Kingdom. Alpha v1 (2017) 89-91

E Bruce Brooks. The Resurrection of Jesus in Mark. Alpha v1 (2017) 81-88

E Bruce Brooks and A Taeko Brooks. The Original Analects. Columbia 1998

Erwin Cook. Agamemnon's Test of the Army in Iliad Book 2 and the Function of Homeric Akhos. American Journal of Philology v124 (2003) 165-198

Engelbert Drerup. Das Fünfte Buch der Ilias. Schöningh 1913

F B Jevons. The Rhapsodizing of the Iliad. Journal of Hellenic Studies v7 (1886) 291-308

Ronald Knox and Joseph Russo. Agamemnon's Test: "Iliad" 2.73-75. Classical Antiquity v8 #2 (Oct 1989) 351-358

W Pachow. A Comparative Study of the Prâtimokṣa. 1955; rev Delhi 2000

T W Rhys Davids. Buddhist-Suttas [SBE v11]. Oxford 1881

Martin L West. The Making of the Iliad. Oxford 2011

William Wrede. The Messianic Secret. 1901; tr Clarke 1971

[6]As cannot be fully argued here, I find that there are not one but two "secrets" in Mark; an illegal and thus covert proclamation of the Davidic Kingdom (see Brooks **Parables**), and a prophecy of Jesus' death and resurrection: a view of Jesus which the disciples will understand only after the Crucifixion (see Brooks **Resurrection**), since that is when that view first arose.

Arguments From Silence

E Bruce Brooks
University of Massachusetts at Amherst
WSWG Note 56rev (10 March 1996)

Arguments from silence have sometimes been thought to be invalid in principle. That is not the case: nonexistence is the correct inference to draw from silence. But the evidence must be read with understanding, and complications must be considered.[1]

Cultural and Textual Factors

Every occupational or other in-group has its own ways of talking, including its own ways of not *having* to talk; its list of things that need not be said, or are "just not said." Thus, a thing might not be mentioned in a text (or included in a tomb) because:

- the text is too short, or the sites too few or too geographically limited, to provide a statistically valid sample
- the thing is not relevant to the immediate discourse
- it is too familiar to require explicit mention
- it is not known to persons at the writer's social level
- it is esoteric, and is thus mentioned only within some inner circle
- it is socially embarrassing, and is thus not commonly mentioned
- it is politically dangerous, and is thus mentioned only obliquely
- it is actually present, but has been misunderstood by modern readers[2]
- the culture does not emphasize it (as, carnage in Chinese battle accounts)
- it is contrary to the ethos of the text (as, victory 勝 in the Chūn/Chyŏu)[3]
- it is not part of relevant ritual practice (the lack of tiger bones in elite Chinese graves does not prove that tigers were then unknown in China)
- it is taboo, and mention is avoided for ritual reasons (as, the personal name of a current or previous Chinese ruler)[4]

Despite its complications in practice, the analytical utility of Chinese taboo avoidance is too well known to require elaborate statement here.[5]

---

[1]One statement of the modern position is Langlois **Introduction** 254f; compare the more positive estimate in Vincent **Historical** 253 and 254, and comment in Lange **Argument** 289.

[2]A thing may be mentioned allusively, or by a name we do not recognize, or by a familiar name in an unfamiliar calligraphic form. We lack the easy virtuosity of the people of that time.

[3]For the contrasting ethos of the warrior and the ruler, see Brooks **Defeat** 189-190 and 198. The warrior wants to have his prowess noticed; the ruler only wants to get the job done.

[4]This is the basic Chinese rule, in families and especially toward rulers, but see n5 below.

[5]But taboo avoidance or nonavoidance can be difficult to interpret. It may not apply equally to all persons, like the contributors to the Lw̌-shř Chūn/Chyŏu, only some of whom observe it; the others may have come from different states, or they may have held lower rank within Chín. For the erroneous later restoration of supposedly tabooed words, see Dubs **History** 2/266-270.

Alpha v1 (2017)

An absence which can be sharply delimited is interpretively stronger, as when a certain idea or cluster of ideas appears in texts only after a certain date.[6] The case for absence is also stronger when something else replaces the missing element.[7]

Political and Institutional Factors

Information flow is resisted by autocratic states. The difficulty of getting a fact into the record is illustrated in the story of the Four Scribes in DJ 9/25:2 (04c). For the state's hatred of low-level information flow, see SJS 2:8 and 2:14 (c0214). For the effectiveness of state suppression, consider the Diatessaron, condemned as heretical by Theodoret of Syria (c423); only one scrap of the Greek text has ever been found. The subculture of dissent has its own opaque literary conventions, and it needs them.[8] Resistance to government necessarily has secrecy as its guiding principle.[9] Those who work in more comfortable circumstances need to be aware of these difficulties.[10]

Of all institutions, the military would seem to have the greatest need for accurate reporting, but the implied expectation is often violated. Misses are recorded as hits; routs as victories. The rule of loyalty prevents criticism of superiors, let alone its inclusion in reports.[11] Government announcements serve government purposes.[12] The more "official" a text, the more compromised it may be as an information source.[13]

Artificial Silence

Where we possess both primary and secondary documents, or early and late ones in the same series, we can sometimes observe both the early suppression and the later elimination of information. The former creates an exception to the rule that earlier evidence is better; the latter confirms the rule.[14] Traditions grow and elaborate, and they may also suppress and discard. I give two examples.

[6]For one set of examples, see Brooks **Alexandrian** 7-10.

[7]The early Analects chapters might be thought too small for the nonmention of the Classics to be significant. What *is* significant is that in those chapters, Confucius is shown as teaching *on a different basis*, making no reference to antiquity at all, but arguing direct from principle.

[8]For a glimpse at the process from the secret police viewpoint, see Vatulescu **Arresting**.

[9]Compare the passwords and countersigns of Mark 11:1-6. The French Resistance official Marc Bloch was arrested and executed through a failure of secrecy among his colleagues (Febvre, in Bloch xviii; itself a cryptic remark, opaque to those who do not know the situation).

[10]As one extreme example, see Slyomovics **Argument**.

[11]See for example O'Kane **Wahoo** 32, 60, 71, 79, 81, 86.

[12]For calculations of when, and how much, to lie to the public, see the staff discussions of Joseph Goebbels, in Boelcke **Secret**. Note the occasional – but only occasional – conclusion that truth is the best propaganda.

[13]I may instance one PhD oral exam, in a year and a place which will remain unspecified. The subject was the Marco Polo Bridge incident of 7 July 1937, when Japanese soldiers fired on Chinese soldiers, the event that touched off WW2 in Asia. The candidate had been asked what her sources were. She replied that she had used official Japanese government documents. The questioner remarked simply: "I was there. It isn't true."

[14]A growth process often supersedes previous growth; see Brooks **Four**.

The Scandal of Shelley. Mary Shelley at first published only the milder of her late husband's poems, to protect his reputation from the socially troublesome content of his other work. The first edition of his letters also avoided reference to his extramarital affairs. As time passed, the more scandalous poems and letters were finally printed. If not for these later editions, we would not be aware of Shelley's less Victorian self. In this case, the later texts more adequately represent the historical figure.

The Atonement. The Gospel of Luke never mentions the Atonement doctrine, and Luke's Acts of the Apostles never shows Paul preaching that doctrine. Comparison with Mark, the basis for Luke's own Gospel, shows that the passages in Mark which refer to that doctrine (Mk 10:45, 14:24) are *omitted by Luke*.[15] Comparison with Paul's letters, of which Luke was aware,[16] shows that Paul insisted on that doctrine. Then Luke in Acts knowingly misrepresents Paul's theology. He clearly did not wish the Atonement to be part of the tradition which he was defining for the Christian future. If we had only Luke, we would not know that the Atonement doctrine had existed. This is a more normal case, where the earlier evidence is better.

Summary

There are many reasons why documents may imperfectly represent an author or incompletely report a historical situation. But be it remembered by the critical historian that if something does not exist, in a certain time and place, *the silence of the record* is the only evidence which that fact is capable of *leaving* in the record.

Works Cited

Marc Bloch. The Historian's Craft. 1949; tr Vintage 1953
Willi A Boelcke (ed). The Secret Conferences of Dr Goebbels. Dutton 1970
A Taeko Brooks and E Bruce Brooks. Defeat in the Chūn/Chyōu. WSP v1 (2010) 189-198
E Bruce Brooks. Alexandrian Motifs in Chinese Texts. SPP #96 (1999)
E Bruce Brooks. The Epistle of Jacob. Alpha v1 (2017) 58-70
E Bruce Brooks. Four Gospel Trajectories. Alpha v1 (2017) 11-12
Homer H Dubs. History of the Former Han Dynasty. 3v Waverly 1938-1955
Paul Elbert. Possible Literary Links Between Luke-Acts and Pauline Letters; in Brodie
    (ed), The Intertextuality of the Epistles, Sheffield (2006) 226-254
Neil Freistat. Illegitimate Shelley. PMLA v109 #3 (1994) 409-423
Roger Ingpen. The Letters of Percy Bysshe Shelley. 2v Pitman 1909
John Lange. The Argument from Silence. History and Theory v5 (1966) 288-301
Charles-Victor Langlois et al. Introduction to the Study of History. 1898; tr Holt 1908
Richard H O'Kane. Wahoo. Presidio 1987
Susan Slyomovics. The Argument from Silence: Morocco's Truth Commission and
    Women Political Prisoners. Journal of Middle East Women's Studies v1 (2005) 73-95
Cristina Vatulescu. Arresting Biographies. Comparative Literature v56 (2004) 243-261
John Martin Vincent. Historical Research: An Outline of Theory and Practice. Holt 1911

---

[15]For a direct argument between the two theological positions, see Brooks **Jacob** 59f.
[16]See Elbert **Links** 229, with further references.

Early Witnesses

The Mandaean Death of John

Charles G Häberl

Rutgers University

(2 March 2016)

The Mandaeans are the major surviving Gnostic group.[1] Their writings, especially those claiming John the Baptist as ancestor, have been dismissed as late, meant to establish a claim that the Mandaeans are a "people of the book" and thus entitled to recognition as a religion under Islam in the 7th century.[2] But Buckley's study of scribal colophons shows that the scribal tradition for at least some texts goes back to the 3rd century.[3] Mandaean tradition, however elaborated over the centuries, is thus of great interest as evidence for a belief apparently ancestral to the first Christianity, one which continued in parallel with Christianity for much of the rest of the century.

The Death of John (Yahya) in Mandaean tradition is an ascent to Heaven, not unlike that which some Christians had claimed for *their* founder. It exists in several versions, which differ (among other things) in the degree of reluctance John shows at leaving his body. In the right-hand volume of the Ginza Rba ("Great Treasure"), which seems to be the earliest of several versions, this concern does appear:[4]

> **Ginza Rba 5:4, 192-193.** Then Manda d'Hayyi said to John, When I put my hand on you, you will depart from your body. John said to Manda d'Hayyi, I have seen you; now I will no longer be here. I have seen and reached you; now I beseech thee in truth. Do not curse me away from you, from the place from which you have come. Prepare me and give me instructions for the great place to which you are going. Have mercy upon me, and reveal to me the mysteries of the kings, about the Great Fruit of the Light, about the anvils and fruits of the Earth, against which they are pressed, about the anvils of the water, against which the living fire spreads, where the Life resides, which is earlier and greater than any other.
>
> [Manda d'Hayyi] undressed him from his clothes in the Jordan, he removed him from his garment of flesh and blood, he clothed him in a robe of splendor and covered him with a good pure turban of light. Manda d'Hayyi continued on his way to the place which is entirely aglow, to the place which is entirely light, and John went with him.
>
> The fish out of the sea and the birds of the two shores of the ocean rallied over the body of John and covered him. When John saw his body, he was troubled about it.

---

[1] For a general introduction, see Buckley **Mandaeans**.

[2] See eg Pallis **Studies**.

[3] Buckley **Stem** 272.

[4] From Drower **Mandaeans** 273-280.

But it is short-lived:

> Then Manda d'Hayyi said to John, Why are you troubled about the flesh and blood from which I removed you? If you want, I will lead you back into it again. Then John said to Manda d'Hayyi, Blessed and praised be the man who stripped the robe of flesh and blood from me, who has redeemed me and freed me! Praise, glory, strengthened and honored is the chosen man, who has clothed me with the garments of splendor and covered me with the good pure turban of light. No, I grieve for my children, who are full of zeal, that I had to leave them there without anyone who can teach them.
>
> Then Manda d'Hayyi said, Whosoever has lived in your mind and in your heart will also live within the hearts and minds of your children. My son, I understand why you grieve.
>
> Then John said to Manda d'Hayyi, "You know even the heart and penetrate the senses. The heart, liver, and kidneys are as plain as the day before you. You split a hair and see what is within it. You understand what is within the light, and what is within darkness." Thus his mouth spoke in glory from the foam of the water and the lapping of the water. Then he took sand from the sea and from the two shores of the ocean, and began to throw it over the body of John. From that day, the burial of the body has been done.[5]
>
> But he was taken and borne to the Realm of Light, and to Shamish and the Lord of Radiance, and joined in the perpetual worship of the Light King.

The Mandaean account of the Death of Adam shows much greater reluctance to leave the body behind. This parallel tradition has affected the Death of John tradition also. An account of the death of John collected by Drower from an informant seemingly shows the one tradition as influencing the other:

> Now, when he had left his body, Yahya looked down and saw his corpse in the water. The birds descended and began to peck at it, for it began to decay. The vulture flew down, and began to peck out the eyes. Yahya gazed at it, and Manda-t-Haiy said, Why gaze on that? That is a corrupt thing of the earth! And Manda-t-Haiy seized earth and buried it. Yahya was glad, for he had loved his earthly body, which we call paghra or 'ostuna, and did not wish it harmed. And the grave still appears above the Jordan like a mound, and the Mandai know it for Yahya's grave.

Works Cited

E Bruce Brooks. The Death of John in Mark. Alpha v1 (2017) 37-38
Jorunn Jacobsen Buckley. The Mandaeans. Oxford 2002
Jorunn Jacobsen Buckley. The Great Stem of Souls. Gorgias 2005; rev 2010
E S Drower. The Mandaeans of Iraq and Iran. Brill 1937
Edmondo Lupieri. The Mandaeans. 1993; tr Eerdmans 2002
Svend Aage Pallis. Mandaean Studies. rev Milford 1926

---

[5]Lupieri **Mandaeans** 236 n29 has suggested, "This institution shows that the redactor of this passage is reutilizing a legend about Adam, for whose corpse it makes sense to speak of first burial." But by contrast, the Ginza account of the death of Adam explicitly mentions that his corpse will remain unburied, unlike that of John.

The Death of John in Mark

E Bruce Brooks

University of Massachusetts at Amherst

(2 March 2016)

The arrest of John the Baptist is noted in passing at Mk 1:14 ("Now after John was delivered up, Jesus came into Galilee, preaching the gospel of God"). Later, to explain a remark of Herod, John's death is narrated in detail, as a flashback:

> **Mk 6:14**. And King Herod heard thereof, for [Jesus'] name had become known, and he said, John the Baptizer is risen from the dead, and therefore do these powers work in him. [15] But others said, It is Elijah. And others said, A prophet, even as one of the prophets. [16] But Herod, when he heard, said, John, whom I beheaded, he is risen.
>
> [17] For Herod himself had sent forth and laid hold upon John, and bound him in prison for the sake of Herodias, his brother Philip's wife, for he had married her. [18] For John said to Herod, It is not lawful for thee to have thy brother's wife. [19] And Herodias set herself against him, and desired to kill him; and she could not; [20] for Herod feared John, knowing that he was a righteous and holy man, and kept him safe. And when he heard him he was much perplexed, and he heard him gladly.
>
> [21] And when a convenient day was come, that Herod on his birthday made a supper to his lords, and the high captains, and the chief men of Galilee, [22] and when the daughter of Herodias herself came in and danced, she pleased Herod and them that sat at meat with him, and the King said to the damsel, Ask of me whatsoever thou wilt, and I will give it thee. [23] And he sware to her, Whatsoever thou shalt ask of me, I will give it thee, unto the half of my kingdom. [24] And she went out, and said to her mother, What shall I ask? And she said, The head of John the Baptizer. [25] And she came in straightway with haste to the King, and asked, saying, I will that thou forthwith give me on a platter the head of John the Baptist.[26] And the King was exceedingly sorry, but for the sake of his oaths, and of them that sat at meat, he would not reject her. [27] And straightway the King sent forth a soldier of his guard, and commanded to bring his head, and he went and beheaded him in prison, [28] and brought his head on a platter and gave it to the damsel; and the damsel gave it to her mother. [29] And when his disciples heard, they came and took up his corpse, and laid it in a tomb.

Mk 6:17-29 is one of the longest consecutive narratives in Mark. It is unusual in other ways too. Despite the exciting, and even erotic, character of the story, there are none of Mark's historical present verbs to heighten its vividness; it is all in the past tense. The figure of John is inconsistent: why did Herod arrest him, if he wanted to hear him? And John as a compelling speaker does nothing to advance the Jesus story. It rather advances the John story, just as Paul's appearances before Roman magistrates in Acts give a sympathetic picture of Christian doctrine, and so advance the Christian cause. The whole point of the story is to make an apologia for John.

Alpha v1 (2017)

I thus suggest that this piece was borrowed *from the parent John tradition*, with which the young Jesus movement was then in contact. If there was such a contact, not only texts, but practices, might have been borrowed. The borrowing of Baptist fasting is in fact predicted *as a future event* in Mk 2:18-20, a clearly interruptive passage:

> **Mk 2:17**. And when Jesus heard it, he saith unto them, They that are whole have no need of a physician, but they that are sick; I came not to call the righteous, but sinners.
>
> [18]. And John's disciples and the Pharisees were fasting, and they come and say unto him, Why do John's disciples and the disciples of the Pharisees fast, but thy disciples fast not? [19] And Jesus said unto them, Can the sons of the bridechamber fast, while the bridegroom is with them? As long as they have the bridegroom with them, they cannot fast. [20] But the days will come, when the bridegroom shall be taken away from them, and then will they fast in that day.
>
> [21] No man seweth a piece of undressed cloth on an old garment, else that which should fill it up taketh from it, the new from the old, and a worse rent is made. [22] And no man putteth new wine into old wineskins, else the wine will burst the skins, and the wine perisheth, and the skins. But they put new wine into fresh wineskins.

Mk 2:21-22 explicitly claims that the Jesus movement is something new, something that cannot be patched onto the old Pharisaic understanding. The passage has little to do with the question of fasting (raised in 2:18-20), and is better seen as summarizing the difference between Pharisaic Judaism and Jesus' Messianic version of Judaism. The Pharisees were preaching to the already righteous. Jesus goes instead to sinners; to those who are not presently righteous, but who, if only they can *become* righteous, will make a difference to the overall righteousness of Israel.

The indication is that 2:18-20 is a later addition, and that, earlier, 2:17 had directly preceded 2:21-22. If we recognize a kinship between the Death of John story and the predicted adoption of customs from the John movement, we will have a Baptist layer, and the whole of that layer must be where its assignable member is.

I conclude by suggesting that attention to the Baptist sect, as a senior Messianic movement with which the Jesus sect shared much, and from which it learned much, may be fruitful, not least by encouraging renewed attention to the Mandaean writings, which represent a much advanced and elaborated tradition[1] deriving from at least one strand of a movement which was contemporary with Jesus, and in whose service Jesus seems to have begun his own career.

And then, "after John was delivered up, Jesus came into Galilee, preaching the Gospel of God" (Mk 1:14). And a second, and divergent, Messianic sect had appeared.

Works Cited

E Bruce Brooks. Salome. Alpha v1 (2017) 94-98

Charles G Häberl. The Mandaean Death of John. Alpha v1 (2017) 35-36

[1]For the later stages of that development, see Häberl **Mandaean**.

The Two Ways

E Bruce Brooks

University of Massachusetts at Amherst

SBL/EGL (Richfield Ohio, 31 March 2011)

The earliest Christianity had no place for the Resurrection of Jesus.[1] It focused on what Jesus had preached: repentance and forgiveness. But repentance for what? What sins might keep us from being saved? The Two Ways text is one answer. It goes back to a Jewish prayer for the Day of Atonement: a list of 22 sins (one for each letter of the Hebrew alphabet, arranged in alphabetic order) for which forgiveness is sought.[2] That list was part of Christianity's heritage in popular Judaism. It is a primary document of the early form of belief and practice to which I here give the name Alpha Christianity.

The list of sins exists in several versions. I here consider only four: Didache 5:1,[3] Mark 7:21-22, Galatians 5:13-6:10,[4] and Barnabas 18:1-20:2. Only the Didache version has a 22-item format, and that version thus probably best reflects the original. I use it below as the basis of comparison with the other lists.

Alpha Christianity. The original list is part of a prayer. That prayer regards law observance as the key to eternal life. Is law observance early in Christianity, or is it (as some have thought) a late heresy? Consider what our earliest Gospel reports Jesus as saying in Mark 10:19, when asked about inheriting eternal life. He answers with five of the Ten Commandments found in Deuteronomy, along with a sixth which is *not* among the Ten. "Thou knowest the commandments: Do not kill (Deut 5:17, Did # 1). Do not commit adultery (Deut 5:18, Did #2). Do not steal (Deut 5:19, Did #5). Do not bear false witness (Deut 5:20, Did #10). Do not defraud (μὴ ἀποστερήσῃς ~ Did #13 δόλος, *not in the Decalogue*). Honor thy father and mother" (Deut 5:16).[5] Jesus in Mark does not preach *himself*; he points to *the Law*, but in a simpler version, minus ceremonial observances like the Sabbath, minus Pharisaic purity complications, and with the addition of a rule against fraud.[6] The Two Ways list *also* prohibits fraud, and Jesus in Mark was thus developing an idea already present in contemporary Judaism. The difference from the Beta theology which was so strenuously preached by Paul (that people are saved by Jesus' death, not by their own works) is fundamental.

[1] For an argument for the later appearance of that doctrine, see Brooks **Resurrection**.

[2] See the argument in Harris **Teaching** 82f.

[3] For the recent recovery of the Didache text, see Niederwimmer 19-26.

[4] Recognized by O'Neill **Recovery** 65f; it interrupts a tirade against circumcision.

[5] Except for filial piety (not in Didache, last in Mark, but urged by Jesus elsewhere in Mark), these are cited in the same order in Deuteronomy, the Didache list, and by Jesus in Mk 10:39.

[6] It has OT precedent (often cited is Lev 6:1-7, but closer is Mal 3:5; Malachi is often quoted in Mark). The Markan Jesus seems to have been sensitive to economic injustice. This non-Ten commandment is suppressed in Mt 19:18-19 and Lk 18:20, probably as a Scripture correction.

The other versions of the Two Ways sin list can be seen to be adapted to the situation of the texts in which they appear. I will consider them in chronological order.

Mark 7:21-22. This follows Jesus' statement in 7:14f, that nothing from outside defiles (thus Pharisee purity rules are irrelevant), but only what comes from inside.[7] Mk 7:20, "And he said, What comes out of a man is what defiles a man." Then follows, in Mk 7:21-22, this list of sins that come from inside a man:

Didache 5:1	Mark 7:21-22
1. **murders** φόνοι	1. evil thoughts διαλογιμοὶ οἱ κακοὶ
2. **adulteries** μοιχεῖαι	2. **fornications** πορνεῖαι
3. lusts ἐπιθυμίαι	3. **thefts** κλοπαί
4. **fornications** πορνεῖαι	4. **murders** φόνοι
5. **thefts** κλοπαί	5. **adulteries** μοιχεῖαι
6. idolatries εἰδωλολατρίαι	6. **covetings** πλεονεξίαι
7. feats of magic μαγεῖαι	7. wickednesses πονηρίαι
8. sorceries φαρμακίαι	8. **deceit** δόλος
9. robberies ἁρπαγαί	9. lasciviousness ἀσέλγεια
10. false witness ψευδομαρτυρίαι	10. an evil eye ὀφθαλμὸς πονηρός
11. hypocrisies ὑποκρίσεις	11. railing βλασφημία
12. double-heartedness διπλοκαρδία	12. **pride** ὑπερηφανία
13. **deceit** δόλος	13. foolishness ἀφροσύνη
14. **pride** ὑπερηφανία	
15. malice κακία	
16. willfulness αὐθάδεια	
17. **coveting** πλεονεξία	
18. foul speech αἰσχρολογία	
19. jealousy ζηλοτυπία	
20. audacity θρασύτης	
21. hauteur ὕψος	
22. boastfulness ἀλαζονεία	

Half of the items on the Mark list have counterparts (here shown in **bold**) on the Didache list. The first four items common to both lists precede the second group of three; otherwise the items are rearranged. Absent are magic (Did #7-8) and crimes without obvious victims or crimes of intent (Did #12 "double-heartedness," #15 "malice," #16 "wilfulness," #20 "audacity," #22 "boastfulness"). Some Didache terms may be combined in Mark: robberies (Did #10) with theft (Did #5 = Mk 3) and haughtiness (Did #21) with pride (Did #14 = Mk #12). The Mark list is almost exclusively ethical. That was the point of the Mark passage in which this list occurs. It turns out that, for the Markan Jesus, sins are *wrongs against other people*.

The Mark list (c45) thus shows some innovation, and a changed idea of sin itself, to focus on actions with a social outcome. That stance is consonant with the economic justice implied by the commandment against fraud (Did #13 = Mk #8, above), which Jesus adds to his reduced Decalogue at Mk 10:19. From a mere presence in the Jewish Atonement prayer, it here gains greater prominence as part of Jesus' social doctrine.

---

[7]For the status of Mk 7:14-23, see in more detail Brooks **Perga** 100.

Galatians 5:13-6:10 interrupts Paul's tirade against circumcision to preach a doctrine of works which is at variance with Paul's doctrine of faith. It is then an interpolation.[8] It appears in all texts of Galatians, and is thus not a scribal corruption. It was most likely added when Paul's letters were edited, sometime after 70,[9] probably to heal the rift between Paul's Beta theory (its battle cry is Romans 3:20-24 and 4:1-3) and the Alphas (whose crisp rejoinder is in Jacob 2:18 and 2:20-24).

That Alpha interpolation lists these "sins of the flesh:"

Didache 5:1	Galatians 5:19-21a
1. murders φόνοι	1. **fornication** πορνεία
2. adulteries μοιχεῖαι	2. impurity ἀκαθαρσία
3. lusts ἐπιθυμίαι	3. licentiousness ἀσελγεια
4. **fornications** πορνεῖαι	4. **idolatry** εἰδωλολατρία
5. thefts κλοπαί	5. **sorcery** φαρμακεία
6. **idolatries** εἰδωλολατρία	6. enmities ἔχθραι
7. feats of magic μαγεῖαι	7. strife ἔρις
8. **sorceries** φαρμακίαι	8. **jealousy** ζῆλος
9. robberies ἁρπαγαί	9. anger θυμοί
10. perjuries ψευδομαρτυρίαι	10. selfishness ἐριθεῖαι
11. hypocrisies ὑποκρίσεις	11. divisions διχοσασίαι
12. double-heartedness διπλοκαρδία	12. sects αἱρέσεις
13. fraud δόλος	13. envyings φθόνοι
14. haughtiness ὑπερηφανία	14. drunkenness μέθαι
15. malice κακία	15. carousings κῶμοι
16. willfulness αὐθάδεια	. . . "and such like"
17. covetousness πλεονεξία	
18. foul speech αἰσχρολογία	
19. **jealousy** ζηλοτυπία	
20. audacity θρασύτης	
21. pride ὕψος	
22. boastfulness ἀλαζονεία	

The Galatians list has few terms in common with the Didache list, but those few are *in Didache order;* they may thus be seen as derived from that list. Civil crimes (murder or perjury) are absent. The rule against fornication is expanded (Gal #1-3). Worship of other gods is forbidden (Gal #4-5, both in Didache), perhaps reflecting the Jerusalem Agreement of early 44 (Acts 15:20, Did 6:3), with its prohibition of idol food. Most of the rest (Gal #6-13) warn of factions in the community, as do Paul's letters (such as 1 Cor 3:1f) and Alpha texts such as Jacob 3:6-4:12.

Barnabas 17 ends plausibly ("Let this, then, be enough"). The text then continues with a Beta-ized version of the Two Ways at 18:1 ("Let us now pass on to another kind of knowledge and instruction"). A 17-chapter version of Barnabas is attested in a 9c Latin manuscript preserved at St Petersburg;[10] it probably represents the original.

---

[8]For the secondary of Gal 5:13-6:10, see again O'Neill **Recovery** 65f.

[9]An editorial addition, 1 Thess 2:13-16, alludes to the destruction of the Temple in 70.

[10]Lake **Apostolic** 1/338.

Despite an initial expression of regard (Barn 1:1-3), Barnabas has no discernible address, and was probably meant as a general letter. In overall strategy, it somewhat resembles the pseudo-Pauline Epistle to the Hebrews. It focuses on the appropriation of Jewish tradition by Christians; among other things, it enjoins the building of a spiritual Temple for the Lord (Barn 16),[11] and ends by saying that nothing has been omitted which is "necessary for salvation" (Barn 17). It thus covers all the teachings which a Gospel might include, except that it is not *structured* as a life of Jesus. Barnabas accepts the Atonement doctrine, and is thus, theologically, a Beta document. Its allegorical style of argument, like that of Hebrews, is Alexandrian.

Barnabas 18-20 (the Two Ways addendum) includes a reference to the Atonement (19:2, "glorify him who ransomed you in death;" no parallel in the Didache version), adjusting the Alpha stance of the Two Ways to the Beta stance of the rest of Barnabas. Its list of sins differs in sequence from the Didache version:

Didache 5:1	Barnabas 20a-d
1. **murders** φόνοι (7)	1. **idolatry** εἰδωλολατρεία (6)
2. **adulteries** μοιχεῖαι (~ 6)	2. **audacity** θρασύτης (20)
3. lusts ἐπιθυμίαι (~ 6)	3. **pride** of power ὕψος δυνάμεως (~ 21)
4. fornications πορνεῖαι(~6)	4. **hypocrisy** ὑπόκρισις (11)
5. thefts κλοπαί	5. **double-heartedness** διπλοκαρδία (12)
6. **idolatries** εἰδωλολατρίαι (1)	6. **adultery** μοιχεία (2)
7. feats of **magic** μαγεῖαι (15)	7. **murder** φόνος (1)
8. **sorceries** φαρμακίαι (14)	8. **robbery** ἁρπαγή (9)
9. **robberies** ἁρπαγαί (8)	9. **haughtiness** ὑπερηφανία (14)
10. perjuries ψευδομαρτυρίαι	10. transgression παράβασις[12]
11. **hypocrisies** ὑποκρίσεις (4)	11. **fraud** δόλος (13)
12. **double-heartedness** διπλοκαρδία (5)	12. **malice** κακία (15)
13. **fraud** δόλος (11)	13. **willfulness** αὐθάδεια (16)
14. **haughtiness** ὑπερηφανία (9)	14. **sorcery** φαρμακεία (8)
15. **malice** κακία (12)	15. **magic** μαγεία (7)
16. **willfulness** αὐθάδεια (13)	16. **covetousness** πλεονεξία (17)
17. **covetousness** πλεονεξία (16)	17. lack of the fear of God αφοβία θεοῦ
18. foul speech αἰσχρολογία (~ 10)	
19. jealousy ζηλοτυπία (~ 6)	
20. **audacity** θρασύτης (2)	
21. **pride** ὕψος (~ 3)	
22. boastfulness ἀλαζονεία (~ 10)	

[11]Barn 16:4-5 "owing to the war it [the Temple] was destroyed by the enemy" makes plain that Barnabas is post-70. Harnack takes Barn 16:4b "at present even the servants of the enemy will build it up again" as a reference to the possibility (c130) of rebuilding the Temple under Roman auspices; Lightfoot **Apostolic** 241 argues otherwise. Barn 4:4 may allude to the Daniel 7:7f prophecy about ten kings subdued by one king; one opinion sees the tenth king as Vespasian (r 69-79). As with the seeming references to contemporary rulers in Revelation, attempts to date Barnabas by these hints have led in different directions.

[12]The term is Pauline (Gal 3:19; Rom 2:23, 4:15, 5:14) and deutero-Pauline (1 Tim 2:14, Heb 9:15). This agrees with the Pauline focus of Barnabas, noted above.

But though the Barnabas list rearranges and abbreviates the Didache list, in substance it is close to it. Specifics are:

- Three sexual offenses (Did #2-4) may have been combined under Barn #6
- Thefts and robberies (Did #5, 9) may have been combined under Barn #8
- Perjuries and fraud (Did #10, 13) may have been combined under Barn #11
- Whether foul speech (Did #18), jealousy (Did #19) and boastfulness (Did #22) may be included under the vague rubric "transgression" (Barn #10) is less clear.
- The category with which Barnabas concludes (lack of the fear of God, #17) is an innovation; it frames the sin of idolatry (Did #6) at the head of the Barnabas list.

The seemingly intentional rearrangements in Barnabas, and its abandonment of the original 22-item format, which is preserved in the Didache version, are conclusive evidence for the directionality Didache > Barnabas. This finding is in agreement with the unquestionably post-Pauline chronological position of Barnabas.

The Two Ways Archetype. So far we have considered only the original sin list. If we go beyond this to compare the Didache and Barnabas versions of the Two Ways tract as wholes, we find that certain parts of each have no counterpart in the other. The rearrangement of material in Barnabas is not confined to the order of items on the sin list; it also transposes material from one chapter to another, so that a full two-column comparison becomes hard to read.[13] But the major sections of the Didache Two Ways which have no clear counterpart in Barnabas are the following:

- Did 1:2b-6. The so-called "sectio evangelica," drawn in part from Matthew and Luke, with verses also from Sirach and other texts.[14]
- Did 3:1-6, the "fence" passage,[15] warns of actions which, though not themselves sinful, may lead to or be the occasion of sin. It represents a rabbinic-style development which is seen also in Matthew 5:21-30.
- Did 6:1-3. This, or part of it, is sometimes included in the Two Ways, but is better regarded as the original beginning of the Didache liturgical manual.[16]

Some Barnabas passages (Barn 19:2a (2), "Glorify him who redeemed you from death)" are not in the Didache version,[17] and are evidence for Beta adjustments in Barnabas. Excising these adjustments gives us our best view of the extended Two Ways tract before its incorporation into either Didache or Barnabas. The author of Barnabas then must have had had access to a pre-Didache form of the Two Ways, implying the survival of that whole tract, not just its sin list, outside the Didache.

[13]For one version of this difficult comparison, see Kraft 134-162.

[14]Also lacking in the Doctrina Apostolorum version. But see note at Did 1:2b, below.

[15]Kraft 146 quotes Pirqe Abot 1:1 "Make a fence around the Torah." This is probably the origin of certain Matthean additions to Luke's Sermon on the Plain (Mt 5:21-48).

[16]For that passage in place in the Didache, see Brooks **Didache** 50f.

[17]"Ransom/redeem" appears in the Didache only at 4:6, where it refers to good deeds counterbalancing evil deeds (for that concept, see Jacob 5:20 "cover a multitude of sins"). In the Didache Eucharist prayers (Did 9:2 "revealed," 9:3 "knowledge γνώσεως revealed," 10:2 "knowledge γνώσεως revealed") Jesus gives *knowledge* of the *way* of salvation (Mk 12:14, "Way of God"). Consistently, Mk 10:19 presents Jesus in the very act of "showing the way."

Independence. We have seen that the Mark, Galatians, and Barnabas lists are all later variants of the original order of the Core Prayer, which is best preserved in the Didache version. Is any of these later versions derived from, or influenced by, another? Or are they independent alterations of a common original? Here are the innovations in the three lists: sins which are not present in the Didache version of the Two Ways:

Mark 7:21-22

1. evil thoughts διαλογιμοὶ οἱ κακοὶ
7. wickednesses πονηρίαι
9. lasciviousness ασέλγεια
10. an evil eye ὀφθαλμὸς πονηρός
11. railing βλασφημία
13. foolishness ἀφροσύνη

Galatians 5:19-221a

2. impurity ἀκαθαρσία
3. licentiousness ἀσελγεια
6. enmities ἔχθραι
7. strife ἔρις
9. anger θυμοί
10. selfishness ἐριθείαι
11. divisions διχοσασίαι
12. sects αἱρέσεις
13. envyings φθόνοι
14. drunkenness μέθαι
15. carousings κῶμοι

Barnabas 20a-d

10. transgression παράβασις[18]
17. lack of the fear of God αφοβία θεοῦ

In a word, no innovation in one of these lists duplicates an innovation in another list. All should thus probably be seen as independently derived, in ways that suited the agenda of the several later writers, from the original Two Ways list.

This attests the pervasiveness of the Two Ways list in Christian consciousness through the first century. The Barnabas version of that list is especially interesting since Barnabas seems to have known the pre-Didache Two Ways *tract*,[19] whereas the Mark and Galatians versions are based on the sin *list*. This list, apart from the tract which later grew up around it, may have continued to be recited in Christian churches, just at it was recited in popular Jewish practice contemporary with Jesus. The version in Barnabas shows us the Two Ways as already expanded into a separate document, and in that form, continuing to enjoy an influential separate existence.

[18]For this term, see again n11. It is not only in its Beta theology that Barnabas is Pauline.

[19]If Barnabas was written in c130 (see n11, above), its author could have known the late (Mattheanized) Didache, but these divergences make the Didache version of the Two Ways a less likely source for Barnabas. It seems rather that both Barnabas and the Didache are seeing the original independent Christianized Two Ways tract.

Translation. Here then is the old Jewish prayer, expanded into a Christian tract.[20] I exclude those parts of the Didache version which are without parallel in Barnabas. These were probably additions inspired by the appearance of the Gospel of Matthew.[21] I note several similarities with another important early text, the Epistle of Jacob.

The Original Didache Two Ways

1:1. There are Two Ways, one of life and one of death, and there is a great difference between the two ways.

1:2a. On the one hand, the way of life is this: First, you love the God who made you; second, your neighbor as yourself.[22] [2b] On the other hand, as many things as you wish not to happen to you, do not do to another.[23]

2:1. And the second command of the Teaching: [2:2]. You will not murder, you will not commit adultery, you will not corrupt children, you will not have illicit sex, you will not steal, you will not practice magic, you will not practice sorcery, you will not murder a child by means of abortion, nor kill one that has been born; you will not desire the things of your neighbor, [2:3] You will not swear falsely, you will not bear false witness, you will not speak evil of anyone, you will not hold grudges. [2:4] You will not be double-minded or double-tongued, for being double-tongued is a snare of death. [2:5] Your word will not be false or empty, but will be fulfilled in action. [2:6] You will not be covetous, nor greedy, nor a hypocrite, nor spiteful, nor arrogant.[24] You will not plot an evil plan against your neighbor. [2:7] You will not hate any one, but some you will reprove, and for others you will pray, and some you will love more than your soul.

3:7a.[25] Be meek.[26] [3:8] Become long-suffering, and merciful, and harmless, and gentle, and good, and one who trembles always at the words that you have heard.[27] [3:9] You will not exalt yourself, and you will not give boldness to your soul. Your soul will not be joined with the haughty, but with just and lowly people you will dwell.[28]

3:10. You will accept the experiences that happen to you as good things,[29] knowing that apart from God, nothing happens.[30]

---

[20]Translation and some notes are drawn from Varner, with the permission of the author.

[21]For more detail on the Mattheanizing of the Didache, see Brooks **Didache**.

[22]Mk 12:28-31, Jesus' answer to the scribe's question about the greatest commandment.

[23]Did 1:2b is required by the Greek. Varner ascribes it to Matthew, but his Golden Rule (derived from Luke) is positive. The source is Analects 12:2 (cf *15:24). Later Western appearances are Tobit 4:15 (a Christian interpolation, not in Sinaiticus) and a legend of Hillel.

[24]Compare Ex 20:13-17 (Varner).

[25]Did 3:1-6, here omitted, are from the Matthean extensions of law in the Sermon on the Mount (Mt 5:21f), and are part of the final Mattheanizing of the text.

[26]Did 3:7b "for the meek shall inherit the earth" is an extension derived from the Beatitude for the Meek (Mt 5:5, no Lukan counterpart).

[27]Compare Isaiah 66:2 (Varner).

[28]Jacob 2:1, "My brethren, hold not the faith [of our Lord Jesus Christ, the Lord of Glory] with respect of persons." The egalitarianism of Jacob is one of its key traits.

[29]Jacob 1:2, "Count it all joy, my brethren, when ye fall into manifold temptations."

[30]Jacob 1:13, "Let no man say, when he is tempted, I am tempted of God, for God cannot be tempted with evil, and he himself tempteth no man."

4:1. My child, the one speaking to you the word of God you will remember night and day,[31] and you will honor him as the Lord. [4:2] And you will seek every day the presence of the saints in order that you may find support in their words. [4:3] You will not cause division, and you will reconcile those who quarrel; you will judge justly, you will not show favoritism when you reprove others for their failings.[32]

4:4. You will not become double-minded, [as to] whether it will be or not.[33]

4:5. Do not become one who, on the one hand, stretches out your hands to receive, or on the other hand, draws them back from giving. [4:6] If you should have something through the work of your hands, you will give it as a ransom for your sins.[34] [4:7] You will not hesitate to give, nor will you grumble when you give, for you know who will be the good paymaster of your reward. [4:8] You will not turn away the one in need, but you will share together all things with your brother, and you will not say that such things are your own, for if you are partners in what is immortal, how much more in mortal things?

4:9. You will not take away your hand from your son or from your daughter, but from youth you will teach them the fear of God.[35] [4:10] You will not command your male or female slave, who are hoping in the same God, in your bitterness, lest they should never fear the God who is over you both; for He does not come to call [to salvation] according to social status, but those whom the Spirit has prepared. [4:11] And you slaves, will be subject to your masters as to the image of God in shame and fear.[36]

4:12. You will hate all hypocrisy, and everything that is not pleasing to the Lord. [4:13] Never forsake the commandments of the Lord, but you will guard the things that you have received, neither adding nor subtracting anything.[37]

4:14. In church you will confess your wrongdoings, and you will not go to your place of prayer with an evil conscience.[38] This is the Way of Life!

---

[31]Compare Heb 13:7 (Varner).

[32]In the primitive Christian community, each member is in principle liable to judge others.

[33]Mk 11:23, "and shall not doubt in his heart, but shall believe that what he saith cometh to pass; he shall have it." Only sincere prayer has a result. Jacob 1:6-7, "But let him ask in faith, nothing doubting, . . . Let not that man think that he shall receive anything of the Lord." The sin here is not uncertainty as such, but lack of faith in God, including God's ability to do what he has promised. Compare the uncertain father of the epileptic boy in Mk 9:14-29.

[34]This is the only appearance of "ransom" in the text. Notice that it is not Jesus who ransoms sinners by his death, but the individual who ransoms *himself* from his sins by doing balancing good deeds. Jacob 5:19-20 ("My brethren, if any among you err from the truth, and one convert him, let him know, that he who converteth a sinner from the error of his way shall save a soul from death, and shall cover a multitude of sins"), *the final passage in that text*. This idea, that individuals can deal with their own sins, is common in later Buddhism, but is rare in early Christianity; these two being the only examples in canonical or paracanonical texts.

[35]This clause corresponds to Barn 19:5d; it may have inspired "lack of the fear of God" at Barn 20:1d (#17 on that list).

[36]Did 4:10-11 are somewhat reminiscent of Col 3:22-4:1 (and its later duplicate, Eph 6:5-9). Those who have felt that the Didache is a 2nd century text naturally conclude that Didache is the borrower, but it may also be that the widely circulated Didache influenced those who composed some of the deutero-Pauline material. I tentatively retain Did 4:10f as original.

[37]Varner cites Deut 4:2 or 12:32.

[38]Note the assumption that *prayer of itself brings forgiveness;* this is the whole logic of the original Jewish prayer on which the Two Ways as we know it is based. Compare Lk 18:13f.

5:1. The Way of Death, on the other hand, is this.

First of all, it is evil and full of accursedness:

1. murders,	5:2. B1. persecutors of the good,
2. adulteries,	B2. hating truth,
3. lusts,	B3. loving a lie,
4. fornications,	B4. not knowing the wages of righteousness,
5. thefts,	B5. not cleaving to the good,
6. idolatries,	B6. nor to just judgement,
7. feats of magic,	B7. those who are alert not for good but for evil,
8. sorceries,	B8. far from being gentle and patient,
9. robberies,	B9. loving empty things,
10. perjuries,	B10. pursuing retribution,
11. hypocrisies,	B11. not showing mercy to the poor,[39]
12. double-heartedness,	B12. not working for the oppressed,
13. fraud,	B13. not knowing the One who made them,[40]
14. arrogance,	B14. murderers of children,
15. malice,	B15. destroyers of what God has formed,
16. willfulness,	B16. turning away from one in need,
17. covetousness,	B17. oppressing the afflicted,
18. foul speech,	B18. advocates of the rich,
19. jealousy,	B19. unjust judges of the poor,
20. audacity,	B20. totally sinful
21. pride,	
22. boastfulness.	

The Two Ways is based on avoidance or forgiveness of sin. Later Christian texts would go on to develop its positive counterpart: *usefulness to others*.

Works Cited

E Bruce Brooks. The Didache. Alpha v1 (2017) 48-57

E Bruce Brooks. The Epistle of Jacob. Alpha v1 (2017) 58-70

E Bruce Brooks. Mark at Perga. Alpha v1 (2017) 99-103

E Bruce Brooks. Paul's Editors. Alpha v1 (2017) 121-126

E Bruce Brooks. The Resurrection of Jesus in Mark. Alpha v1 (2017) 81-88

E Bruce Brooks. Time Depth in Mark. Alpha v1 (2017) 73-80

J Rendel Harris. The Teaching of the Apostles. Johns Hopkins 1887

James A Kleist. The Didache [Ancient Christian Writers]. Paulist 1948

Robert A Kraft. The Didache and Barnabas [The Apostolic Fathers v3]. Nelson 1965

Kirsopp Lake. Apostolic Fathers I [Loeb]. Harvard 1912

J B Lightfoot. Apostolic Fathers. Macmillan 1891

J C O'Neill. The Recovery of Paul's Letter to the Galatians. SPCK 1972

Kurt Niederwimmer. The Didache. 2ed 2003; Fortress [Hermeneia] 1998

William Varner. The Way of the Didache. University Press of America 2007

William O Walker Jr. Evidence for Interpolation in Paul. Alpha v1 (2017) 17-22

[39]The enmity of rich and poor is a major theme in Jacob; see Brooks **Jacob** 58f.

[40]This echoes Did 1:2a, and confirms that passage as part of the original Didache.

The Didache

E Bruce Brooks

University of Massachusetts at Amherst

SBL/NE (Newton MA, 20 April, 2007)

The Epistle of Jacob[1] and the Didache ["Teachings"] are two surviving examples of guidance texts sent to the early churches. The Epistle is part of the NT canon, but the Didache, though it had been known to exist, was discovered only in 1873 by Archbishop Bryennios.[2] Discussion about its date centers on passages where the Didache is close to Matthew. Are they integral, in which case the text is post-Matthean and late? Or secondary, in which case its *earliest state* is pre-Matthean and thus early? I here argue that the Matthean elements in the Didache are secondary, and that the core attests an early form of Christian belief and practice, one which I have elsewhere[3] called Alpha, in contrast to the Beta Christianity preached by Paul.

Text. The chief witness is the Bryennios manuscript, written in 1056. Others are the POxy 1782 fragments (late 4c) and a 5c Coptic fragment (BrMus Or 9271) containing Did 10:3b-12:2a, probably an extract. The Didache, as we can now see, was incorporated, not without Beta additions, in Apostolic Constitutions 7 (late 4c). The long title of the Didache is "Teachings of the Twelve Apostles," and its inclusion in that compendium suggests its ongoing importance in the early churches.

Ending. The Didache consists of three parts: (1) Did 1-5, the Two Ways, originally a separate tract,[4] addressed to believers; (2) Did 6-15, a manual of instruction for administering sacraments and receiving Apostolic visitors, addressed to church leaders and organized by the itemizing formula perì dé; and (3) Did 16, the "Apocalypse," again addressed to believers and thus again contrasting with the central section. The Bryennios manuscript ends in the middle of a sentence, at 16:8a. Aldridge has noticed that the ApCon version of the Didache extends beyond that point, and seems to preserve verses lost from that manuscript. These I number as Did 16:8b-11.[5]

---

[1] For a detailed analysis and reconstruction, see Brooks **Jacob**.

[2] For details on this and other manuscripts, see Niederwimmer **Didache** 19-26.

[3] Brooks **Two** 39.

[4] For this part, see Brooks **Two**. The present study deals with the other two parts

[5] I follow Aldridge **Lost**, except that with support from Boniface, which lacks it, and since Aldridge himself (p10) suspects that it "may be a later addition," I regard his Did 16:12, "And they shall rejoice in the Kingdom of God, which is in Christ Jesus" (p15) as a Beta addition in ApCon. The preceding Did 16:11, the last line of the text, "to inherit those things which eye hath not seen, nor ear heard, nor have entered into the heart of man, such things as God hath prepared for them that love him," occurs also in 1 Cor 2:9, where it is treated as a quote. If, as I here argue, the Didache Apocalypse is late, it postdates 1 Cor, and doubtless derives from it. What Paul thought he was quoting is uncertain (Moffatt, following Jerome, suggests a free rendition of Isaiah 64:4; Fitzmyer considers and rejects this and several other possibilities).

With these adjustments, the Didache originally ended this way:[6]

16:8a. Then the world will see the Lord coming upon the clouds of Heaven,
[8b] the angels of his power, in the throne of his kingdom,

16:9. To condemn the Devil, the deceiver of the world, and to render to every one *according to his deeds*.

16:10. Then shall the wicked go away into everlasting punishment, but *the righteous shall enter eternal life*,

16:11. to inherit those things which eye hath not seen, nor ear heard, nor have entered into the heart of man, such things as God has prepared for them that love him.[7]

Given the probably secondary nature of this Matthean Apocalypse at the end, and the special character of the Two Ways tract at the beginning (and since both are addressed to believers rather than to church leaders), it is probable that the part in the middle, which provides liturgical guidance for local church leaders, is the original Didache. From here on, I will focus on that probably original Didache.

Form. The liturgical section of the Didache (6:1-15:4) falls into two parts, a first part organized by the itemizing formula perì dé ("as for, now concerning"),[8] and a second part where that idiom does not occur. The first perì dé passage, 6:3, deals with permissible food. The last perì dé marker is at 11:3 ("Now concerning apostles and prophets"). But where does that passage end? We may notice the contradiction between *forbidding* long residence of apostles in Did 11:5 ("But if ever he should remain three [days], he is a false prophet") and *allowing* it in Did 12:3 ("but if, on the other hand, he wishes to settle down among you"). Then somewhere between 11:5 and 12:3 should come the break between the original "perì dé ordered list and the later additions, which lack that idiom. 12:3 ("if, on the other hand") is linked to 12:2 ("if, on the one hand"), and so 12:2 must also be outside the perì dé zone. The original "apostles" guideline then seems to end at 12:1. It makes a very satisfactory conclusion:

12:1. And everyone coming in the name of the Lord,
Let him be received, and then, having put him to the test,
You will know, for you will have understanding of right and left.

In other words, the local leaders, instructed by the preceding counsel, will be able to judge for themselves whether their visitor is after all a false apostle.[9]

---

[6]In these lines, I italicize a distinctive Alpha tenet: the role of good vs evil deeds at the Last Day (see Brooks **Two**; **Jacob** passim). Faith vs works as the key to salvation was at issue between Paul in Romans 3:20-24, 4:1-3 and Jacob at 2:18, 2:20-24.

[7]tr Aldridge. Varner 100 arrives at a slightly different solution of the ending problem.

[8]Also used as an organizing principle in 1 Cor, where it marks answers to questions raised by the Corinthians ("now concerning the matters about which you write), at 7:1 (sex and marriage), 7:25 (the unmarried), 8:1 (food offered to idols), 12:1 (spiritual gifts), 16:1 (the collection for Jerusalem), and 16:12 (the visit of Apollos). Mitchell **Concerning** has shown that this topic marker need not imply a previous list of questions, rather, it introduces "a new topic, the only requirement of which is that it is readily known to both writer and reader" (p236). That will nicely cover the case in the Didache. It does not lessen the likelihood that authoritative guidance on these subjects was much desired by the leaders of the local churches.

[9]Here, I suggest, are the "false Christs" of whom the Markan Jesus warns in Mk 13:5-6.

Matthean parallels exist at several points in this section. They can be excised without damage to continuity, and I suggest that they were added later, in order to keep the text current with Matthew, which, as things appeared to the proprietor[10] of the Didache, had by then become the authoritative account of Jesus. Thus we have phrases like "as the Lord commanded in his Gospel" (Did 8:2, followed by the Matthean version of the Lord's Prayer), or "As the Lord has said concerning this" (followed by Jesus' comment "Do not give dogs what is holy," unique in Mt 7:6). Note, however, that the text also regards Old Testament pronouncements as Words of the Lord; thus we have as part of one Eucharistic prayer, following mention of God's servant Jesus, the line "To you is the glory forever," which is from Isaiah 52:13.[11]

How does one prove the secondarity of the Matthew echoes? One way is to give the text *without* the Mattheanisms, to see if it stands on its own without them, or if they are instead the framework on which the rest of the text has been assembled. I carry out that experiment below, the Mattheanisms being set at the right margin.

Does everyone realize the importance of the moment at which we have arrived? Here is one of the oldest documents in Christianity, distributed to the house churches to guide them in their relations with the occasional apostolic visitors, and in the correct handling of regular observances: baptism, the Eucharistic remembrance, and the issue (always present when Jews and Gentile synagogue-followers met together) of what foods were acceptable. As we watch this advice being given, we can get an idea of how these churches were organized, what they did, and what they awaited.

———————··•··———————

The Core Didache[12]

The perì dé itemization markers are printed in **bold**; subheads have been supplied.

[INTRODUCTORY WARNING]

6:1. See to it that no one leads you astray from this way of teaching, since he is teaching you apart from God.[13]

6:2. For, on the one hand, if you are able to bear the whole yoke of the Lord, you will be perfect, But if, on the other hand, you are not able, that which you are able, do this.[14]

---

[10]I use "proprietor" to denote the person in charge of the text: composing it, sending it out, and updating it from time to time as might be necessary.

[11]The Jesus-centeredness of the early Jesus movement is largely a myth of the later Jesus movement. The prophets of old were not thought to be speaking for themselves, but for God, and Jesus, regarded as a prophet by his followers, was also seen as speaking the word of God.

[12]With the author's permission, the translation here used is that of William Varner.

[13]The early churches, with their Jewish background and their still-Jewish orientation, felt that they were *obeying the will of God*, not that they were following commands of Jesus.

[14]The "whole yoke of the Lord" is the full requirements of Jewish law, including the purity rules which the Markan Jesus so clearly opposed. The Didache takes what might be called a middle view: Do all you can, but at least the minimum. Two examples then follow.

[FOOD]

6:3. **Concerning Food**, bear that which you are able,[15] but from the food sacrificed to idols, especially keep away, for it is the worship of dead gods.

[BAPTISM]

7:1. **Concerning Baptism**,[16] baptize this way. After you have said all these things beforehand, immerse in the name of the Father, and of the Son, and of the Holy Spirit[17] in flowing water. [7:2] But if you[18] do not have flowing water, immerse in another water, and if you are not able to so in cold, in warm; [7:3] and if you should have neither, pour water on the head three times in the name of the Father, and of the Son, and of the Holy Spirit.

[FASTS][19]

8:1. [Rules on Fasting, cf Mt 6:16][20]

[PRAYER]

8:2-3. [Rules on Prayer, cf Mt 6:9-13][21]

[THE THANKSGIVING MEAL]

9:1. **Concerning the Thanksgiving Meal**, give thanks this way. [9:2] First, concerning the cup: "We give you thanks, our Father, for the holy vine of your servant David, which you revealed to us through your servant Jesus.[22] To you is the glory forever."

---

[15]The implication is that Jewish food laws apply by default, but are no longer crucial; the important thing is to avoid anything that might be construed as worship of other gods. This is essentially the ruling given in Luke's version (Ac 15:20, 29) of the Jerusalem conference.

[16]As in 1 Peter, which with Beare and others I regard as in origin a baptismal homily, the Christian life begins with baptism, considered not only as a symbolic purification from sin (the tradition of John the Baptist), but also as a rite of Christian entry. It is thus entirely appropriate as the first part of this section of the Didache, which gives instruction to local church leaders.

[17]This "Trinitarian" formula, here and in Mt 28:19, has been much discussed. Mt 28:11-20 is Matthew's replacement for the missing ending of Mark (which by Mk 14:28 and 16:7 featured an appearance of Jesus in Galilee); it contradicts Matthew's main narrative, in which Jesus appears in Jerusalem (for Jerusalemization in the Gospels, see Brooks **Four** 12). John's baptism was a sign of reconciliation with God; the addition of Jesus, as guiding from Heaven, is present already in Mk 13:31 (cf Mt 28:29, "Lo, I am with you always"); baptism in the Spirit is present in Mk 1:8 ∥ Mt 3:11. The later homoousia discussion (the degree of identity between Jesus and God) is not in view, and there is no reason to see this formula as anything but early Jesus tradition. Perhaps it was such an early tradition that was drawn on by Matthew in trying to envision, in Mt 28:11-20, what Mark might have said in his missing ending.

[18]The "you" in Did 7:1 is singular; in 7:2-4 it is plural. This has been thought to imply a complex history of Didache baptismal advice (Garrow **Dependence** 94f, with reconstruction). I do not regard this as a necessary inference.

[19]There was no original Didache topic for fasts. The rule on fasting before baptism was part of the instructions for baptism; the later material was thus inserted into the baptism section.

[20]Note the recurrent motif of permissible relaxation of a known ideal procedure.

[21]The Matthean form of the Lord's Prayer is followed by a line not in Matthew: "For yours is the power and the glory forever." Varner 48f notes that this "doxology" or ascription of glory recurs at Did 9:3 and 10:5, and concludes that it is "similar to a common ending to prayers in the Jewish liturgy that survive until today." It may be ascribed to the Didache author himself.

[22]Note that in this formula, Jesus is the one whose teaching *revealed* the way to salvation, not, as in later Beta Christian doctrine, the one whose death *achieved* salvation for believers.

9:3. **And Concerning the Broken Bread**: "We give you thanks, our Father, for the life and knowledge[23] which you revealed to us through your servant Jesus. To you is the glory forever." [9:4] "Just as this bread was scattered over the mountains, and was gathered together and became one,[24] in this way may your church be gathered together from the ends of the earth into your Kingdom. Because yours is the glory and the power, through Jesus Christ forever." [9:5] And let no one eat or drink from your thanksgiving meal except those baptized in the name of the Lord.

For also the Lord has said concerning this:
"Do not give what is holy to the dogs" [Mt 7:6][25]

10:1. And after being filled, give thanks in this way: [10:2] We give you thanks, holy Father, for your holy name, which you have caused to dwell in our hearts, and for the knowledge and faith and immortality which you revealed to us through your servant Jesus. To you is the glory forever. [10:3] You, almighty Master, created all things for the sake of your name. Both food and drink you have given to people for enjoyment, in order that they might give thanks. But to us you have graciously bestowed spiritual food and drink and eternal life through your servant. [10:4] Before all things, we give you thanks because you are powerful; to you is the glory forever.

10:5. Remember, Lord, your church, to save her from every evil, and to perfect her in your love, and to gather her together from the four winds,[26] the sanctified into your Kingdom which you prepared for her; Because yours is the power and the glory forever.

10:6. May grace come, and may this world pass away! Hosanna to the God of David![27] If anyone is holy, let him come! If anyone is not, let him repent! Maranatha![28] Amen!

---

[23]The nonmention of the blood of Jesus is crucial to the position. Jesus is important to this Jewish sect because, amid the many Jewish rules, he has indicated what is essential to salvation. It is at this point that Gnostic Christianity diverges. The Gnostics, like the Alpha Christians, did not believe in a Resurrection, and still less in an Atonement interpretation of Jesus' death. The Alphas sought to escape this troublesome world; so did they. Where the Gnostics differed was in rejecting the Second Coming of Jesus and the final one-time End of the World, and seeking instead an individual escape from a world which they regarded as evil. The Antichrist myth (a personification of the evil presiding over this world) may represent the influence of early Gnostic conceptions on the mainstream; its first appearance in the canon is at 2 Thess 2:6-12.

[24]The ingathering of the saved at the Last Day is already present in Mk 13:27.

[25]A not wholly appropriate later insertion of an admittedly striking Matthean phrase.

[26]This is usually referred to Mt 24:31, but the "four winds" of Mk 13:27 will suffice.

[27]The promise to David was part of Jesus' Messianic claim; he argues in Mk 12:35f that the Messiah need not be a descendant of David (as Jesus was not; popular enthusiasm later had its way, and Matthew and Luke give Jesus a genealogy reaching back to David). Says one after Jesus' death, "we had hoped that he was the one to redeem Israel" (Lk 24:21); one who sees him restored to life asks, "Lord, will you at this time restore the kingdom to Israel?" (Ac 1:6).

[28]In the Greek original, μαρὰνἀθά. This is the Aramaic ejaculation prayer "Come, Lord," hoping for the return of Jesus. The return of Jesus, and the appearance of the End Days, was the core of early Christian expectation. It is sobering to realize that this central prayer of the early churches is almost unknown in extant texts. Paul, cursing (anathema) the Alpha Christians in 1 Cor 16:22, follows up with μαραναθά in 16:23 (the only time in the NT when this prayer occurs in its Aramaic form), as if to say, "May the Lord indeed come, and condemn you for your errors." The prayer appears in translated form in Rev 22:20, its only other NT appearance.

10:7. But allow the prophets to give thanks as much as they wish.[29]

11: 1. Therefore, whoever teaches you all these things said previously, receive him. [11:2] If, on the other hand, the one teaching, if he has been turned, and should teach another doctrine for the destroying [of these things], do not listen to him. But if it is for the bringing of righteousness and knowledge of the Lord, receive him as the Lord![30]

[VISITING APOSTLES]

11:3. **Concerning the Apostles and Prophets** in accord with the decree of the gospel,[31] act thus:

11:4. Every apostle coming to you, let him be received as the Lord, [5] but he will not remain except for one day, and if there is need, also another, but if ever he should remain three, he is a false prophet. [6] And when he departs, let the apostle take nothing except bread [that he needs] until he is [next] lodged. If, however, he asks for money, he is a false prophet.[32]

11:7. And every prophet speaking in the Spirit you should not test or judge, for every sin will be forgiven, but this sin will not be forgiven.[33] [8] But not everyone speaking in the Spirit is a prophet, but only if he has the behavior of the Lord. Therefore, from their behavior will be known the false prophet and the prophet.

11:9. And every prophet ordering a table in the Spirit, will not eat from it, but if he does, he is a false prophet. [10] And every prophet teaching the truth, if he does not do what he preaches, he is a false prophet. [11] And every prophet who has been put to the test and is genuine, and who acts for the earthly mystery of the church, but not teaching to do what he himself does, he shall not be judged by you, for he has his judgement from God, for so the ancient prophets also acted.

11:12. But whosoever should say in the Spirit, "Give me silver," or any other thing, you will not listen to him. But if he should say to give to others in need, let no one judge him.

12:1. And everyone coming in the name of the Lord, let him be received, and then, having put him to the test, you will know, for you will have understanding of right and left.

We may pause here to note the end of the text as it originally existed. Its last word on its last subject (the reception of visiting apostles) in effect turns the question over to the locals: they must now handle it themselves. Later came an extension, providing guidance for the case of the apostle (one thinks of Paul) who chooses to stay longer.

---

[29]Fixed prayers should not inhibit the prayers of inspired persons, as in Paul's churches.

[30]This anticipates the next section, on receiving apostles. Its concern for "another doctrine" is new, since only practice, not doctrine in the usual sense, has so far been set forth.

[31]Not here a written text, but the teaching as apostolically preached. For this general use of the word, see Mk 1:14f, 10:29, 13:10, and 14:9.

[32]The apostles are not to carry money, but to rely on local hospitality (Mk 6:8).

[33]Denial of the Holy Spirit is the unforgivable sin in Mk 3:29. (The wording in Mt 12:32 is slightly, but I believe trivially, closer).

The Didache Extension
This material is not organized by perì dé markers, and is thus later than the preceding.

[THE RESIDENT APOSTLE]
12:2. If, on the one hand, the one coming is passing through, help him as much as you are able. He will not remain, however, among you except for two or three days, if there should be a need. [3] If, on the other hand, he wishes to settle down among you, and if he is a craftsman, let him work and let him eat.[34] [4] If, on the other hand, he does not have a craft, according to your own understanding, plan beforehand how he will live among you as a Christian, without being idle. [5] If, on the other hand, he does not wish to behave in this way, he is a Christ-peddler. Beware of such ones!

13:1. And every genuine prophet wishing to settle down among you is worthy of his food.

> [2] Likewise, a genuine teacher is worthy,
> just as the laborer, of his food [Mt 10:10][35]

13:3. So you shall take every first fruits of the produce from the wine vat and threshing floor, of both cattle and sheep, and you will give the first fruits to the prophets, for they themselves are your high priests. [4] But if you do not have a prophet, give it to the poor. [5] But if you should make bread, take the first fruits and give according to the commandment.[36] [6] Similarly, when you open a jar of wine or oil, take the first fruits, and give it to the prophets. [7] And of silver and of clothing and of every possession, take the first fruits, as it seems good to you, and give according to the commandment.

[A CEREMONY OF RECONCILIATION]
14:1. And on the Lord's Day of the Lord,[37] when you are gathered together, break bread and give thanks, having before confessed your failings, so that your sacrifice may be pure. [2] However, let no one having a conflict with his comrade come together with you, until they have been reconciled,

> In order that your sacrifice may not be defiled [Mt 5:23-24].[38]

[3] for this [sacrifice] is that which was spoken by the Lord, "In every place and time, offer to me a pure sacrifice, because I am a great King," says the Lord, "and my name will be wondrous among the Gentiles" [Mal 1:11, 14].[39]

[APPOINTED LOCAL AUTHORITIES]
15:1. Appoint then, for yourselves, overseers and deacons worthy of the Lord,[40] gentle men, and not money lovers, and truthful and tested, for they likewise conduct among you the ministry of the prophets and teachers. [2] Do not then look down upon them, for they themselves are your honored ones, along with the prophets and teachers.

---

[34]Work is exactly what Paul did. He continually emphasizes that, during his longer stays, he has not been a burden on his hosts (1 Thess 2:9, 1 Cor 9:3-7).

[35]The intruded Matthean quote merely echoes the preceding Didache line.

[36]This is a reference to the conventional Jewish practice of alms-giving.

[37]For this curious locution, see Tidwell **Didache XIV:1** (1999).

[38]The Matthean quote in 14:2b merely underlines what was already complete in 14:1.

[39]Malachi is frequently quoted in the early texts; including the earliest of them, Mk 1:2.

[40]See Php 1:1 for these offices, and 1 Tim 3:2-10 for many of the qualifications listed here.

[INTERNAL DISCIPLINE]

15:3. And correct one another, not in anger but in peace.

As you have it in the Gospel [Mt 18:15-18].[41]

And to everyone wronging another, let no one speak to him, nor let anyone hear from you about him, until he repents.

[4] And do your prayers and alms and all your actions as you have it from the Gospel of our Lord [Mt 6:1-4, 5-15].[42]

———————•••••———————

Like the Epistle of Jacob, not to mention Jude [Judas], the extended Didache ends with a comment on the erring brother. Still later there was added an Apocalypse, partly based on Matthew,[43] perhaps an attempt to make the text complete by giving advice on an urgent question: the end of the world.[44] Here is that added Apocalypse:

16:1. Be watchful over your life; do not let your lamps be quenched, and do not let your waists be unguarded [Mt 25:8, Lk 12:35?]. But be prepared, for you do not know the hour in which our Lord is coming [Mk 24:42]. [16:2] And frequently be gathered together, seeking what is appropriate for your souls, for the whole time of your faith will not benefit you unless you are perfected in the end time. [16:3] For in the last days, the false prophets and corrupters will be multiplied, and the sheep will be turned into wolves, and love will be turned into hatred. [16:4] For when lawlessness increases, they will hate each other and they will persecute and they will betray each other [Mt 24:10-12]. Then will appear the world-deceiver as a son of God, and he will do signs and wonders [Mt 24:24], and the earth will be delivered into his hands, and he will do unlawful things that never have happened from eternity. [16:5] Then the human creation will come into the fiery test, and many will be led into sin and will perish, but the ones remaining firm in their faith will be saved [Mt 24:10, 13) by the curse itself. [16:6] And then the signs of the truth will appear [Mt 24:30]: first, a sign of an opening in heaven, then a sign of a trumpet sound [Mt 24:30, 1 Thess 4:16], and the third sign will be a resurrection of dead ones, [16:7] but not of all [the dead], but as it was said, "The Lord will come and all the holy ones with him" [Zech 14:5, 1 Thess 3:13]. [16:8a] Then the world will see the Lord coming atop the clouds of Heaven [Mt 24:30, 26:64, Dan 7:13].

[16:8b][45] . . . with the angels of his power, in the throne of his kingdom, [16:9] to condemn the Devil, the deceiver of the world, and to render to every one according to his deeds. [16:10] Then shall the wicked go away into everlasting punishment, but the righteous shall enter eternal life, [16:11] to inherit those things which eye hath not seen, nor ear heard, nor have entered into the heart of man, such things as God has prepared for them that love him.

Thus we reach the end of the final form of the Didache.

---

[41]A merely decorative reference to Matthew. The wording in 2 Tim 2:25 is actually closer.

[42]This Matthean quote is however integral; it brings the Didache section to an end.

[43]For that argument, see Verheyden **Eschatology** 214-215.

[44]"By the curse itself." On problems as their own solution, see Jacob 1:2-4.

[45]This is the portion supplied by Aldridge, given in his translation.

Date

The Didache core advises churches on conducting ceremonies between Apostolic visits. The first section of the core shares the decision on food prohibitions which there is reason to believe was promulgated from Jerusalem in the year 44,[46] and that section may thus be dated to that year. What about the rest of the core? In the Epistle of Jacob, general advice is also preceded by what looks like a response to a particular situation:

Jacob Sections[47]	Didache "peri de" Sections
§2. **Response to Persecution**	§2 (6:3). **Food rules**
§3. Avoid personal friction	§3 (7:1). Baptism
§4. Avoid social distinctions	§4 (9:1). The thanksgiving meal
§5. Avoid doctrinal differences	§5 (9:2). The Cup
§6. Together await the End	§6 (9:3). The Bread
§7. Mutual support	§7 (11:3). Apostles and Prophets

It seems likely that the §2 parts of both texts were later additions, placed first because of their urgency and importance. The Did 6:1-2 introduction (§1) echoes advice at the end (11:33-12:1) on the distinguishing of true from false Apostles. The two together framed the Didache core, and continued to do so after the addition of Did 6:3.

The end of the Didache extension, Did 15:1-2, deals with self-governance, the choosing of bishops and deacons *from among the church members*. The qualities looked for in Did 15:1-2 may be compared to passages in two of the Pastoral Epistles:

> **Did 15:1**. Appoint then for yourselves bishops and deacons worthy of the Lord: **gentle** men and **not money lovers** ἀφιλαργύρους and truthful and **tested**.

> **Titus 1:5** . . . and appoint elders in every city, as I gave thee charge; [6] if any man is blameless, the husband of one wife, having children that believe, who are not accused of riot or unruly. [7] For the bishop must be blameless, as God's steward, not self-willed, not soon angry, no brawler, not greedy of filthy lucre αἰσχροκερδῆ, [8] but given to hospitality, a lover of good, sober minded, just, holy, self-controlled, holding to the faithful word which is according to the teaching, that he may be able to both exhort in the sound doctrine and to convict the gainsayers.

> **1 Tim 3:2**. The bishop therefore must be without reproach, the husband of one wife, temperate, sober-minded, orderly, given to hospitality, apt to teach, [3] no brawler, no striker, but **forbearing**, not contentious, **no lover of money** ἀφιλάργυρον; [4] one that ruleth well his own house, having [his] children in subjection with all gravity . . . [6] not a novice . . . [8] Deacons in like manner must be grave, not double-tongued, not given to much wine, not greedy of filthy lucre, [9] holding the mystery of the faith in a pure conscience. [10] And let these also first be **proved**, then let them serve as deacons.

1 Timothy retains some details from Titus and adds others. It is in the added 1 Timothy details, not those inherited from Titus, that contacts with the Didache qualities occur. The Didache has thus skipped the second Pastoral, and made contact with the third.[48]

---

[46]For the date and nature of this important event, see Brooks **Jerusalem** 109.

[47]This list, with the addition of §2, is summarized from that in Brooks **Jacob** 69.

[48]See Easton **Pastoral** 17f for the sequence 2 Tim > Tit > 1 Tim.

The Didache thus (1) begins as a guide to church elders, Did 6:1-2, 7:1-12:1; (2) inserts 6:3, a line announcing the Jerusalem ruling of the year 44; (3) adds 12:2-14:3, on apostles who stay beyond three days, to provide for extended visits such as those of Paul in the 50's; (4) preposes the ethical Two Ways tract, perhaps in response to the cessation of Jacob's newsletter after 57; (5) adds 15:1-3 on church self-government, which has points of contact with the post-Pauline Pastoral Epistles of the 70's; and (6) adds a Matthean Apocalypse at the end, imitating the two new Gospels, and making the Didachd itself a sort of Gospel, with Matthean and Lukan touches throughout.

The Didache formation process might then look something like this:

40's	original ceremonial core	Did 6:1-2 7:1-12:1
45	food rule update inserted	Did 6:3
50's	deals with apostles remaining longer	Did 12:2-14:3
c60?	adds ethical Two Ways tract at beginning	Did 1-5
c75?	prescribes for church self-government	Did 15:1-3
c80?	adds Apocalypse; general Mattheanizing	Did 16 etc

Forty years is possible, but it is a long time for one person to be in charge of a text. Perhaps the Didache was, or became, an institutional enterprise. As to his (or its) location, anything between Ephesus and Syria could explain the external affinities.

Works Cited

Robert E Aldridge. The Lost Ending of the Didache. VC v53 (1999) 1-15

E Bruce Brooks. Four Gospel Trajectories. Alpha v1 (2017) 15-16

E Bruce Brooks. The Epistle of Jacob. Alpha v1 (2017) 58-70

E Bruce Brooks. Jerusalem and Paul. Alpha v1 (2017) 104-109

E Bruce Brooks. The Two Ways. Alpha v1 (2017) 39-47

Burton Scott Easton. The Pastoral Epistles. Scribner 1947

Joseph A Fitzmyer. First Corinthians. Yale 2008

Alan J P Garrow. The Gospel of Matthew's Dependence on the Didache. Clark 2004

J Rendel Harris. The Teaching of the Apostles. Johns Hopkins 1887

Clayton N Jefford (ed). The Didache in Context. Brill 1995

C N Jefford and S J Patterson. A Note on Didache 12:2a (Coptic). Second Century 7 (1989-90) 65-75

F Stanley Jones and Paul A Mirecki. Considerations on the Coptic Papyrus of the Didache; in Jefford **Didache** 47-87

James A Kleist. The Didache [Ancient Christian Writers #6]. Paulist 1948

Margaret M Mitchell. Concerning περι δε in 1 Corinthians. NovT v31 (1989) 229-256

Jerome Murphy-O'Connor. 2 Timothy Contrasted with 1 Timothy and Titus. RB v98 (1991) 403-418

Kurt Niederwimmer. The Didache. 2ed 1993; Fortress [Hermeneia] 1998

Neville L A Tidwell. Didache XIV:1 (ΚΑΤΑ ΚΥΡΙΑΚΗΝ ΔΕ ΚΥΡΙΟΥ) Revisited. VC v53 (1999) 197-207

Huub van de Sandt (ed). Matthew and the Didache. Royal van Gorcum 2005

William Varner. The Way of the Didache. University Press of America 2007

Joseph Verheyden. Eschatology in the Didache and the Gospel of Matthew; in van de Sandt **Matthew** 193-215

The Epistle of Jacob

E Bruce Brooks

University of Massachusetts at Amherst

SBL/ New England (Newton MA, 20 Apr 2007)

This letter of advice to churches has been called Jewish and Christian; it is now collegial, now abusive; it meanders thematically. Efforts have been made to clarify it by dividing it into sections. I construe it as overlaid by later authorial additions. Three topics are notably suspect: (1) rich versus poor, (2) hearing versus doing; or in effecrt, faith versus works, and (3) complaints against the tongue. They occur at more than one place, they interrupt their context, and they sometimes use strong language.

1. Rich versus Poor

This first appearance of the rich (note "so also shall the rich man") is mild enough, but even it interrupts a discourse on the acceptance of persecution:

> Ja 1:2. Count it all joy, my brethren, when ye fall into manifold **temptations**, [3] knowing that the proving of your faith worketh patience . . . [7] For let not that man think that he shall receive anything of the Lord, [8] a doubleminded man, unstable in all his ways.
>
> > [9] But let the brother of low degree glory in his high estate, [10] and the rich, in that he is made low, because as the flower of the grass he shall pass away [11] For the sun ariseth with the scorching wind and withereth the grass and the flower thereof falleth, and the grace of the fashion of it perisheth; so also shall the rich man fade away in his goings.[1]
>
> [12] Blessed is the man that endureth **temptation**, for when he hath been approved, he shall receive the crown of life . . .

Ja 1:12 resumes the topic of Ja 1:8 – understanding and enduring persecution.

---

[1] Ja 1:9-11 is treated as a section (not, let me emphasize, as an interpolation) by Ropes, Moffatt, Dibelius, Easton, Reicke, Balz/ Schrage, Laws, Davids, Wall, Moo, and Hartin.

In Ja 2:1f, rich and poor are members of the same congregation, and are cautioned against social prejudice. Into that gentle advice, there intrudes a sudden note of hatred:

Ja 2:1. My brethren, hold not the faith[2] with **respect of persons**. [2] For if there come into your synagogue a man with a gold ring, in fine clothing, and there come in also a poor man in vile clothing, [3] and ye have regard to him that weareth the fine clothing . . . [4] do ye not make distinctions among yourselves, and become judges with evil thoughts? [5] Hearken, my beloved brethren, did not God choose them that are poor as to the world to be rich in faith, and heirs of the Kingdom which he promised to them that love him? [6a] but ye have dishonored the poor man.

[6b] Do not the rich oppress you, and themselves drag you before the judgement seats? [7] Do they not blaspheme the honorable Name by which ye are called?

[8] Howbeit, if ye fulfil the royal law, according to the Scripture, Thou shalt love thy neighbor as thyself, ye do well, [9] but if ye have **respect of persons**, ye commit sin, being convicted by the law as transgressors . . .[3]

The main text argues against **respect of persons** in the community. Ja 2:6b-7 does not; it curses the rich as outsiders and blasphemers. It is intrusive in context, and is thus presumptively late. Ja 2:1-6a / 8-9f, into which it intrudes, is presumptively earlier.

In Ja 4:13-5:6 there suddenly comes a long denunciation of the merchants:

Ja 4:12b. But who are thou that **judgest thy neighbor**?

[13] Come now, ye that say, Today or tomorrow we will go into this city, and spend a year there, and trade, and get gain, [14] whereas ye know not what shall be on the morrow . . .[5:1] Come now, ye rich, weep and howl for your miseries that are coming upon you . . . [4] Behold, the hire of the laborers who mowed your fields, which is of you kept back by fraud, crieth out, and the cries of them that reaped have entered into the ears of the Lord of Sabaoth. [5] Ye have lived delicately on the earth, and taken your pleasure; ye have nourished your hearts in a day of slaughter. [6] Ye have condemned, ye have killed, the righteous one; he doth not resist you.[4]

[7] Be patient therefore, brethren, until the coming of the Lord. Behold, the husbandman waiteth for the precious fruit of the earth, being patient over it, until it receive the early and latter rain. [8] Be ye also patient; establish your hearts, for the coming of the Lord is at hand. [9] Murmur not, brethren, one against another, **that ye be not judged**; behold, the Judge standeth before the doors. [10] Take, brethren, for an example of suffering and patience, the prophets who spake in the name of the Lord. [11] Behold, we call them blessed that endured . . .

A speech against **judging** is here interrupted by a tirade against the rich.

---

[2]Ja 2:1b ["of our Lord Jesus Christ, the Lord of Glory"], with 1:1b ["and of the Lord Jesus Christ"], the only two mentions of Jesus in the Epistle, are probably post-authorial additions meant to qualify the Epistle for the emerging Christian canon. See Spitta 7-8, Mayor cxc-cxcv, Easton 20f.

[3]For the reference of Ja 2:8 back to 2:6a, see Dibelius 141f. Ja 2:6b-7 are treated as a unit by Dibelius, Laws, and Moo.

[4]For a classic expression of oppression of the righteous poor by the wicked rich, see Psa 10.

With these faults of the rich in mind, we may turn back to 4:1-10, which like 4:13f condemns the pursuit of wealth as enmity with God, and like the milder 1:9-11 contrasts the coming exaltation of the poor with the coming humiliation of the rich. That passage occurs in a context reproving criticism and enmity among brothers:

> Ja 3:17. But the wisdom that is from above is first pure, then peaceable; gentle, easy to be entreated, full of mercy and good fruits, without variance, without hypocrisy. [18] And the fruit of righteousness is sown in **peace** for them that make peace.
>
>> [4:1] Whence come wars and whence fightings among you? Come they not hence, of your pleasures that war in your members? [2] Ye lust, and have not; ye kill and covet and cannot obtain, ye fight and war; ye have not, because ye ask not. [3] Ye ask and receive not, because ye ask amiss, that ye may spend it in your pleasures. [4] Ye adulteresses, know ye not that the friendship of the world is enmity with God? Whosoever therefore would be a friend of the world maketh himself an enemy of God. [5] Or think ye that the scripture speaketh in vain? Doth the spirit which he made to dwell in us long unto envying? [6] But he giveth more grace. Wherefore the scripture saith, God resisteth the proud, but giveth grace to the humble. [7] Be subject therefore unto God, but resist the devil, and he will flee from you. [8] Draw nigh to God, and he will draw nigh to you. Cleanse your hands, ye sinners, and purify your hearts, ye double minded. [9] Be afflicted and mourn and weep; let your laughter be turned to mourning and your joy to heaviness. [10] Humble yourselves in the sight of the Lord, and he shall exalt you.
>
> [11] **Speak not one against another**, brethren. He that speaketh against a brother, or judgeth his brother, speaketh against the law, and judgeth the law, but if thou judgest the law, thou art not a doer of the law, but a judge . . .

The interrupting diatribe, is not against those who cause friction in the group, but against those who sin by indulging desires; or in other words, by devoting themselves to the pleasures available to the rich.

Summary. We have now examined five passages mentioning the rich, either alone or in contrast with the poor. Their sequence in the Epistle is:

- 1:9-11. Fading of the rich, exaltation of the poor [*interruptive*]
- 2:1-6a, 8-13. Against social discrimination between rich and poor
- 2:6b-7. Oppressions of the rich against the brethren [*interruptive*]
- 4:1-10. Worldly desires lead to evil [*interruptive*]
- 4:13-5:6. Denounces the arrogance of the merchants [*interruptive*]

These passages are different in character (one mild, the others harsh; one even speaks of the rich as murderers). They would not work well if joined as a single chapter in a discourse. The author returns to his subject more than once, and prefers to scatter his statements against the rich across the epistle, perhaps to give them wider exposure and thus greater emphasis. That we do not know. The passage likely to be earliest of them is the mild 2:1-6a and its continuation in 2:8-13. The harsh and probably later 1:9-11 now precedes this in the epistle, as though to update the theme with greater emphasis. We will see this "preposing" pattern again.

We will also see the long passage 4:13-5:16 again; on that second occasion not as an interpolation, but as a passage into which *something else* seems to be interpolated.

2. Hearing versus Doing

Ja 1:22-25 interrupts a discourse against anger and ill speaking:

Ja 1:19. Ye know this, my beloved brethren, but let every man be swift to hear, slow to speak, slow to **wrath**; [20] for the wrath of man worketh not the **righteousness** of God. [21] Wherefore putting away all filthiness and overflowing of wickedness, receive with meekness the implanted **Word**, which is able to save your souls.

[22] But be ye doers of the **Word** and not hearers only, deluding your own selves. [23] For if anyone is a hearer of the Word and not a doer, he is like unto a man beholding his natural face in a mirror, [24] for he beholdeth himself and goeth away, and straightway forgetteth what manner of man he was. [25] But he that looketh into the perfect law, the law of liberty, and so continueth, being not a hearer that forgetteth but a doer that worketh, this man shall be blessed in his doing.

[26] If any man thinketh himself to be **religious**, while he bridleth not his **tongue** but deceiveth his heart, this man's religion is vain. [27] Pure religion and undefiled before our God and Father is this: to visit the fatherless and widows in their affliction, and to keep oneself unspotted from the world.

The use of a catchword ("Word") from the context is a common device, meant to make an interpolation seem more topically consecutive than it is. The text before and after contrasts what is righteous with the anger of the individual.

Ja 2:18-26, a diatribe against those who claim that faith[5] is sufficient without works, follows a milder statement which, like Ja 2:1-6, criticizes neglect of the poor:

Ja 2:14. What doth it profit, my brethren, if a man say he hath faith, but have not works? Can that faith save him? [15] If a brother or sister be naked and in lack of daily food, [16] and one of you say unto them, Go in peace, be ye warmed and filled, and yet ye give them not the things needful to the body, what doth it profit? [17] Even so faith, if it have not works, is **dead** in itself.

[18] Yea, a man will say, Thou hast faith and I have works; show me thy faith apart from thy works, and I by my works will show thee my faith. [19] Thou believest that God is one; thou doest well: the demons also believe, and shudder. [20] But wilt thou, know, O vain man, that faith apart from works is barren? [21] Was not Abraham our father justified by works, in that he offered up Isaac his son upon the altar? [22] Thou seest that faith wrought with his works, and by works was faith made perfect, [23] and the Scripture was fulfilled which saith, And Abraham believed God, and it was reckoned unto him for righteousness, and he was called the friend of God. [24] Ye see that by works a man is justified, and not only by faith. [25] And in like manner was not also Rahab the harlot justified by works, in that she received the messengers, and sent them out another way? [26] For as the body apart from the spirit is dead, even so faith apart from works is **dead**.

With the previous group in mind, the second part of this looks like a harsher update and explanation of the first part; note the repetition of the catchword "dead."

[5]Faith in what? For Mark's Jesus, faith that God will keep his promises. For the late Paul, acceptance of the proposition that Jesus' death has power to confer salvation.

The last passage, on doing, is interpolated into one previously considered:[6]

> Ja 4:13. Come now, you that say, Today or tomorrow we will go into this city, and spend a year there, and trade and get gain, [14] whereas ye know not what shall be on the morrow. What is your life? For ye are a vapor that appeareth for a little time, and then vanisheth away. [15] For that ye ought to say, If the Lord will, we shall both live and do this or that. [16] But now ye glory in your vauntings; all such glorying is evil.
>
> > [17] To him therefore that knoweth to do good and doeth it not, to him it is sin.
>
> [5:1] Come now, ye rich, weep and howl for your miseries that are coming upon you. [2] Your riches are corrupted and your garments are moth-eaten.

This criticism of those who hold back from doing the good they know they should do sits awkwardly in the long denunciation of those who are simply pursuing gain.

On Doing. We have in all four passages, which occur this way in the text:

- 1:22-25. Looking in a mirror [*interruptive*]
- 2:14-2:17. Neglecting one's duty to the poor
- 2:18-26. Example of Abraham proves need for works [*a harsh continuation*]
- 4:17. Knowing and not doing [*interruptive*]

As with the Rich and Poor theme, treated above, these passages are rather different in character (one mild, and at least one notably harsh). They would not work well if grouped together as one chapter in a discourse. Of the four, the earliest is probably the mild 2:14-17. The stronger 1:22-25 has been positioned to precede this, as though by way of update. If this "preposing" device is a pattern, we have seen it before.

3. Against the Tongue

The material surrounding Ja 3:5b-8 sees the tongue as capable of speaking good or evil, and asks that it be controlled. 3:5b-8 instead calls it uncontrollable:

> 3:5a. So the **tongue** also is a little member, and boasteth great things.
>
> > [5b] Behold, how much wood is kindled by how small a fire! [6] and the **tongue** is a fire; the world of iniquity among our members is the tongue, which defileth the whole body . . . [8] But the tongue can no man tame; a restless evil, full of deadly poison.
>
> [9] Therewith bless we the Lord and Father, and therewith curse we men, who are made in the likeness of God. [10] Out of the same mouth cometh forth both blessing and cursing. My brethren, these things ought not so to be.

The middle passage is incompatibly drastic, and may be an interpolation.[7]

All three groups seem to be later additions to an earlier text. One test of that proposal is to see if the text without the suspect passages makes sense in its own right. To apply that test, a reconstruction of Jacob follows on the next two pages.

---

[6]Given the position of 4:17 (from the Doing group) as interpolated into a passage from the Rich group (4:13f), it follows that the Doing group is later than the Rich group. For its absolute dating, in terms of the controversy with Paul, see p79 below

[7]Ja 3:5b-8 is treated as a unit by Moffatt. Many others recognize a 5a/b topic break.

4. The Reconstructed Original Epistle of Jacob
Minus interpolations, with topical subheadings supplied in brackets.

[§1. OPENING SALUTATION]

[1:1] Jacob, a servant of God, to the twelve tribes which are of the Dispersion, greeting.

[§2. STEADFASTNESS IN TRIALS]

[1:2] Count it all joy, my brethren, when ye fall into manifold temptations; [3] Knowing that the proving of your faith worketh patience. [4] And let patience have [its] perfect work, that ye may be perfect and entire, lacking in nothing. [5] But if any of you lacketh wisdom, let him ask of God, who giveth to all liberally and upbraideth not; and it shall be given him. [6] But let him ask in faith, nothing doubting: for he that doubteth is like the surge of the sea driven by the wind and tossed. [7] For let not that man think that he shall receive anything of the Lord; [8] a doubleminded man, unstable in all his ways.

[1:12] Blessed is the man that endureth temptation; for when he hath been approved, he shall receive the crown of life, which [the Lord] promised to them that love him. [13] Let no man say when he is tempted, I am tempted of God; for God cannot be tempted with evil, and he himself tempteth no man: [14] but each man is tempted, when he is drawn away by his own lust, and enticed. [15] Then the lust, when it hath conceived, beareth sin: and the sin, when it is fullgrown, bringeth forth death. [16] Be not deceived, my beloved brethren. [17] Every good gift and every perfect gift is from above, coming down from the Father of lights, with whom can be no variation, neither shadow that is cast by turning. [18] Of his own will he brought us forth by the Word of truth, that we should be a kind of firstfruits of his creatures.

[§3. AGAINST ANGER]

[1:19] Ye know [this], my beloved brethren. But let every man be swift to hear, slow to speak, slow to wrath; [20] for the wrath of man worketh not the righteousness of God. [21] Wherefore putting away all filthiness and overflowing of wickedness, receive with meekness the implanted Word, which is able to save your souls.

[1:26] If any man thinketh himself to be religious, while he bridleth not his tongue but deceiveth his heart, this man's religion is vain. [27] Pure religion and undefiled before our God and Father is this, to visit the fatherless and widows in their affliction, [and] to keep oneself unspotted from the world.

[§4. EQUALITY OF PERSONS]

[2:1] My brethren, hold not the faith with respect of persons. [2] For if there come into your synagogue a man with a gold ring, in fine clothing, and there come in also a poor man in vile clothing; [3] and ye have regard to him that weareth the fine clothing, and say, Sit thou here in a good place; and ye say to the poor man, Stand thou there, or sit under my footstool; [4] Do ye not make distinctions among yourselves, and become judges with evil thoughts? [5] Hearken, my beloved brethren; did not God choose them that are poor as to the world [to be] rich in faith, and heirs of the kingdom which he promised to them that love him? [6] But ye have dishonored the poor man.

[2:8] Howbeit if ye fulfil the royal law, according to the scripture, Thou shalt love thy neighbor as thyself, ye do well: [9] but if ye have respect of persons, ye commit sin, being convicted by the law as transgressors. [10] For whosoever shall keep the whole law, and yet stumble in one [point], he is become guilty of all. [11] For he that said, Do not commit adultery, said also, Do not kill. Now if thou dost not commit adultery, but killest, thou art become a transgressor of the law. [12] So speak ye, and so do, as men that are to be judged by a law of liberty. [13] For judgment [is] without mercy to him that hath showed no mercy: mercy glorieth against judgment.

[§5. AGAINST JUDGING OTHERS]

[**3:1**] Be not many teachers, my brethren, knowing that we shall receive heavier judgment. [2] For in many things we all stumble. If any stumbleth not in word, the same is a perfect man, able to bridle the whole body also. [3] Now if we put the horses' bridles into their mouths that they may obey us, we turn about their whole body also. [4] Behold, the ships also, though they are so great and are driven by rough winds, are yet turned about by a very small rudder, whither the impulse of the steersman willeth. [5a] So the tongue also is a little member, and boasteth great things. [9] Therewith bless we the Lord and Father; and therewith curse we men, who are made after the likeness of God: [10] out of the same mouth cometh forth blessing and cursing. My brethren, these things ought not so to be. [11] Doth the fountain send forth from the same opening sweet and bitter? [12] Can a fig tree, my brethren, yield olives, or a vine figs? Neither [can] salt water yield sweet.

[3:13] Who is wise and understanding among you? let him show by his good life his works in meekness of wisdom. [14] But if ye have bitter jealousy and faction in your heart, glory not and lie not against the truth. [15] This wisdom is not [a wisdom] that cometh down from above, but is earthly, sensual, devilish. [16] For where jealousy and faction are, there is confusion and every vile deed. [17] But the wisdom that is from above is first pure, then peaceable, gentle, easy to be entreated, full of mercy and good fruits, without variance, without hypocrisy. [18] And the fruit of righteousness is sown in peace for them that make peace.

[**4:11**]. Speak not one against another, brethren. He that speaketh against a brother, or judgeth his brother, speaketh against the law, and judgeth the law; but if thou judgest the law, thou art not a doer of the law, but a judge. [12] One [only] is the lawgiver and judge, [even] he who is able to save and to destroy: but who art thou that judgest thy neighbor?

[§6. PATIENCE IN AWAITING THE END]

[**5:7**]. Be patient therefore, brethren, until the coming of the Lord. Behold, the husbandman waiteth for the precious fruit of the earth, being patient over it, until it receive the early and latter rain. [8] Be ye also patient; establish your hearts: for the coming of the Lord is at hand. [9] Murmur not, brethren, one against another, that ye be not judged: behold, the judge standeth before the doors. [10] Take, brethren, for an example of suffering and of patience, the prophets who spake in the name of the Lord. [11] Behold, we call them blessed that endured; ye have heard of the patience of Job, and have seen the end of the Lord, how that the Lord is full of pity, and merciful.

[5:12] But above all things, my brethren, swear not, neither by the heaven, nor by the earth, nor by any other oath: but let your yea be yea, and your nay, nay; that ye fall not under judgment.

[§7. MUTUAL SUPPORT IN THE COMMUNITY]

[**5:13**] Is any among you suffering? Let him pray. Is any cheerful? Let him sing praise. [14] Is any among you sick? Let him call for the elders of the church; and let them pray over him, anointing him with oil in the name of the Lord: [15] and the prayer of faith shall save him that is sick, and the Lord shall raise him up; and if he have committed sins, it shall be forgiven him. [16] Confess therefore your sins one to another, and pray one for another, that ye may be healed. The supplication of a righteous man availeth much in its working. [17] Elijah was a man of like passions with us, and he prayed fervently that it might not rain; and it rained not on the earth for three years and six months. [18] And he prayed again; and the heaven gave rain, and the earth brought forth her fruit.

[5:19] My brethren, if any among you err from the truth, and one convert him, [20] let him know, that he who converteth a sinner from the error of his way shall save a soul from death, and shall cover a multitude of sins.

5. Comments on the Reconstruction

Main Purpose. Dibelius suggested that the genre of Jacob was paraenesis.[8] In the general sense of ethical guidance, the reconstructed text agrees, if we remember that this guidance is given to communities in a specific situation of belief and expectation. All but §2 (on persecution) counsel amity in community life, and holding oneself ready for the expected End. The unity of that advice shows up as follows:

- §3. Avoiding the friction of **personal** grievances: all are members
- §4. Avoiding **social** distinctions: God has chosen all
- §5. Avoiding **doctrinal** differences: God will decide
- §6. Patience in awaiting the End
- §7. Mutual support in prayer and forgiveness

It would not be too much to say that §3-5 censure worldly distractions, based on personal ambition or animus, and that §6-7 remind hearers not of what divides them, but of what holds them together: common expectation of the End, and concern for the welfare of others, including those who have yielded to temptation and left the flock. All of §3-7 might be reduced to a sentence: Leave all to God, and await God fervently.

Persecution. §2 is more circumstantial. It urges steadfastness in adversity, and offers understanding (not through teaching, but through prayer) of the persecution. It is vain to search the record for a formal Roman persecution of Christians. None is known, and none are required. From the beginning, Christian communities were in tension with their immediate context in the Jewish synagogues (whence the vigorous persecutions of Paul) and in their own house churches, with their Greek neighbors (whence the changes later recommended in the Haustafeln or domestic codes).[9] Probably the original text consisted of the §3-7 paraenesis, and the persecution counsel of §2 was a response to some later emergency.[10]

The Theology of Jacob as here reconstructed is readily summarized:

- The chief fact about the world is that it will soon end in a final judgement.[11]
- The right of judgement, both now and later, belongs to God alone.
- Attachment to the world is itself an evil; it leads to sin and eternal death.
- Love within the community is required of its members.
- Avoidance of sins is insufficient; there must also be positive good.
- Prayer for specific results is the individual's means of contact with God.
- God forgives even apostasy, if forgiveness is earnestly sought.

Developmentally, much of this has parallels in Mark and, and some aspects, notably the growing emphasis on poverty as virtue, is further developed in Luke.

---

[8]Dibelius 3, "a text which strings together admonitions of general ethical content." Dibelius 11 then uses this to explain the zigzag character of Jacob: "Associated with this [lack of design] is yet another characteristic of paraenetic literature: the repetition of identical motifs in different places within a writing." No. Ethical advice need not be offered by scatterbrains.

[9]These codes are integral in the Deutero-Paulines, but interpolated in the genuine Paulines. They abandon elements of the originally distinctive character of the Christian communities.

[10]It may correspond to a stratum in Mark which first mentions "persecutions;" see below.

[11]The ejaculatory Aramaic Maranatha prayer ("Come, Lord"), mentioned in Didache 10:6, was the primary prayer of the early Christian communities, who awaited the end of the world.

6. Comments on the Later Additions

In these passages, the text seems to be responding to emergencies. What provoked the intensification of Ja 3:5b-8 was probably an increase of doctrinal factionalism, a problem which is also condemned in Paul's letters from the late 50's (eg 1 Cor 1:6f). The other two crises are economic and doctrinal:

The Rich in Mark and Paul. One of Mark's devices for introducing new matter into his text is to change the scene, often from public preaching to a private discourse with the disciples.[12] In some of these second scenes, the disciples are criticized for their lack of understanding; in others, they are simply puzzled or astonished at what they have heard or seen. Both imply the addition of late material to the original Mark. One "Twelve" interpolation in Mark is about the problem of the rich:

> **Mk 10:21.** And Jesus looking upon him loved him, and said to him, One thing thou lackest: go, sell whatsoever thou hast, and give to the poor, and thou shalt have treasure in Heaven, and come, follow me. [22] But his countenance fell at the saying, and he went away sorrowful, for he was one that had great possessions.
>
> > [23] And Jesus looked round about, and saith unto his disciples, How hardly shall they that have riches enter into the Kingdom of God! [24] And the disciples were amazed at his words. But Jesus answereth again, and saith unto them, Children, how hard is it for them that trust in riches to enter into the kingdom of God! [25] It is easier for a camel to go through a needle's eye, than for a rich man to enter into the Kingdom of God. [26] And they were astonished exceedingly, saying to him, Then who can be saved? [27] And Jesus looking upon them saith, With men it is impossible, but not with God, for all things are possible with God.

The absolute exclusion of *all* rich from Heaven comes only in the inset passage, which corresponds in severity to the harsher of the Jacob interpolations on this subject.

Mk 10:23f is late in Mark, but it is not in the *last* strata, which date from 44/45.[13] I will not here suggest a specific date for Mk 10:23f, but the point for our purposes is that it attests the same situation in the churches (the departure and enmity of the rich) as do the harsher of the Jacob passages against the rich. The preceding Mk 10:17f, with its sad vignette of a man burdened by wealth, seems to correspond typologically to the milder of the items in that Jacob stratum.[14] The inference is that Mark and Jacob are evolving in the same direction, and probably at more or less the same time.

The theme of rich versus poor is faint in Paul (eg 1 Cor 1:26f, "not many mighty, not many noble"), perhaps because the problem assumed a less severe form in the metropolitan churches, but it does seem to exist there also.

---

[12]For the classic case of Mk 4:10f, see Brooks **Reader** 26-27.

[13]For the last strata, see Brooks **Time**.

[14]With due caution, we may note that the disaffection of the rich, and their condemnation by the Christian leadership, is remembered in emblematic form in Acts 5:1-11, the story of Ananias and Sapphira. Logically, holding all property in common (as in Acts) is not the same as a command to divest oneself of all wealth (as in Mark). But the two may be related.

Faith versus Works in Mark and Paul. The issue is the Atonement doctrine; the idea that Jesus' death saves individuals by atoning for their sins. For Paul, "faith" is not trust in God's promise, but *acceptance of the assertion that Jesus' death saves*.

The Atonement doctrine, whose keywords are "ransom" and "blood," appears only in two brief passages in Mark, here italicized:

- Mk 10:45a. For the Son of Man came not to be ministered unto, but to minister, [45b] *and to give his life a ransom for many.*
- Mk 14:22. And as they were eating, he took bread, and when he had blessed it, he brake it, and gave to them, and said, Take ye: This is my body. [23] And he took a cup,. . . [24] *And he said unto them, This is my blood of the Covenant, which is poured out for many.*[15]

The "and to give" in 10:45, which is extraneous to what precedes, may mark a later addendum by Mark, and so may the "And he said unto them" of 14:24.[16] In general, so little developed is the Atonement idea in Mark that it seems reasonable to conclude that these two phrases are late within the formation process of the text.

In his late epistles, Paul insists on the primacy of the Atonement interpretation, and the irrelevance of "works of the Law" to salvation. The Alpha Christians instead relied on the Law in the reduced form in which Jesus himself [Mk 10:19] had left it to them. Here are the relevant passages from Paul and Jacob, structured as a dialogue:

- Rom 3:20-24. Because by works of the law shall no flesh be justified in his sight, for through the Law cometh the knowledge of sin. [21] But now apart from the Law a righteousness of God hath been manifested, being witnessed by the law and the prophets, [22] even the righteousness of God through faith in Jesus Christ unto all them that believe, for there is no distinction; [23] for all have sinned, and come short of the glory of God, [24] being justified freely by his grace through the redemption that is in Christ Jesus.
  - Ja 2:18. Yea, a man will say, Thou has faith and I have works; show me thy faith apart from thy works, and I by my works will show thee my faith.
- Rom 4:1-3. What then shall we say that Abraham our forefather hath found according to the flesh? [2] For if Abraham was justified by works, he hath whereof to glory, but not toward God. [3] For what saith the scripture? "And Abraham believed God, and it was reckoned unto him for righteousness."
  - Ja 2:20-24. But wilt thou know, O vain man, that faith apart from works is barren? [21] Was not Abraham our father justified by works, in that he offered up Isaac his son upon the altar? [22] Thou seest that faith wrought with his works, and by works was faith made perfect, [23] and the scripture was fulfilled which saith, "And Abraham believed God, and it was reckoned unto him for righteousness, and he was called the friend of God." [24] Ye see that by works a man is justified, and not only by faith.

This two-way argument most likely is from c57, the probable date of Romans.

---

[15]Luke 22:20 omits the italicized phrase; see Brooks **Silence** 26. 1 Cor 11:25 also lacks it, perhaps a Lukan gesture of Paul's editors (the interruptive 1 Cor 11:23-32 is interpolated). Matthew 26:26 clarifies it doctrinally: "which is poured out for many, *unto remission of sins.*"

[16]The Lukan account of the Last Supper has been heavily sacramentalized; for the "Western Non-Interpolation" passages on which this conclusion turns, see Metzger **Textual** 164f.

If so, then the history of the Atonement doctrine is something like the following:

• Devised in Jerusalem by theorists who explained Jesus' death as sacrifice, thus (in their view) ennobling it. This would have been in the early 40's.

• Reflected in Mark, the Jerusalem Gospel (Mark was himself a resident of Jerusalem, and knew the Galilean career of Jesus only at second hand),[17] at about that time. (The latest material in Mark is c45). Still in the early 40's.

• Perhaps known to Paul as early as 1 Thess 1:10b, "Jesus, who delivereth from the wrath to come,[18] but if so, it has not yet eclipsed the older salvation scenario (2:12 "to the end that ye should walk worthily of God;" 4:3 "For this is the will of God, even your sanctification, that ye abstain from fornication"). This takes us to the year 51, the probable date of 1 Thess.

• Increasingly adopted by Paul as central to his view of salvation, and argued as such in 1 Cor 5:7f, Gal 1:3f, and the passages of Romans above quoted. Survivals of the repentance and forgiveness idea persist (Rom 2:4, 2 Cor 7:10) simply as part of Paul's inherited doctrine. This takes us to about the year 57.

• Vigorous and animated response to Paul by Jacob, probably also in c57.[19]

The rise and spread of the Atonement doctrine thus covers something like 15 years, beginning from Jerusalem and moving outward.[20] It was controversial when it did appear. Efforts were apparently made, in editing Paul's letters, to damp down this all too divisive controversy between Alpha and Beta Christians.[21]

7. Date

The c57 skirmish with Paul is the latest datable event in the formation of Jacob; everything else is earlier. Jacob reflects the crisis of the rich, which also registers in late passages in Mark. The bulk of Jacob must be earlier than these two encounters, and should be ascribed at minimum to the early 40's, or quite possibly to the late 30's. This agrees with the conclusion earlier reached, that the formation period of Jacob is parallel to Mark at its early end, and earlier than Luke at its later end.

The purpose of Jacob was to guide the churches between visits of itinerant preachers; it is intrinsically a text of the Apostolic Age. The end of that Age, with the deaths of Paul (c60) and Peter (c64), opened a new era, when the churches organized themselves around their own leaders, as the post-Pauline Pastoral Epistles authorize. The Epistle of Jacob would have had little function in that different context.

---

[17]The knowledge of Jerusalem, and of details of Jesus' days there, imply a Jerusalem author for Mark. The vagueness of Mark's Galilee information agrees with that Jerusalem location.

[18]1 Thess 5:9f "through our Lord Jesus Christ, [10] who died for us" may be interpolated.

[19]Commentators have hesitated to acknowledge this tension within Christianity, but the similarity in wording and example, and the sense of engagement on both sides, I believe, make this interpretation inevitable. Neither Paul nor Jacob is talking in abstract terms.

[20]Nothing in this Jewish concept of atoning sacrifice implies derivation from Greco-Roman civilization. It is otherwise with Paul's conception of baptism, which involves participation in the death and resurrection of Jesus; in effect, a baptism in blood (1 Cor 10:16), and not, as with John the Baptist and the first Christians, a symbol of forgiveness gained by repentance.

[21]Such as the insertion of Alpha material into Gal 5:13–6:10 see Brooks **Two** 43.

8. Influence

It has been claimed that Jacob and the late Synoptics draw on "early paraenetic tradition." I here suggest that this Epistle, which on its own account was distributed to churches around the Mediterranean world, *is itself* that early paraenetic tradition.

If so – if Jacob was the newsletter of early Christianity; addressed not to one church but to all the local churches for guidance between visits from circuit preachers, the people whose interim manual of procedure was the Didache – then traces of it should be visible in later Christian writings. And they are. Here are a few:[22]

Jacob		Later Texts	
• Ja 1:2-4	=	Rom 5:3	we rejoice in our sufferings
• Ja 2:5	=	1 Cor 1:27	God chose the foolish to shame the wise
• Ja 3:12	=	Mt 7:16	no fig tree yields . . .
• Ja 5:12	=	Mt 5:37	let your oaths be Yea and Nay
• Ja 5:19f	=	Jude 22	[both end with advice about erring brothers]

Often noted parallels between Jacob and such late texts as 1 and 2 Clement and the Shepherd of Hermas (all written in Rome) do not imply a Roman origin for Jacob. The Epistle is a general letter, and was sent to churches all over the Mediterranean world. Its influence will very naturally have soaked into the tradition of those early churches, both in Rome and elsewhere.

Parallels between Jacob and the Qumran documents[23] are probably best interpreted as implying a common background in contemporary Jewish paraenesis.

9. Author

The usual choice is the Lord's Brother, who was prominent at Jerusalem some time after the killing of the liberal Jacob of Zebedee. The liberal Jacob had decided that Gentiles need not keep Jewish food rules (thus legitimizing shared meals), but the conservative Lord's Brother later sent agents to Antioch to reverse that liberal ruling, and once again, in effect, forbid communal meals including both Jews and Gentiles.[24] It was this reversal (and Cephas' submission to it) that so enraged Paul in Gal 2:11-14.

The good Greek[25] of the Epistle has been thought to argue against Jacob the Brother as its author.[26] And it does. That literary Greek was taught in Galilee does not prove that the Brother learned it. The likely author is Jacob of Alphaeus, listed in Mark among the Twelve, probably the brother of Levi of Alphaeus. Levi was a tax collector: not merely literate, but *functional as an official* in a Greek-speaking bureaucracy.

[22]For the web of similarities between Jacob and 1 Peter, see Johnson 54f

[23]See Verseput. Similarly, Harris has shown that the core of the Two Ways text is a Jewish prayer; see Brooks **Two**. The c57 date for the last layer of Jacob precludes influence from other texts with which it has also been compared: Matthew, Luke, Hebrews, 1 Clement, and Hermas.

[24]The riddle of the two Jacobs, in my view, has been solved by Beare **Sequence** 305f.

[25]Or sometimes even playful Greek; see Yoder φαῦλος.

[26]See eg Dibelius 17; Easton 6, Allison 19. A similar argument occurs with the authorship of 1 Peter, which is written in a conspicuously literate Greek, and for that reason is also best considered as not a work of the person with whom it identifies itself.

For Jacob the brother of Levi, with the same advantages of upbringing as Levi, writing literate Greek would present no problem. As Levi's brother, Jacob may have succeeded him as office manager in Galilee. This would make him the obvious person to direct the affairs of the scattered churches between apostolic visits. His membership in the earliest Christianity contrasts with Jacob the Brother's hostility to Jesus in his lifetime (Mk 3:31f) and his hostility toward Gentile converts, and to accommodations of doctrine made in their behalf, in the Brother's own years of power (Gal 2:12).

10. Envoi

I will give the last word to Joseph Mayor: "I have endeavored to show that the Epistle is a natural product of pre-Pauline Christianity" (page clxxxix). Precisely so. A pre-Pauline Christianity that ends in a shouting match with Pauline Christianity.

Works Cited

Dale C Allison Jr. James. Bloomsbury 2013

Horst Balz und Wolfgang Schrage. Die Katholischen Briefe. Vandenhoeck 1980

Frank W Beare. The Sequence of Events in Acts 9-15 and the Career of Peter. JBL v62 #4 (1943) 295-306

E Bruce Brooks. Arguments from Silence. Alpha v1 (2017) 30-32

E Bruce Brooks. The Reader in the Text. Alpha v1 (2017) 25-29

E Bruce Brooks. The Resurrection of Jesus in Mark. Alpha v1 (2017) 81-88

E Bruce Brooks. Salome. Alpha v1 (2017) 94-98

E Bruce Brooks. Time Depth in Mark. Alpha v1 (2017) 73-80

E Bruce Brooks. The Two Ways. Alpha v1 (2017) 39-47

Peter H Davids. The Epistle of James. Eerdmans 1982

Martin Dibelius (rev Heinrich Greeven). James. 1964; tr Fortress 1976

Burton Scott Easton. The Epistle of James; in The Interpreter's Bible v12, Abingdon (1957) 1-74

J Rendel Harris. The Teaching of the Apostles. Johns Hopkins 1897

Patrick J Hartin. James, First Peter, Jude, Second Peter. Liturgical 2006

Luke Timothy Johnson. The Letter of James. Yale 1995

Sophie Laws. The Epistle of James. Hendrickson 1980

Joseph Mayor. The Epistle of St James. 3ed Macmillan 1913

Bruce M Metzger. A Textual Commentary on the Greek New Testament. 2ed UBS 1994

James Moffatt. The General Epistles. Hodder & Stoughton 1928

Douglas J Moo. The Letter of James. Eerdmans 2000

Bo Reicke. The Epistles of James Peter and Jude. Doubleday 1964

James Hardy Ropes. The Epistle of St James. Clark 1916

Friedrich Spitta. Der Brief des Jakobus; in Zur Geschichte und Litteratur des Urchristentums, Vandenhoeck (1896) 2/1-239

Donald J Verseput. Wisdom, 4Q185, and the Epistle of James. JBL v117 (1998) 691-707

Robert W Wall. Community of the Wise. Trinity 1997

Keith L Yoder. Adjectival φαῦλος in James 3:16. Alpha v1 (2017) 9-10

Adverbial πόθεν in Mark 12:37

E Bruce Brooks

University of Massachusetts at Amherst

(10 Oct 2004)

Problem. In Mark 12:37, Jesus points out that David (in Psalm 110) speaks of the Christ as his "Lord," and asks, And whence is he his *son?* The Synoptic Gospels Mark, Matthew, and Luke have these versions of the question,

Mk 12:37	καὶ πόθεν αὐτοῦ ἐστιν υἰὸς	and whence is he his son?
Mt 22:45	πῶς υἰὸς αὐτοῦ ἐστιν	how is he his son?
Lk 20:41	καὶ πῶς υἰὸς αὐτοῦ ἐστιν	and how is he his son?

Now, πόθεν is related to πῶς by the suffix -θεν "from," whence the "whence" of the above translation.[1] Both words occur elsewhere in Mark. Except in this passage, neither is substituted for the other in Matthew or Luke, nor is either replaced by the other in manuscripts. Pershbacher gives "how, in what way" as a meaning of πόθεν, and cites these two examples of that meaning:

Mk 8:4   How can one feed these people with bread here in the desert?

Mk 12:37 How is he his son?

The first can be construed spatially ("from what source," thus "where are we going to get all that bread from?"). For the second, that interpretation is less obvious.[2] The commentators accordingly wrestle with it. Swete 289 cites Demosthenes Crown 242: οὐκ ἔστι ταῦτα. . . πόθεν, for the equation whence = how. Rawlinson 175 "it is better to take the words as meaning 'in what sense, then, is he his son.'" Taylor 492: "πόθεν (6:2, 8:4*) is used in the sense of πῶς, 'how?' . . . The question is ironical."

Solution. I suggest that it is literal. Jesus says, in effect, "I have cited David for my claim that the Christ is David's Lord. From *where* (from what equal authority)[3] can you show that he is his son?" Jesus has a text to cite, while his opponents have none. So he wins – and with a certain flair, having posed an unanswerable question.[4]

If this nuance is not understood, then πόθεν is indeed a solecism: spatial πόθεν where nonspatial πῶς would be better Greek. This is how it is treated by Matthew and Luke, and also by many manuscripts. Some manuscripts (Sinaiticus uncorrected, Freer, Family 1, Family 13) go further, and harmonize Mark to Luke.

[1] Blass §104 "Adverbs in θεν" answer the question "whence."

[2] Arndt 686 lists only Mk 12:37 as a Synoptic example of meaning #3 "of cause or reason how, why, in what way;" so also Danker 838. This category may actually be empty; see below.

[3] So understood by Gundry (1993) 718f, but without visible effect, since later commentators still expound "how:" Perkins (1995), Evans (2001), Witherington (2001), Edwards (2002), Boring (2006), Yarbro Collins (2007), Stein (2008), and Marcus (2009).

[4] For another example of classical wit see Brooks **Interrogative** 54, and further n6 below.

Synoptic Implications. Mark's crudities are often altered by Matthew and Luke; the directionality of those alterations is one of the arguments for the Synoptic sequence Mk > Mt, Lk.[5] The Matthew and Luke parallels to Mk 12:37 would count as such corrections, of seemingly wayward πόθεν to conventionally correct πῶς – except that here, the corrections are erroneous: they are based on a misreading. Mark's Greek is quite adequate to his purpose, and in Mk 12:37 he has given us a momentary glimpse of a Jesus lively in debate, and scoring a point by what amounts to wit.[6]

As for the theory that Mark, far from being the oldest Gospel, is a conflation of Matthew and Luke, let it be assumed that πῶς would here be better Greek than πόθεν. Having before him those two Gospels, all the supposed conflator Mark has to do to write presentable Greek is to retain the πῶς which is present in both his sources. Instead, he gratuitously deviates into the supposedly incorrect πόθεν.

Whence this deviation?

Works Cited

Willoughby C Allen. The Gospel According to St Matthew. 3ed T & T Clark 1912
William F Arndt et al. A Greek-English Lexicon of the New Testament. Chicago 1957
Friedrich Blass et al (ed Funk). A Greek Grammar of the New Testament. Chicago 1961
M Eugene Boring. Mark. Westminster 2006
E Bruce Brooks. Four Gospel Trajectories. Alpha v1 (2017) 11-12
E Bruce Brooks. Interrogative Yēn 焉 and Aň 安 in Jwāngdž. WSP v1 (2010) 52-54
Frederick William Danker. A Greek-English Lexicon . . . [BDAG]. 3ed Chicago 2000
James R Edwards. The Gospel According to Mark. Eerdmans 2002
Craig A Evans. Mark 8:27-16:20. Nelson 2001
Robert H Gundry. Mark. Eerdmans 1993
John Hawkins. Horae Synopticae. 2ed Oxford 1909
Joel Marcus. Mark 8-16. Yale 2009
Pheme Perkins. The Gospel of Mark [New Interpreters Bible v8]. Abingdon 1995
Wesley J Perschbacher (ed). The New Analytical Greek Lexicon. Hendrickson 1990
A E J Rawlinson. The Gospel According to St Mark. Methuen 1925; 4ed 1936
Robert H Stein. Mark. Baker 2008
Henry Barclay Swete. The Gospel According to St Mark. Macmillan 1898; 3ed 1927
Vincent Taylor. The Gospel According to St Mark. Macmillan 1959
Ben Witherington III. The Gospel of Mark. Eerdmans 2001
Adela Yarbro Collins. Mark. Fortress 2007

---

[5]For passages in Mark likely "to give offence" and thus to have been altered by the other Synoptists, see Hawkins **Horae** 117f. For the priority of Mark, see also Brooks **Four**.

[6]Is there a hint of personal satisfaction as Jesus delivers this line? If so, changing witty πόθεν to routine πῶς might be meant to reduce it. Signs of human emotion in Jesus are often suppressed in the later Gospels. To the Hawkins 119 list of passages "seeming . . . unworthy of [Jesus]," which includes Mk 3:5 (anger at the Pharisees) and 10:14 (indignation at the disciples), one might add Mk 1:41 "moved with pity" (or its variant, "was angered"), 1:43 "sternly charged [the leper]," and 10:21 "Jesus, looking upon him, loved him," all of which are absent in the parallel passages in Matthew and Luke. See further Allen xxxi-xxxii.

Time Depth in Mark

E Bruce Brooks

University of Massachusetts at Amherst

(13 Jan 2012)

The story of the Syrophoenician Woman (Mk 7:24-30) implies that the Jesus movement did not include Gentiles ("dogs"), but Mk 13:10 says that the End will not come until the Gospel is preached "unto all the nations." Jesus in Mk 13:7-8, 24-31 lists signs that will precede the End Time (Mk 13:7-8, 24-31), but in Mk 13:32-37 he says it will come unexpectedly, *without* warning signs. If Mark made this up, he is an incompetent storyteller. If he culled it from sources, he is an indiscriminate scavenger.

The third option is that the Gospel of Mark has time depth; that it was written over an extended period, and that the additional materials reflect new developments in Christian thought during that period. If so, then *Mark is an accretional text*, the result of a growth process which extended over years, and offers us a witness to those years. I here explore two accretional sequences, and identify the span of years in question.

1. The Gentile Mission

The following are the only mentions or hints of the Gentile Mission in Mark:

• (G1) **Mk 7:24-30** (the Syrophoenician Woman) takes the position that Gentiles may benefit, *but only incidentally*, from the healing work of Jesus.

• (G2) **Mk 5:1-20** (the Gerasene Demoniac) features a healed Gentile who offers to follow Jesus, but is told instead *to witness to his own people.*

• (G3) **Mk 8:1-9** (the Feeding of Four Thousand), a doublet of the Feeding of Five Thousand (Mk 6:34-44), accepts Gentiles (symbolized by the 7 baskets of leftovers, 7 or 70 being a universal symbol) as *of equal status with Jews.*

• (G4) **Mk 9:38-40** (the Strange Exorcist), with Hilgenfeld (1850),[1] accepts a Gentile mission (Paul) *outside the organizational control of the Twelve*, against the objections of the original Apostles (represented by John).[2]

• (G5) **Mk 13:10**, The End will come when "all nations" are evangelized. Gentile converts are now *essential to the plan of salvation.*[3]

Save perhaps for G4, no two of these can possibly reflect the same situation.

---

[1]Hilgenfeld's identification has not gone unchallenged. Meyer called it "exaggerated ingenuity" (p149). It was again proposed by Loisy in 1912, and again ridiculed by Rawlinson in 1925 as "too fantastic to deserve serious consideration" (p129). Cranfield in 1959 called it "fantastic" (p309). No later commentator known to me even mentions it.

[2]This exactly matches the enmity felt for the Twelve by Paul himself, who sneeringly calls them "pillars" (Gal 2:9), or "super-Apostles" (2 Cor 11:5, 12:11). Compare the sad 1 Cor 9:2.

[3]For a contrary view, see Kilpatrick **Gentile** 157, "There is no preaching to the Gentiles in this world, and there is no interest in their fate in the world to come."

Alpha v1 (2017)

Typologically, then, the various G passages form a time sequence. There is direct evidence that G4 (Mk 9:38-40) is at least later than its immediate context:

Mk 9:37. Whosoever shall receive one of such little children in my name receiveth me, and whosoever receiveth me, receiveth not me, but him who sent me.

[38] John said unto him, Teacher, we saw one casting out demons in thy name, and we forbade him, because he followed not us. [39] But Jesus said, Forbid him not, for there is no man who shall do a mighty work in my name, and be able quickly to speak evil of me. [40] For he that is not against us is for us. ·

[41] For whosoever shall give you a cup of water to drink, because ye are Christ's, verily I say unto you, he shall in no wise lose his reward.

The thematic continuity between 9:37 and 9:41 (discipleship) is obvious;[4] so is the interruptive character of Mk 9:38-40. It follows that Mark was not scrambled together on one occasion; rather, some passages were added after others were in place.

2. The Markan Apocalypse, Mk 13:3-37

Mark 13 has been studied by Taylor (**Mark** 636-644), who finds a whole series of answers to the question, When will the End come, each stacked on the preceding as this fundamental Christian expectation underwent disappointments and adjustments. Even *asking* the question implies doubt. Taylor notes the separateness of 13:10, but does not identify it as a layer. That it is an interpolation, and thus later, is obvious:

Mk 13:9. But take ye heed to yourselves, for they shall deliver you up to councils, and in synagogues shall ye be beaten, and before governors and kings shall ye stand for my sake, for a testimony unto them.

[10] And the Gospel must first be preached unto all the nations.

[11] And when they lead you to judgement, and deliver you up, be not anxious beforehand what ye shall speak, but whatsoever shall be given to you in that hour, that speak ye, for it is not ye that speak, but the Holy Spirit. [12] And brother shall deliver up brother to death, and the father his child, and children shall rise up against parents and cause them to be put to death. [13] And ye shall be hated of all men for my name's sake, but he that endureth to the end, the same shall be saved.

Mk 13:10 has nothing whatever to do with the surrounding warning on persecution, and we thus have two layers: that warning, and the requirement that the Gospel must be universally preached before the End can come. Labeling these as separate layers, and transferring a few verses to Taylor's oldest (A) layer,[5] we have:

- (A1) **Mk 13: 5-8, 21-31** (Signs of the Parousia), **Taylor A**, augmented
- (A2) **Mk 13: 9, 11-13** (Warnings of Persecution), **Taylor B**
- (A3) **Mk 13:14-20** (The Abomination of Desolation), **Taylor C**, reduced
- (A4) **Mk 13:32-37** (No One Knows the Time), **Taylor D**, reduced
- (A5) **Mk 13:10** (The Necessity of the Gentiles), no separate label in Taylor

For an outline of how these look as successive interpolations, see the following page.

---

[4]So also Wellhausen (76) and Montefiore (1/220f). This and other passages here identified as "interpolations" are not scribal corruptions, since they appear in all manuscripts.

[5]Specifically, 13:21-23 from Taylor's C, and 13:28-31 from Taylor's D, to Taylor's A.

Here is the whole accretion process, with some passages slightly abbreviated:

A1 [5] Take heed that no man lead you astray. [6] Many shall come in my name, saying "I am he" and shall lead many astray. [7] And when ye shall hear of wars and rumors of wars, be not troubled; these things must needs come to pass, but the End is not yet. [8] For nation shall rise against nation, and kingdom against kingdom; there shall be earthquakes in divers places; there shall be famines; these things are but the beginning of travail.

A2 [9] But take ye heed to yourselves, for they shall deliver you up to councils, and in synagogues shall ye be beaten, and before governors and kings shall ye stand for my sake, for a testimony unto them.

A5 [10] And the Gospel must first be preached unto all the nations.

A2 [11] And when they lead you to judgement and deliver you up, be not anxious beforehand what ye shall speak, but whatsoever shall be given to you in that hour, that speak ye, for it is not ye that speak, but the Holy Spirit. [12] And brother shall deliver up brother to death, and the father his child, and children shall raise up against parents, and cause them to be put to death. [13] And ye shall be hated of all men for my name's sake, but he that endureth to the end, the same shall be saved.

A3 [14] But when ye see the abomination of desolation standing where he ought not (let him that readeth understand), then let them that are in Judaea flee to the mountains, [15] and let him that is on the housetop not go down, nor enter in, to take anything out of his house, [16] and let him that is in the field not return back to take his cloak. [17] But woe unto those that are with child and to them that give suck in those days! [18] And pray ye that it not be in the winter. [19] For those days shall be tribulation, such as there hath not been the like from the beginning of the creation which God created until now, and never shall be. [20] And except the Lord had shortened the days, no flesh would have been saved, but for the elect's sake, whom he chose, he shortened the days.

A1 [21] And then if any man shall say unto you, Lo, here is the Christ, or Lo, there, believe it not. [22] For there shall arise false Christs and false prophets, and shall show signs and wonders, that they may lead astray, if possible, the elect. [23] But take ye heed; behold, I have told you all things beforehand. [24] But in those days, after that tribulation, the sun shall be darkened, and the moon shall not give her light, [25] and the stars shall be falling from heaven, and the powers that are in the heavens shall be shaken. [26] And then shall they see the Son of Man coming in clouds with great power and glory [27] And then shall he send forth the angels, and shall gather together his elect from the four winds, from the uttermost part of the earth to the uttermost part of Heaven . . . [30] Verily I say unto you, This generation shall not pass away, until all these things be accomplished. [31] Heaven and earth shall pass away, but my words shall not pass away.

A4 [32] But of that day or that hour knoweth no one, not even the angels in Heaven, neither the Son, but the Father. [33] Tale ye heed, watch and pray, for ye know not when the time is. [34] as a man, sojourning in another country, having left his house, and given authority to his servants, to each one his work, commanded also the porter to watch. [35] Watch, therefore, for ye know not when the lord of the house cometh, whether at even, or at midnight, or at cockcrowing, or in the morning, [36] lest coming suddenly he find you sleeping. [37] And what I say to you I say unto all: Watch.

• *All Five Mark 13 Apocalyptic Strata, A1-5* •

It thus appears that A1 simply gives the signs of cosmic upheaval that will precede the End. Then was added A2 (warning of persecutions that would precede the End), and later A3 (the Caligula threat), quickly followed by A4 (the compensation for the failed Caligula prediction, with its command to forget about signs, and just watch). The final A5, which pushed the End into the distant future, in effect canceling the previous expectation of an imminent end,[6] was then inserted into A2.

With the Abomination passage, we come to a major crux in NT study. Does it predict the fall of Jerusalem in 70, or anticipate the sacrilege of Caligula in 40? (Caligula had ordered that his statue be worshiped in Jewish temples). The answer to this question makes a 30-year difference in the date we assign to Mark. We may recall the protest that Caligula's demand elicited. The Alexandrians (Josephus Ant 18/8:2-9) sent Philo to plead their case at Rome; Caligula's generals protested against it. Matthew identifies "abomination of desolation" as referring to Daniel (11:31, 12:11), recalling the intrusion of a "heathen altar" into the Temple by Antiochus IV Epiphanes in 0168 (Taylor 511f), and Mark begs us to spot it ("let him that readeth understand"). All told, the Caligula interpretation thus seems literarily unproblematic.[7]

Caligula was assassinated in early 41, and the feared desecration never came off. But the failed prediction was in the text. How to deal with it? To eliminate it would admit error, and weaken the Gospel as an authority text.[8] Instead, Mark *blunted* the earlier prediction, denying that the End would be preceded *by any signs whatsoever*; it would come unexpectedly. That denial is A4. It radically reverses the idea of signs. Instead, the End will come *without warning*, and all must be constantly in readiness.

The Caligula threat was in 40. The hope that it will not come in winter (Mk 13:18, part of A3) implies that an alternative (autumn) still existed, hence this passage may be very closely dated to the summer of 40. The passage in response to the death of Caligula, our A4, could not have been written before 41, but was then urgent, as a correction of A3. It follows that the earlier A1 and A2 predictions must predate 40, and should thus be assigned to the Thirties. This dating will presently be supported.

---

[6]The continued nonappearance of the End Days was obviously a problem for the Jesus sect, who prayed for it constantly (with the Aramaic Maranatha, or "Come, Lord"). Members died, and every death intensified the problem. By the end of the century, outsiders were laughing at the Jesus people for the obvious failure of their hope. 2 Peter 3:3-13, "Where is the promise of his coming? For, from that day that the fathers fell asleep, all things continue as they were from the beginning of the creation." The response in that text is to point out that "one day is with the Lord as a thousand years." This pushes the End even further into the future. That it directly contradicts Jesus in Mk 13:30, "Verily I say unto you, This generation shall not pass away until all these things be accomplished," does not matter; the need is to save that hope *somehow*.

[7]The Gospel writers were not such fools. When one of them wants to describe the conquest of Jerusalem by Titus, the result will be more like Lk 21:20, *Luke's replacement* for Mk 13:14. For an extended discussion of the Caligula interpretation of Mk 13:14, see Crossley **Date** 27f.

[8]During its formation period, Mark's Gospel was not widely published, but was known in its immediate vicinity. Updated versions were probably circulated to those churches as they came out, much like the Epistle of Jacob (see Brooks **Jacob** for the several layers of that text). Any elimination of previously familiar material would have been noticed, and would have impugned the authority of the whole Gospel in the eyes of its early recipients.

Our next task is to identify other passages which are associated with any of these, and can be put in the same stratum, and to relate the G and A sequences to each other. For a start, the last items in each series (G5 and A5) *are the same passage.*

3. Passages Associated with the G Series

G1 (The Syrophoenician Woman). The story proper is flanked by two travel passages, Mk 7:24 (to Tyre) and 7:31 (back circuitously to Galilee).[9] We should regard these three consecutive passages as constituting one unit: Mk 7:24-31. Thus:

> Mk 7:24. Journey to the vicinity of Tyre
> Mk 7:25-30. Healing the Woman's daughter
> Mk 7:31. Journey back to Galilee

G2 (The Gerasene Demoniac). In imitation (more exactly, in refutation) of the Twelve-Only Feeding of Five Thousand, this Gentiles-Also passage is associated with a sea miracle. It should probably be construed as including that miracle:

> Mk 4:35-41. Stilling of the Storm (Journey to Gerasa[10])
> Mk 5:1-20. Exorcism of the Gerasene Demoniac
> Mk 5:21. Journey back to Galilee

G3 (Feeding of Four Thousand). This is framed with a symmetrical pair of highly distinctive spit healings. It directly follows the story of the Syrophoenician Woman:

> Mk 7:32-37.   Spit Healing of a Deaf Man
> Mk 8:1-9.   Feeding of Four Thousand (Parallel to the Five Thousand)
> Mk 8:10.   Journey to Dalmanutha
> Mk 8:11-12.   Pharisees ask a Sign; they are refused[11]
> Mk 8:13.   Journey back to "the other side"
> Mk 8:14-21.   Symbolism of the Baskets of Fragments Taken Up[12]
> Mk 8:22-26.   Spit Healing of a Blind Man at Bethsaida

There is also a discontinuous passage which is out of context where it is, and evidently belongs with this one:

> Mk 6:52   Misunderstanding the Loaves (compare 8:14-21)

G4 (The Strange Exorcist). No obviously associated passages.

G5 = A5 (All Nations). No obviously associated passages, but see at A5, below.

---

[9]The return itinerary has been held up to ridicule. But Jesus was a marked man, and as 1:45 tells us, after one of his healings he became generally known, and "could no more openly enter into a city [where the Roman police presence was greater], but was without in desert places." If a black activist, returning to the US from Africa, enters not at New York but through Canada, will that roundabout itinerary be laughed at by modern journalists? I suspect it will not.

[10]As Origen established by direct inspection, the actual locale of this incident was Gergesa. There is no harm, for present purposes, in retaining Mark's mishearing.

[11]For this interpolation, see below.

[12]A direct comparison of the two Feeding miracles, giving away the number symbolism. That this explanation is the core of the matter is seen in the fact that the explanation is nearly as long as the Feeding narrative itself. Mk 8:15 (the Leaven of Herod) is probably an intrusion into this passage, and should be excluded for analytical purposes.

4. Passages Associated with the A Series

A1 (Signs of the End). No obviously associated passages.

A2 (Warning of Persecutions). Not distinctive; the Jesus sect had endured early persecution from the zealot Paul, and continued to do into the 2nd century. Other mentions are in 4:17 and 10:30, both of them interpolated passages, which may tentatively be associated with A2.

A3 (Caligula). No obviously associated passages.

A4 (Refusal of a Sign). The assurance (13:30) that the End will come within the lifetimes of some present is repeated in 9:1, an appendage to what precedes it; both statements are emphasized with "Verily." Another refusal of a sign is at 8:11-12, with which 8:10 should be associated as a preliminary journey. This group was noticed above as interpolated in context; here is the relational implication.

A5 = G5 (All the Nations). No obviously associated passages. But accepting the account of Luke (in Acts), that Mark went to Antioch and later on campaign with Paul, his conviction as to the importance of Gentile converts was sincere. Then the passages, mostly parenthetical, by which he sought to adapt his text for non-Jewish hearers, will have come soon afterward, and are a Layer Z, which I date to the following year, 45.[13] They are Mark's final touches on his Gospel. A list[14] would include:

Explanations of Jewish customs and beliefs or adaptation to non-Jews:
- 2:27. In effect abolishes Sabbath rules
- 7:3-4. Explains Jewish washing of hands and food-preparation vessels
- 7:19b. A universalizing statement, that all foods are permissible
- 12:18b. Identifies the Sadducees as not believing in resurrection
- 14:12b. Defines the First Day of Unleavened Bread as the time when the Passover lambs are sacrificed

Translations of Aramaic phrases or Semitic words:
- 3:17b. Boanerges = "sons of Thunder" [epithet of the Zebedees]
- 5:42b. Talitha cumi = "little girl, rise" [word of healing]
- 7:11b. Corban = "dedicated [to God]"
- 7:34b. Ephphatha = "be opened" [word of healing]
- 14:36b. Abba, "father"
- 15:22b. Golgotha = "the place of a skull"
- 15:34b. Eloi, Eloi, lama sabachthani = "My God, my God, why hast thou forsaken me?" [last words of the crucified Jesus]

Passage G1, the first grudging acceptance of Gentiles, must be later than the Twelve passages (3:13-19, 6:7-13, and 6:30, plus small phrases) and the Feeding of Five Thousand (6:31-44), since both, *with their Twelve symbolism*, imply a Jews-only movement. So also, the first Apocalyptic Answer, A1, must respond to an Apocalyptic Question, which cannot have been asked until doubt about the expectation of the End had arisen. Thus, *not even the first members* of these series are original in Mark.

---

[13]Not an unprecedented suggestion; Johannes Belser (**Einleitung**, 1901) gives the date 44. Mark, as an accretional text, *has no single date;* I regard Belser's 44 as a final completion date.

[14]Borrowed from Brooks **Perga**.

5. Overview: Strata So Far Identified

Twelve Stratum. Mk 3:13-19, 6:7-13, and 6:30, plus small phrases; 6:31-44.
G1: 7:24-31 (Must follow any passages referring to the Twelve; see p78).
G2. 4:35-5:21.
G3. 7:32-8:9, 8:13-26, 6:52 (for the last, see p77).
G4. 9:38-40.
G5 = A5. 13:10.
A1. 13:3-8, 21-31.
A2. 13:9, 11-13.
A3. 13:14-20.
A4. 13:32-33, 8:10-12, 9:1 (Must follow the G3 stratum).
A5 = G5. 13:10.
Z. 2:27, 3:17b, 5:42b, 7:3-4, 7:11b, 7:19b, 7:34b, 12:18b. 14:12b, 14:36b, 15:22b, and 15:34b (Aramaic and other translations; Mark's final adjustments.

6. Appendix: Paul as Exorcist

The Strange Exorcist of Mk 9:38f is not an unauthorized *preacher of the Gospel*, but an unauthorized *exorcist of demons*. Did Paul exorcize? Mk 6:13 makes clear that the Twelve had power over demons: "And they cast out many demons, and anointed with oil many that were sick, and healed them."[15] We do not usually think of Paul as an exorcist, but exorcisms are deeds of power, and Paul *does* claim power:

> • **1 Cor 2:4**. And my speech and my preaching were not in persuasive words of 'wisdom, but in *demonstration of the Spirit and of power*, [5] that your faith should not stand in the wisdom of men, but in the power of God.[16]

Another self-testimony to Paul's powers is:

> • **2 Cor 12:12**. Truly the signs of an apostle were wrought among you in all patience, *by signs and wonders and mighty works*.

Paul also claims this power as available to others, as a working of the Spirit:

> • **1 Cor 12:7**. But to each one is given the manifestation of the Spirit to profit withal. [8] For to one is given through the Spirit the word of wisdom and to another the word of knowledge . . . [10] and to another *workings of miracles*, and to another prophecy, and to another discernings of spirits . . .

"Miracles" will cover the required territory. The match seems sufficiently good.[17]

---

[15]Anointing with oil does not figure in the healings of Jesus in Mark, but is recommended for the elders of the local churches in Jacob 5:14 (for the date of this text, see Brooks **Jacob**). Together with wine, an antiseptic, it is applied to a wounded man by the Good Samaritan. For parallels between Jacob and the Two Ways text preserved in the Didache, see Brooks **Two**. These two early documents in part inhabit the same time frame as the letters of Paul; indeed, the final stratum of Jacob directly and sarcastically contests Paul's theology of atonement.

[16]This is orthodox teaching; the healings and exorcisms of Jesus are regularly ascribed to the power of God (eg Mk 5:19, "tell them how great things the Lord hath done for thee").

[17]Acts 16:16 shows Paul exorcising a "pythonic" spirit (a spirit of prophecy), but this might be Lukan invention based on Paul's letters. For Luke's knowledge of Paul, see Walker **Acts**.

7. Conclusion

Mark is early and accretional. Its earliest layers predate Paul; one late layer is contemporary with him, and attests his independent preaching.

Two fixed dates are the A3 response to the Caligula threat in (40), and the A4 response to its nonoccurrence (41). A third is the prediction of the death of Jacob and/or John Zebedee in Mk 10:35-45. The death of Jacob, as told by Luke in Acts, was in retaliation for the liberal ruling given to the Antioch deputation; that ruling in effect eliminated the dietary laws, considered essential by the Temple authorities. The death of Herod Agrippa I, who attacked the Christian leaders to please his Jewish subjects, was seen as punishment for this persecution.[18]

The date of Herod's death was 44, probably the same year as the persecution. Mark's last adjustments may reasonably be ascribed to the next year, 45. At that point, his Gospel was complete, and it remained only to distribute it more widely.

Works Cited

Frank W Beare. The Sequence of Events in Acts 9-15. JBL v62 (1943) 295-305

Johannes Belser. Einleitung in der Neuen Testament. Herder 1901

E Bruce Brooks. Acts-Luke. Alpha v1 (2017) 143-157

E Bruce Brooks. The Epistle of Jacob. Alpha v1 (2017) 58-70

E Bruce Brooks. Mark at Perga. Alpha v1 (2017) 99-103

E Bruce Brooks. The Resurrection of Jesus in Mark. Alpha v1 (2017) 81-88

E Bruce Brooks. The Two Ways. Alpha v1 (2017) 39-47

C E B Cranfield. The Gospel According to St Mark. Cambridge 1959; 3ed 1966

James G Crossley. The Date of Mark's Gospel. Clark 2004

Morton S Enslin. "Luke" and Paul. JAOS v58 (1938) 81-91

Morton S Enslin. Once Again, Luke and Paul. ZNW v61 (1970) 254-255

Adolf Hilgenfeld. Das Markus-Evangelium. Breitkopf & Härtel 1850

G D Kilpatrick. The Gentile Mission in Mark and Mark 13:9-11; in Nineham (ed), Studies in the Gospels, Oxford (1955) 145-158

John Knox. Acts and the Pauline Letter Corpus; in Keck and Martyn (ed), Studies in Luke-Acts, Abingdon (1966) 33-50

Alfred Loisy. L'Évangile selon Marc. Nourry 1912

Heinrich August Wilhelm Meyer. Critical and Exegetical Handbook to the Gospels of Mark and Luke. 5ed 1867; tr 2v Clark 1880.

C G Montefiore. The Synoptic Gospels. 1909; 2ed 2v Macmillan 1927

A E Rawlinson. The Gospel According to St Mark. Methuen 1925

Vincent Taylor. The Gospel According to St Mark. Macmillan 1952

William O Walker Jr. Acts and the Pauline Corpus Reconsidered. JSNT v24 (1985) 2-23; in Porter et al (ed), The Pauline Writings, Clark (1995) 55-74

Julius Wellhausen. Das Evangelium Marci. 2ed Reimer 1909

---

[18]For the dates, unraveled from the Acts/Galatians accounts (another famous crux in New Testament scholarship), see Beare **Sequence**.

The Resurrection of Jesus in Mark

E Bruce Brooks

University of Massachusetts at Amherst

SBL/NE (2006)

I have noted elsewhere[1] that Mark includes material of different date. Some passages there considered proved to be part of larger strata. I here take up another set of passages which cohere in that way: those which predict or describe Jesus' bodily resurrection after three days in the tomb. Surprisingly, there are only five of them:

- Three recognized Passion Predictions, Mk 8:31-33, 9:31b–32, 10:32b–34[2]
- A less often recognized fourth Passion Prediction, Mk 9:9b-13
- The Empty Tomb story, the whole ending of extant Mark, 15:40-16:8

There are signs that these are interpolated and thus late in Mark: that the story of the Resurrection – the Empty Tomb story – is a later theory and not a historical memory. At the end, I ask, Does Mark also preserve an *earlier* account of Jesus' death?

The Four Passion Predictions

These can be removed without damage to context. So can many passages in Mark. More important, they *interrupt* or *contradict* their context. Here is a contradiction:

Mk 8:27. And Jesus went forth, and his disciples, into the villages of Caesarea Philippi, and on the way he asked his disciples, saying unto them, Who do men say that I am? [28] And they told him, saying, John the Baptist; and others, Elijah; but others, One of the prophets. [29] And he asked them, But who say ye that I am? Peter answereth and saith unto him, Thou art the Christ. [30] And he charged them that they should tell no man of him.

> [31] And he began to teach them that the Son of Man must suffer many things, and be rejected by the elders and the chief priests and the scribes, and be killed, and after three days rise again. [32] And he spake the saying openly. And Peter took him and began to rebuke him. [33] But he turning about, and seeing his disciples, rebuked Peter, and saith, Get thee behind me, Satan; for thou mindest not the things of God, but the things of men.

In Mk 8:27f Peter acclaims Jesus as the Christ (Messiah), the coming King of Israel. In 8:31-33, he hears Jesus' prediction of his coming death, and rejects it.

The word "Christ" (Anointed) evokes the national Messiah of Psalm 2:2 (a passage quoted about Jesus in Mk 1:11). Peter had expected a living King; he got suffering and death instead. *This is a radical reversal of expectation.* No wonder he protested.[3]

---

[1]Brooks **Time**.

[2]No others are considered, for instance, in Strecker **Predictions** 1968.

[3]For this common literary device of objection *within the story*, in which the objection of current readers is projected back into the story, and there answered, see Brooks **Reader**.

And here is an interruption:

> **Mk 9:30**. And they went forth from thence, and passed through Galilee, [31a] and he would not that any man should know it.
>
> > [31b] For he taught his disciples, and said unto them, The Son of Man is delivered up into the hands of men, and they shall kill him, and when he is killed, after three days he shall rise again. [32] But they understood not the saying, and were afraid to ask him.
>
> [33] And they came to Capernaum, and when he was in the house he asked them, What were ye reasoning on the way? [34] But they held their peace, for they had disputed one with another on the way, who was the greatest. [35] And he sat down, and called the Twelve, and he saith unto them, If any man would be first, he shall be last of all, and servant of all.

So, what happened? Either (1) the disciples argued who was the greatest, a discussion unheard by Jesus, who has to ask them; or (2) Jesus taught them about his death and resurrection, in which case he knows what happened, and the 9:33 question is absurd.

The absurdity can be cured by the removal of the middle passage; that is, 31b-32 is interruptive. In context, it is also inconsistent: 9:33f implies an earthly kingdom over which Jesus rules, and in which he has favors to dispense, whereas 31b-32 instead implies an earthly death of Jesus, leading to a Resurrection, not to an earthly realm. *These cannot be part of the same perception of Jesus.* Then 31b-32 is inconsistent as well as interruptive. These are standard signs of an interpolation.

In the next example, I omit Mk 10:35-45, the request of the Zebedees for preferred positions in the Kingdom. This is a remake of Mk 9:34-35, above, and amounts to predicting the death of Jacob Zebedee, a prediction which was fulfilled in early 44, when, as Acts 12:1-3 tells us, he was killed by Agrippa I, a response to his and other leaders' authorizing Gentile commensality. It is the latest datable passage in Mark.

With that adjustment, the rest of the context reads as follows:

> **Mk 10:32a**. And they were on the way, going up to Jerusalem, and Jesus was before them, and they were amazed, and they that followed were afraid.
>
> > [10:32b] And he took again the Twelve and began to tell them the things that were to happen unto him, [33] saying, Behold, we go up to Jerusalem, and the Son of Man shall be delivered unto the chief priests and the scribes, and they shall condemn him to death, and they shall deliver him unto the Gentiles, [34] and they shall mock him, and shall spit upon him, and shall scourge him, and shall kill him, and after three days he shall rise again.
>
> [46] And they come to Jericho, and as he went out from Jericho, with his disciples and a great multitude, the son of Timaeus, Bartimaeus, a blind beggar, was sitting by the wayside. [47] And when he heard that it was Jesus the Nazarene, he began to cry out and say, Jesus, thou son of David, have mercy on me . . .

Again the Davidic touch. If the Jesus party were on their way to attempt something daring in the Temple, the disciples' fear is intelligible, along with their awe of Jesus, whom they will have regarded as the Anointed One, the foreseen and present Messiah. The party in 10:32a (and 46) is large, but in 10:32b, Jesus speaks *only to his disciples*. That contrast is another detail tending to separate 10:32a from 10:32b and following.

The above are the usual Three Passion Predictions. The less noticed fourth is:

Mk 9:2. And after six days Jesus taketh with him Peter and Jacob and John, and bringeth them up into a high mountain apart by themselves, and he was transfigured before them, [3] and his garments became glistering, exceeding white, so as no fuller on earth can whiten them. [4] And there appeared unto them Elijah with Moses, and they were talking with Jesus. [5] And Peter answereth and saith to Jesus, Rabbi, it is good for us to be here, and let us make three tabernacles, one for thee, and one for Moses, and one for Elijah. [6] For he knew not what to answer, for they became sore afraid. [7] And there came a cloud overshadowing them, and there came a voice out of the cloud, This is my beloved Son, hear ye him. [8] And suddenly looking round about, they saw no one any more, save Jesus only with themselves. [9a] And as they were coming down from the mountain, he charged them that they should tell no man what things they had seen.

> [9b] save when the Son of Man should have risen again from the dead. [10] And they kept the saying, questioning among themselves what the "rising again from the dead" would mean. [11] And they asked him, saying, How is it that the scribes say that Elijah must first come? [12] And he said unto them, Elijah indeed cometh first, and restoreth all things, and how is it written of the Son of Man, that he should suffer many things and be set at nought? [13] But I say unto you, that Elijah is come, and they have also done unto him whatsoever they would, even as it is written of him.

[14] And when they came to the disciples . . .

Mk 9:9a is a perfectly satisfactory ending to the mysterious vision of Jesus on the mountain. Mk 9:14 picks up the narrative of the descent from the mountain, and continues with the story of the epileptic boy. Mk 9b-13, coming between, is intrusive, and thus, by the standard criterion which we are here applying, is also later in date.

Mk 9:2-9a is a vision of Jesus transfigured. The presence of Moses and Elijah has two meanings. First, Moses was important to Jesus in his legislative role (in opposition to the Pharisees)[4] and Elijah to his Messianic role (in contemporary thought, Elijah was the chief prophet of the Messiah); they symbolize the Law and the Prophets, the tradition which Jesus had purged of Pharisaic legal overgrowth and reoriented along Minor Prophet lines, and sought to bring about on earth. Second, both were regarded (Moses in the noncanonical Assumption of Moses;[5] Elijah in 2 Kings 2:11) as having ascended direct to Heaven at their death, without suffering the corruption of burial. The implication is that Jesus has indeed died – in contrast with the pure Messianic expectation seen in the above passages – but was not buried at all. Quite the contrary, he has ascended direct to Heaven, as had Moses and Elijah. This minority tradition we will meet again, in material to be considered below.

---

[4]See, for example, Jesus' accusation in Mk 7:9-13, that the Pharisees contravene the law of Moses with their own legal extensions and contrivances.

[5]Montefiore 2/207 has seen, if not exploited, the relevance of these texts to this passage. For the assumption of Moses in later Judaism, see Josephus Ant 4/48:323-326, which even deals with the contradiction with the canonical tradition of Moses' death (Deut 24:5f). The idea of Moses' assumption may be a popular development from the clouds which envelop Moses when he talks to God. For references to the rabbinic literature, see Vermes **Jesus** 186f.

The Empty Tomb

Mk 15:40–16:8, the Empty Tomb, fulfils the Resurrection predictions, and probably belongs to the same layer. It depicts Jesus' burial and his bodily Resurrection after three days. It has been challenged as a later addition. Grant in 1943 (p179) argued that Mark originally ended with the centurion's acknowledgement of Jesus as Son of God in Mk 15:39. Kirby 2002 notes that the Parable of the Vineyard, Mk 12:1-12, depicts Jesus' fate as having his body tossed out of the city and buried in an unmarked grave. Yarbro Collins 2007 argues on other grounds for the absence of the Empty Tomb story in what she calls the Pre-Markan Passion Narrative; which she ends at Mk 15:38.[6] These arguments agree with the above finding, that the Passion Predictions are secondary in Mark. So the tradition of Jesus' Resurrection after Three Days does indeed exist in Mark, *but only in passages which seem to be later additions to the text.*

The Deaths of Jesus

If the Resurrection After Three Days is a later development within Christianity,[7] how *did* the life of Jesus end? We have seen that other ideas of Jesus' end are envisioned in Mark: the earlier expectations to which the repeated Passion Predictions are juxtaposed, *as though they were intentional correctives of what precedes them:*

- Mk 8:27-30. **Messiah Expectation** / Mk 8:31-33. Resurrection Correction
- Mk 9:30, 33f. **Messiah Expectation** / Mk 9:31b-32. Resurrection Correction
- Mk 10:32a. **Messianic Argument** / Mk 10:32b-34. Resurrection Correction
- Mk 9:2-9a. **Jesus in Heaven** / Mk 9:9b-13. Resurrection Correction

The Messiah Expectation did not come off, and Jesus was crucified as a failed candidate for the title "King of the Jews." The other option to which the Burial and Resurrection predictions stand opposed is the Jesus who ascended direct to Heaven. As above noted, the vision of Mk 9:2-9a links Jesus with persons believed to have ascended to Heaven at the time of their deaths. That tradition survives in Luke, when Jesus address the Repentant Thief:

- **Lk 23:43**. "Verily I say unto thee, Today shalt thou be with me in Paradise."

This contradicts the rest of Luke's Passion story, and is probably not a late innovation. It more likely reflects an early tradition which had become secure in popular affection.

These two options may be combined as follows: Jesus died as a disappointed national Messiah, but ascended direct to Heaven at his death, to return in glory later.

The Davidic Messiah

How could anyone write an account of Jesus that ends with his failure as Messiah? *Yet this is what Mark does.*[8] The only credible answer is that this is what happened:

---

[6]She ends the "Pre-Markan Passion Narrative" at 15:38, the Rending of the Veil. I see no difference, other than nomenclature, between "Pre-Markan" and a label such as "Mark A."

[7]In context, part of a general divinization process; see Brooks **Four** 11.

[8]Still agreeing with Yarbro Collins **Mark** 819 that the Gospel originally ended at Mk 15:38.

Notice how much of that outcome survives in Mark:

- **Mk 2:25-28**. Jesus invokes the example of David to justify plucking the grain
- **Mk 4:1-9, 21-33**. Jesus preaches the coming Kingdom in veiled terms[9]
- **Mk 10:47**. Blind Bartimaeus calls on "Jesus, thou Son of David" to heal him
- **Mk 11:1-10**. Jesus' disciples stage his entry into Jerusalem so as to evoke Zech 9:9 ("riding on an ass"); the crowd acclaims "the Kingdom of David"
- **Mk 11:11**. Jesus and his party inspect the Temple and return to their lodging
- **Mk 11:15, 17**. Jesus purifies the Temple by driving out the moneychangers (it was at the Temple that God was expected to return to Israel; Mal 3:1)
- **Mk 11:16**. Jesus' party prevent commercial access to the Temple grounds
- **Mk 12:35-37**. He argues that the Messiah need *not* be a descendant of David[10]
- **Mk 15:2**. Jesus acknowledges his intent before Pilate ("You have said so")
- **Mk 15: 9, 12, 18, 32**. Jesus is mocked by Jews and Romans as a Messianic pretender, "the King of the Jews [or Israel]"
- **Mk 15:26**. The inscription on the Cross reads, "King of the Jews"
- **Mk 15:34**. Jesus dies feeling that he has been abandoned by God

There is also the passage where Jesus' friends think him demented:

Mk 3:19b. And he cometh into a house. [20] And the multitude cometh together again, so that they could not so much as eat bread. [21] And when his friends heard it, they went out to lay hands on him, for they said, He is beside himself.

[22] And the scribes that came down from Jerusalem said, He hath Beelzebub, and, By the Prince of Demons casteth he out the demons . . . [30] because they had said, He hath an unclean spirit.

[31] And there come his mother and his brethren, and, standing without, they sent unto him, calling him. [32] And a multitude was sitting about him, and they say unto him, Behold, thy mother and thy brethren without seek for thee. [34] And looking round on them that sat round about him, he saith, Behold, my mother and my brethren! [35] For whosoever shall do the will of God, the same is my brother, and sister, and mother.

If Jesus had become convinced of his Davidic Messiah role, the concern of his friends and family for his sanity was entirely justified. We might thus add Mk 3:19b-21 and 31-35 to the list of Davidic passages in Mark.

Now notice the pattern of Mk 3:22-30, "scribes from Jerusalem." The theme is interruptive (not Jesus' sanity, but his being in league with Satan). Further, it is also situationally at odds with its context.[11] If we remove it, the concern of Jesus' family and friends join to make a consistent story. Here too, a Davidic passage is interrupted *by something else*, and the implication is that the Davidic passage is the earlier.

---

[9]For the Mark 4 parables, see further Brooks **Parables**.

[10]Popular tradition soon supplied Jesus with Davidic credentials (Mt 1:1f, Lk 3:23f).

[11]Johannes Weiss puts it neatly. "3:20 geht Jesus in ein Haus, 3:31-35 ist die Scene im Hause gedacht, wo aber sind die γραμματεῖς 3:22? auch im Hause?" (**Älteste** 165).

Another Interpolation. Consider also the two endings to the story of Plucking Grain on the Sabbath. No story needs two endings; which one is the original? Jesus' defense of his disciples' actions consists of a citation of a Davidic precedent, when David and those with him, being in need, entered the House of God and ate the Bread of the Presence, "and gave also to them that were with him" (see 1 Sam 21:1-6). As the conclusion to that statement, we have these two possibilities:

• **Mk 2:27**. And he said unto them, The Sabbath was made for man, not man for the Sabbath.
• **Mk 2:28**. So that the Son of Man is Lord even of the Sabbath.

Of the two, it is 2:28, the Son of Man passage (notice the link ὥστε "so that," as in a logical demonstration), that connects with what precedes, and is the proper ending.

The other argument against 2:27 is textual: it is missing in Matthew and Luke, and also in Codex Bezae. A similar situation was noticed by Westcott and Hort for nine passages which they call "Western Non-Interpolations:" early additions to the good ancestor of Codices Vaticanus and Sinaiticus, but absent in the even better ancestor behind Bezae. Mk 2:28 is not among the Westcott/Hort list of Nine, but it qualifies by their criteria. Besides, if the universalistic 2:27 were original, it is hard to see why it would have been omitted by copyists, but easy to see why it might have been added by a scribe as a wider remake of the narrow Davidic argument. It is then the Davidic ending which is original, and the universal one which is later.

The Messianic Expectation survives in Luke. A disciple asks the risen Jesus,

Ac 1:6. Lord, dost thou at this time restore the kingdom to Israel?

. . . as if Jesus' death were a mere delay in his Messianic program. In Ac 1:7, Jesus fobs them off: that is no longer a proper subject for discussion. And why is it not? Because *the movement's theory of its leader has moved on,* as Ac 1:8 spells out.

The Direct Ascent

This is the other model which the Resurrection predictions oppose. Of what did it consist? From Mark and other texts, we learn that Jesus' disciples fled at his arrest, and returned to Galilee. Then one of them, probably Peter,[12] had a vision of Jesus in Heaven; the Jesus movement had a rationale for continuing. It was at that moment that Christianity began. This vision *was unexpected*, as in the two stories which show Peter and others back in Galilee and going fishing, *without any thought* of seeing Jesus.[13] Matthew's completion (Mt 28:15-20) of Mark's mutilated ending[14] has the Eleven (minus Judas) go to Galilee, "unto the mountain where Jesus had appointed them." This mountain vision may be derived from the mountain vision of Mk 9:2-8.[15]

---

[12]So Paul (or his editors) in 1 Cor 15:5.

[13]One version is in Jn 21, a later addition to that Gospel; the other is the conclusion to the incompletely preserved Gospel of Peter (Elliott 158).

[14]That the present ending of Mark is defective is implied by scribal attempts (not to mention that of Matthew) to supply it. See Metzger **Textual** at Mk 16:9-20, and n19 below.

[15]First suggested by Wellhausen **Marci** 71.

The other suggestive point is that some stories of the bodily resurrected Jesus include incidents in which he also appears or disappears like a spirit. In Lk 24:13-31, the risen Jesus is recognized by two companions as he breaks bread (as though to eat, a proof of physicality), *but then immediately vanishes*. In Lk 24:36-37, Jesus *suddenly appears* to the disciples, and does in fact eat, but later, outside the city, he suddenly "*was carried up to Heaven*" (24:51). This oscillating mixture might result from the overlay of a later tradition (the tangible Jesus) on an earlier one (the spiritual Jesus).

It is easy to see how the idea of the bodily return of Jesus might have arisen. A claim of a body touched is stronger than a claim of a vision seen, and might have been added to strengthen the Resurrection claim.[16] Since resurrection on the Sabbath would offend Jewish sensibilities, a three-day interval is needed (crucified on Friday, remaining buried on Saturday, bodily risen on Sunday), perhaps with support from the story of Jonah.[17] Finally, the reappearance of Jesus in Jerusalem (rather than Galilee, as had been predicted in Mk 14:28 and in Mk 16:7), fits the Jerusalemizing tendency which may be seen in all the Gospels.[18] Of these conflicting accounts, the spiritual and the bodily resurrection, the bodily resurrection version, with its Jerusalem associations, is thus probably the later.

Mark actually narrates neither the Galilee vision nor the Jerusalem Resurrection. Instead, the Gospel breaks off at a narratively and grammatically impossible place.[19] If the story had continued after 16:8, it would have told of the bodily Resurrection in Jerusalem, and ended (as Mk 14:28 predicts) with Peter's vision of Jesus in Galilee.

Which of these two mutually incompatible outcomes was earlier in Mark? To that, there can be only one philologically satisfactory answer. Since the predictions of the Galilee appearance are *interpolated into* the story of the Jerusalem appearance, it is inevitable that the Jerusalem appearance, the Empty Tomb story, was added first, and that the Galilee vision, was added still later, in a position at the end of the text. Since the Gospel of Mark shows many signs of being a Jerusalem production (the Gospel is precise and detailed about events occurring in or near Jerusalem, including the passwords of the Jesus party as they staged the Entry Into Jerusalem or arranged a place for the party to eat the Passover; and the names of some prsons present at the Crucifixion, *and their children*, but vague about names of persons or the sequence of events in distant Galilee), it is plausible that, at one point in the evolution of the text, the Jerusalem version of the Resurrection was the last thing in the Gospel.

[16]Even the bodily-resurrection claim was to be challenged, as we see in Mt 27:62-68.

[17]Mt 16:4 adds "Jonah" to Mk 8:12; see also Mt 12:38-42 ‖ Lk 11:29-32.

[18]See Brooks **Four** 12.

[19]Knox **Ending** (1942) 22, "To suppose that Mark originally intended to end his Gospel in this way implies both that he was totally indifferent to the canons of popular story-telling, and that by pure accident he happened to hit on a conclusion which suits the technique of a highly sophisticated type of modern literature. The odds against such a coincidence . . . seem to me to be to be so enormous as not to be worth considering." Manson **Studies** (1962) 30, "while ἐφοβοῦντο γάρ may conceivably be the end of a sentence, it cannot well be the end of a Gospel, or even of a paragraph. We must suppose that the end of the Gospel is lost, and that the additional verses which appear in our manuscripts are attempts to repair the damage."

Summary

We find that the material in Mark tells more than one story of the death of Jesus. If taken in the sequence indicated by the interpolation evidence, the Davidic stratum (ending at 15:38) preceded the Resurrection stratum, and this in turn was followed by an account of the Galilee vision. What has happened to produce this situation?

(1) The vision of Peter, back in Galilee, saved the Jesus movement from extinction in the wake of Jesus' unanticipated death. Jesus *was still in existence*, and in Heaven; not buried in the earth. The vision of Mk 9:2-9a, as above noted, in which Jesus appears with earlier figures who had also ascended direct to Heaven on their death, and never seen burial and corruption, is Mark's first version of the Galilee vision, placed *at the center* and not the end of his story. (2) Impressed by the later idea of a Jerusalem Resurrection, Mark of Jerusalem *adds it to the end of his text*. (3) Still later, he adds an account of the Galilee vision at the end of his text, and inserts predictions of that episode (Mk 14:28 and 16:7) into his account of the Jerusalem Resurrection. (4) For whatever reason, this new ending does not survive in the final canonical text.

Many locations have been proposed for Mark, but I venture to add one more:

Mark is the Jerusalem Gospel.

The idea of Jesus' death in the seemingly oldest strata of Mark, which attach no theological importance to it, agrees with the early belief to which I have elsewhere[20] given the name Alpha Christianity, a belief which makes no use of the Resurrection, or of any other theory based on Jesus' death.

Works Cited

E Bruce Brooks. Four Gospel Trajectories. Alpha v1 (2017) 15-16

E Bruce Brooks. The Reader in the Text. Alpha v1 (2017) 25-29

E Bruce Brooks. Salome. Alpha v1 (2017) 94-98

E Bruce Brooks. Mark's Parables of the Kingdom. Alpha v1 (2017) 89-91

E Bruce Brooks. Time Depth in Mark. Alpha v1 (2017) 73-80

E Bruce Brooks. The Two Ways. Alpha v1 (2017) 39-47

Frederick C Grant. The Earliest Gospel. Abingdon 1943

Peter Kirby. The Case Against the Empty Tomb. JHC v9 (2002) 175-202

Wilfred Lawrence Knox. The Ending of St Mark's Gospel. HTR v35 (1942) 13-23

T W Manson. Studies in the Gospels and Epistles. Westminster 1962

C G Montefiore. The Synoptic Gospels. 1909; 2ed 2v Macmillan 1927

Georg Strecker. The Passion and Resurrection Predictions in Mark's Gospel. Interpretation
    v22 (1968) 421-442

Geza Vermes. Jesus the Jew. Collins 1973

Johannes Weiss. Das Älteste Evangelium. Vandenhoeck 1903

Julius Wellhausen. Das Evangelium Marci. 2ed Reimer 1909

Adela Yarbro Collins. Mark. Fortress 2007

---

[20]Brooks **Two** 39.

Mark's Parables of the Kingdom

E Bruce Brooks
University of Massachusetts at Amherst
(14 June 2013)

One long stretch of Jesus teaching in Mark is the Parables of the Kingdom, 4:1-33. At the end Mark tells us, "and with *many such* parables (παραβολαῖς; similitudes, not story parables) spake he the word unto them, as they were able to hear it." So this is an assemblage of *typical* parables, and not a consecutive sermon. I here take up the reinterpretation of the first parable given in Mk 4:10-20, and its implications.

Meaning. Most of the parables[1] describe the small growing large, or the hidden revealed. It is not hard to see these as reflecting covert preaching of the Messianic Kingdom which would soon exist in its fullness. Covert, because realizing God's promise to David in real time would involve expulsion of the Romans, who were concerned to prevent anything of the kind. Messianic, because that is the charge on which Jesus was later executed by those same Romans.[2] Here are the Mk 4 parables:

4:3-9. Parable of the Sower: Only some seed yields fruit
4:21-23. There is nothing secret that will not be revealed
4:26-29. The seed will grow secretly until the harvest comes
4:30-32. The tiny mustard seed grows to give shelter to the birds of the air

Reinterpretation. The Parable of the Sower is evidently addressed to the crowd, but 4:10-20 (suddenly addressing the disciples) intrudes to *eliminate* the crowd; it says that *only* the disciples can understand Jesus' preaching (and they, not all that clearly).[3] So far the reinterpretation of the Sower. But what is it that is being reinterpreted? What did the Sower Parable originally mean? It means what 4:10-20 says it means: it encourages those spreading the Word but finding their efforts sometimes unavailing.

But 4:10-20 restricts understanding to the *disciples*, whereas the parable as written *encourages the crowd*. Then it originally *envisioned many as preaching the Word.*[4] The issue is the contrast between contact preaching (each convert tells others) and the orderly preaching of the Apostles. Mk 4:10-20 has been seen as rebuking the disciples.[5] Rather, its function is to *reject the crowd* as carriers of the Word.

---

[1]The exception is the ethical 4:24-25 (The Measure You Give), which has no Kingdom symbolism, and belongs instead to Mark's poverty theme. See the Appendix.

[2]For this conclusion, doubtless uncomfortable to many, see Brooks **Resurrection** 86f.

[3]By Mk 4:12b, it is not intelligible to the crowds: "and hearing they may hear and not understand, lest haply they should turn again, and it should be forgiven them" (Isaiah 6:9-10). That is, *Jesus intends to be misunderstood* – easily the most repugnant statement in the Bible.

[4]Räisänen **Messianic** 140, "If one pays attention to the contents of the parables in Mk 4, they look like consolation and admonition for a community engaged in mission." Exactly so.

[5]As at first (Mk 4:13) it somewhat seems to do; see Weeden **Mark** 27-29.

Contact Missionarizing

We can test this by considering a point which the commentaries do not address: What is the meaning of sixtyfold? A preacher makes a convert. That convert counts as 1 (if a household, maybe 6). There is no way he could register as 30, or 60, or 100. *With contact missionarizing, the case is different.* Probably some converts *do* merely count as 1; they carry the Word no further. But fruitful individuals will tell others and persuade the village (30), the neighbors together will persuade the next village (60), and both villages together, a bigger village (100). Their fruitfulness more than offsets the failures, who do not accept the Word at all, or do so only temporarily.

Early Preaching. What evidence supports this idea of contact missionarizing? Consider the list of early bishops in Apostolic Constitutions 7:46; the evidence consists of the *gaps* in that survey. ApCon holds that Apostolic connections are necessary for the doctrinal soundness of the churches. It gives, for each church listed, its first bishop and the Apostle who appointed him. The evidence is the churches which are *not* mentioned, or whose Apostolic credentials are fantastic. Unmentioned are Armenia, Cyprus, Corinth, Damascus, Edessa, Ethiopia, Philippi, Sinope, and Thessalonica. Mentioned but fantastic is Caesarea, whose bishops are said to be Luke's Zacchaeus and Theophilus, plus Acts' Cornelius, none of whom ever existed.

Many centers included what I call Alpha (pre-Resurrection) Christians. From Alexandria came Apollos, who (Ac 18:24-26) had to be reinstructed by Priscilla and Aquila before he could preach Pauline doctrine. Paul in Romans (3:20-24, 4:1-3)[6] clearly argues with people who do not share his doctrines; note the curse on them, the ἀνάθεμα, at 1 Cor 16:22. As for the Christians of Sinope, as late as the early 2c they preserved a Christianity indistinguishable from the recommendations of the Didache, the Epistle of Jacob, and the Jesus of the early layers of Mark.[7]

There is very little surviving evidence of this earliest missionarizing, but what does exist seems to be consistent. It suggests an early wildfire spreading of the Word, as distinct from the more organized approach which we might associate with the Twelve.

The Twelve, as Eduard Meyer saw (**Ursprung** 1a/264-291), are extraneous in Mark. Meyer envisioned a Twelve Source, for which there is no scenario. They are instead likely to be later interpolations, updating Mark in this organizational sense. How do we know they are interpolated? Because this Twelve passage is interpolated:

> **Mk 6:6b**. And he went round the villages teaching.
>
> > [7] And he calleth unto him the Twelve, and began to send them forth by two and two, and he gave them authority over the unclean spirits . . .
>
> [14] And King Herod heard thereof, for his name had become known, and he said, John the Baptizer is risen from the dead, and therefore do these powers work in him.

Herod looks past the Twelve and reacts to Jesus' preaching. Then when Mk 6:14 was written, Mk 6:7-13, the Sending of the Twelve, *was not yet part of the text.*

---

[6]Bitterly contested by the Epistle of Jacob 2:18, 2:20-24. Jacob is an Alpha document.

[7]See respectively Brooks **Didache**, Brooks **Jacob**, and Brooks **Pliny**.

We have now reached this position: (1) The Mk 4 parables are an assemblage, not a sermon. They covertly preach a coming Kingdom of God, not to mislead the crowds (to whom Jesus appeals: "Who hath ears to hear, let him hear"), but to keep the Messianic Plan from reaching the ears of the Roman authorities. (2) This appeal to the crowd as spreaders of the Word was later reinterpreted in Mk 4:10-20 to restrict knowledge of Jesus' message to an accredited elite. (3) We know that Mk 4:10-20 is interpolated because it interrupts the series of parables, it involves a sudden change of audience, and it imposes an elite meaning on the first parable. (4) We know that the Twelve or their precursors, the likely beneficiaries of the elite reading of Mk 4:10-20, are themselves interpolated in Mark, one example being Mk 6:7-13, noted above.

What this implies is early contact missionarizing, which perhaps because of its lack of structure went fast and far: Rome in the west, Sinope in the north, Alexandria in the south. Apostolic tradition either knows nothing of this effort, or else has filled the gap with fantastical inventions (Caesarea) or known but post-Neronian leaders (Rome).

Appendix: Mark 4:24-25

This is the only one of the Mark 4 Parables that is not a metaphor of the coming of the Kingdom, or the spread of the Word concerning it. It reads as follows:

> **Mk 4:24**. And he said unto them, Take heed what ye hear: with what measure ye mete it shall be measured unto you, and more shall be given unto you. [25] For he that hath, to him shall be given, and he that hath not, from him shall be taken even that which he hath.

There are two things wrong with this as one of the Mark 4 Parables. First, as an ethical pronouncement, it is at odds with the covert parables of the Kingdom. Second, a small point, the command to hear comes at the beginning, and not, as in the earlier parables, at the end ("Who hath ears to hear, let him hear," Mk 4:9 and 4:23).

An economic analogue to Mk 4:24-25 is Mk 10:29-30 (the second of two addenda to the Rich Young Man story, 10:17-22), where Jesus says that those who lose family or property *will receive it again* as communal brotherliness and community property. The point of the Woman with Two Mites (12:41-44) is that even a tiny divestment counts as large. 10:29-30 and 12:41-44 are reinforced by the emphatic Verily (Ἀμὴν), and together with 4:24-25, may be taken as constituting a Poverty (P) layer in Mark.

That late idea is much further developed in Luke, whose Sermon in the Plain preaches a discipleship of complete divestment.

Works Cited

E Bruce Brooks. The Didache. Alpha v1 (2017) 48-57

E Bruce Brooks. The Epistle of Jacob. Alpha v1 (2017) 58-70

E Bruce Brooks: Luke's Sermon on the Way. Alpha v1 (2017) 167-179

E Bruce Brooks. Pliny at Pontus. Alpha v1 (2017) 209-214

E Bruce Brooks. The Resurrection of Jesus in Mark. Alpha v1 (2017) 81-88

Eduard Meyer. Ursprung und Anfänge des Christentums. 2v Cotta 1921, 1923

Heikki Räisänen. The Messianic Secret in Mark. 1976; tr T & T Clark 1990

Theodore J Weeden Sr. Mark: Traditions in Conflict. Fortress 1971

Josephus and Mark

Brad McAdon
University of Memphis
SBL/EGL (17 March 2017)

The author of our canonical Mark may have been influenced by several texts: Paul's letters (especially Romans, 1 Corinthians, Galatians, and 1 Thessalonians), Josephus's *Antiquities* Book 18, and the Septuagint. If so, there will be significant implications concerning the historicity of Mark's John the Baptist narratives, the dating of canonical Mark, and Mark's compositional practices. I here take up the Josephus possibility. There are two principal Markan passages.

The Introduction of John at the beginning of the Gospel, Mk 1:4-6:

• There are several thematic similarities between Mk's narrative of JB's baptism and proclamation and Josephus's account of the same (see the table on the next page). These similarities need to be explained.

• There are significant differences between Mk's narrative of JB's baptism and proclamation and Josephus's account of the same. These differences can be explained if Mark used Josephus for his model and then Christianized John to serve his (Mark's) rhetorical ends.

• There is a chronological incongruity. Josephus seems (1) to place John's baptism after Jesus's activity and (2) to date John's death in 36 CE, which is several years later than the NT seems to date his activity and death.

The Death of John in Mk 6:14-29:

• The number of specific details within these similarities are striking, and suggest dependence. Moreover, the fact that Josephus's *Antiquities* 18 is the only extant source that includes narrative material on the Herodian family, a Philip, Herod Antipas, Herod Antipas and Herodias's relationship, John's criticism of this relationship, John's baptism, arrest, imprisonment, and death strongly suggest dependence one way or the other. If, for example, Mark did not know and use *Antiquities* 18, this would mean that he must have had access to and used some other source material for these narrative components of John's baptism and death including specific details about the Herodian family – including ambiguity about a Philip – and John's baptism, arrest, and death that is extremely similar in content to, if not identical to, *Antiquities* 18. So far, we know of no such source.

Some of the Implications:

• Historicity of John the Baptist narratives in Mark

• Dating of the composition of Mark

• Contribution to understanding more about the final author of Mark's compositional practices.

Josephus's Antiquities Book 18	Narrative Theme	Mark
John Surnamed the Baptist	John's name	John the Baptist (1:4)
Jews and others too	Attracts audiences	All in Judea, the Jerusalemites
Exhorted Jews to join in baptism	John's proclamation	Proclaiming a baptism
Aroused by his sermons	John was persuasive	All baptized, confessing sins
When others joined the crowds	Herod disturbed	By what he heard from John
"a good man"	John was . . .	"a good and holy man"
Brought in chains to Machaerus	John's arrest	"after John had been arrested"
Relationship detailed	Herod and Herodias	Relationship briefly mentioned
Was previously married	Her previous marriage	Was previously married
Herod II (correct)	Her previous husband	Philip (incorrect)
Herodias's daughter's husband	Philip	Herodias' first husband
Traditional/religious reasons	Marriage criticized for	Traditional/religious reasons
Implicit reference	Lev 18:16, 20	Implicit reference
Fear of future sedition	Reason for arrest	Criticism of marriage
Identified as Salome	Herodias's daughter	Not named

Discussion
After the EGL Meeting

Question: The Herods were public figures. John's movement, Mark and Josephus agree, was also public. Are not both relying on common knowledge, whence the many similarities in their accounts, but with varying emphasis? As an example of varying emphasis ("reason for arrest"), criticizing Herod's marital irregularities was seditious, since it challenged the legitimacy of his rule. Is it likely that Mark knew nothing of these matters, went to Josephus to learn of them, and then miscopied Josephus?

The Author: It does not follow that the detailed narrative material in Mark and Josephus was public / common knowledge. If it were common knowledge, why is it that our only extant sources of this detailed narrative material are Mark and Josephus? As the table above indicates, Philip is just one of the many similar themes in the John the Baptist narratives between Mark and Josephus. Josephus's description of Herod Antipas's brother Philip just prior to his explanation of Herodias's first husband Herod, who was also a brother of Antipas (*Ant* 18:106-110), is obscure enough for a sometimes inexact reader and writer like Mark to confuse Philip with Herod.

There are reasonable reasons why Josephus would not use Mark as his source. I am not aware of reasonable reasons why Mark would not use Josephus.

Salome

E Bruce Brooks

University of Massachusetts at Amherst

(21 Feb 2011)

The usual picture of Jesus wandering over Galilee does not include details such as food and lodging. Who paid the bills? The short answer seems to be: rich women.[1] Officially, under Greco-Roman law, women were subject to fathers, husbands, or sons. The economic facts were sometimes different. As witness the case of Salome.

The Women at the Cross. According to Mark 15:40-41, these women witnessed the crucifixion of Jesus: "both Mary Magdalene and Mary the mother of Jacob the less and of Joses, and Salome; who when he was in Galilee, followed him and ministered to him; and many other women that came up with him unto Jerusalem." Notice the flashback to Galilee; it is their *ministering there* that defines them for Mark. Further:

> • **Mk 15:47**. And Mary Magdalene and Mary the mother of Joses beheld where he was laid.
> • **Mk 16:1**. And when the Sabbath was past, Mary Magdalene and Mary the mother of Jacob, and Salome, brought spices, that they might come and anoint him.

That is, two located the tomb, but all three came to anoint Jesus. In Luke we have:

> • **Lk 23:49**. And all his acquaintance, and the women that followed with him from Galilee, stood afar off, seeing these things . . .
> • **Lk 23:55**. And the women, who had come with him out of Galilee, followed after, and beheld the tomb, and how his body was laid.
> • **Lk 24:1**. But on the first day of the week, at early dawn, they came unto the tomb, bringing the spices which they had prepared . . . [9] and returned from the tomb and told all these things to the eleven . . . [10] Now they were Mary Magdalene, and Joanna, and Mary the mother of Jacob; and the other women with them told these things unto the apostles.

There are always three, but their names are partly different. Elsewhere in Luke:

> • **Lk 8:1**. And it came to pass soon afterwards that he went about through cities and villages, preaching and bringing the good tidings of the Kingdom of God, and with him the Twelve, [2] and certain women who had been healed of evil spirits and infirmities: Mary that was called Magdalene, from whom seven demons had gone out, [3] and Joanna the wife of Chuza Herod's steward, and Susanna, and many others, who ministered unto them of their substance.

That is, the economic function has been transferred to a slightly different group, introduced earlier, some of whom are said to have been *previously healed by Jesus*. They are no longer *benefactors*, but *beneficiaries*, of Jesus. Jesus is supreme.

---

[1] For rich women as donors in Judaism, see Brooten **Women** 141f, 157f.

In Lk 8, then, Mary the mother of Jacob and Salome were replaced by Joanna and Susanna, but in Lk 24, the mother of Jacob is again restored to the group at the Cross. This is something often seen: an author makes a change, but not *consistently*, and a detail in the original text reappears in the derivative text.[2] The intermittent consistency of the rewrite is one way we can distinguish it from the earlier version. Luke puts this Galilee information where it belongs chronologically, and reidentifies the women. But Luke's changes are not maintained, and the earlier tradition of the Women at the Cross shows through when Luke reaches that point in the rewritten narrative. This is one way we know that Luke is later than Mark.[3]

So far Luke. The Women at the Cross passage in Matthew reads this way:

> • **Mt 27:55**. And many women were there beholding from afar, who had followed Jesus from Galilee, ministering unto him; [56] among whom was Mary Magdalene, and Mary the mother of Jacob and Joses, and the mother of the sons of Zebedee.

Matthew here subtly eliminates Mark's Galilee information (Mark: "who *when he was in Galilee*, followed him and ministered to him"); in Matthew, their ministering is confined to the present journey. Matthew also omits Salome's name and contrasts the Jacobs in another way. Mark tells us that one Jacob is "the less;" Matthew tells us that the other Jacob is the son of Zebedee – a far more important figure.

Matthew may have felt uncomfortable with the name Salome,[4] and in his later references to the Women at the Cross, she drops out altogether, leaving the two Marys:

> **Mt 27:61**. And Mary Magdalene was there [at the burial], and the other Mary, sitting over against the sepulcher.
>
> **Mt 28:1**. Now late on the Sabbath day, as it began to dawn toward the first of the week, came Mary Magdalene and the other Mary to see the sepulchre.

---

[2] For further examples of this phenomenon, see Goodacre **Fatigue**.

[3] Another reason may be Luke's inclusion of "Joanna, the wife of Chuza Herod's steward." Joanna appears nowhere else in the early literature, and her high political connection may be a result of Lukan social reaching. It would have been very advantageous to the early Christians to have this degree of acceptance in high places. Luke in Acts shows Paul as kindly received by many of the Romans before whom he appears, perhaps a further instance of this technique, meant to show that Christianity is harmless to Rome. Php 4:22 ("those of Caesar's household greet you") claims similar connections. This letter is genuine, but the personalia of all the letters are subject to tampering; in this case, probably by Paul's editors (see Brooks **Philippi** 112), who wished to make both Paul and Christianity more acceptable to Rome.

[4] Salome, the daughter of Herodias (Josephus Ant 18/5:4; Mk 6:17-29 does not name her), had by her dancing brought about the death of John the Baptist. Herodias' hatred for John was due to his disapproval of her divorce from a first husband to marry Herod Antipas (Josephus Ant 18/5:1). Salome married Philip the Tetrarch, and after his death, her kinsman Aristobolus, whose kingdoms were in Chalcis and Armenia (Josephus Ant 18/5:4; her image appears with his on coins of those realms). She may have shared her mother's hatred of John, and perhaps John's disciple Jesus, who also held strict views on divorce (emphasized in the Synoptics and in 1 Cor 7:11-13). Except for Mk 15:40 and 16:1, the name Salome never appears in the NT.

Nor does Matthew name Salome when he has *her* ask Jesus for a favor. Here is Mark:

> **Mk 10:35**. And there came near unto him Jacob and John the sons of Zebedee, saying unto him, Teacher, we would that thou shouldest do for us whatsoever we shall ask of thee.

But in Matthew, who inserts her into the story, her name does not appear:

> **Mt 20:20**. Then came to him the mother of the sons of Zebedee with her sons, worshiping him and asking a certain thing of him.

The following request for positions of power is the same in both cases.

The Families. Mark's "Jacob the less" is the Jacob who is *not* the son of Zebedee. From the Mk 3:16-19 list, he is Jacob of Alphaeus, the brother of Levi of Alphaeus; Levi is called by Jesus to be a disciple in Mk 2:14. We then have these parentages:

- Alphaeus and Mary > Levi (one of the Five), Jacob (one of the Twelve) and Joses
- Zebedee and Salome > Jacob and John (two of the Five, included in the Twelve)

These families between them supplied four of the principal followers of Jesus. We are also informed that the wives (but, as far as we are told, apparently not the husbands) were among the supporters – the day-to-day infrastructure – of the Jesus movement.

The Other Brothers among the early Jesus followers are Peter and Andrew. They were not rich. Mk 1:16-18 describes them as "casting a net" and leaving the "nets" when Jesus calls; they are seemingly working from shore, not from a boat. By contrast, Jacob and John do have boats (Mk 1:19) and employ other hands (Mk 1:20). Peter lived in his wife's mother's house; his wife accompanied him on mission (1 Cor 9:5). The economic base of both was then her mother, seemingly a widow with property.[5]

Jacob and John may have felt that their wealth entitled them to higher status than Peter. Paul and Acts both imply that at Jerusalem Jacob Zebedee *was* superior to Peter. It is thus reasonable that Jacob was the first to be killed by Herod Agrippa I in c44. Peter, who escaped, was apparently next on the hit list.[6]

Mythical Development. If from the Markan women at the tomb (Mary Magdalene, Mary of Alphaeus, and Salome of Zebedee), we follow Matthew in removing Salome, we have left two Marys and a blank. The blank promptly attracted a replacement. Given the increasing prominence of Jesus' mother in successive Gospels,[7] it was not unlikely that developing tradition would push her into Salome's slot, giving Three Marys. This is exactly what happens. In John, only Mary Magdalene is named among the women at the tomb, but as witnesses to the Crucifixion, John has Three Marys: "[Jesus'] mother; his mother's sister, Mary the wife of Clopas; and Mary Magdalene" (Jn 19:25).[8] John's inclusion of Jesus' mother is sentimentally satisfying, but it is also mythologically predictable. It is probably not based on better information.

[5]We should not forget, in this connection, the mother of John Mark of Jerusalem, whose evidently large house was a rendezvous point for Christians in Jerusalem (Ac 12:12-17).

[6]Mk 10:39, cf Ac 12:1-3.

[7]For this early tendency, see Brooks **Four** 15, "The Mary Trajectory."

[8]The relationship is obviously fantastic; no family would have two daughters named Mary.

Economic Aspects. Traditions add, and traditions also discard. Matthew, in having the mother of Jacob and John make their request for them (though Jesus' plural "you" in Mt 20:22, as though addressing the brothers themselves, implies the earlier story),[9] has relieved them of the onus of personal ambition. The women's "ministering" in Galilee also gets attenuated over time. As we have seen, it is transferred to another group of three in Lk 8:3, and is absent altogether in Matthew and John. That Jesus and company had to be fed and otherwise supported in their travels may have been too earthy a fact to survive in the increasingly ethereal (and Cross-centered) Jesus image which later tradition preferred to construct for itself.

The Apocryphal Salome

Salome never recurs in the NT after her cameo role in Mark. In the apocryphal literature, she becomes (1) a disciple, who shares attributes with Mary Magdalene,[10] or slightly later, (2) an acquaintance of the family at the time of Jesus' birth.

Salome the Disciple is a parallel to the Gnostic development of Mary Magdalene, for which see the Gospel of Mary.[11] Here is Salome as a disciple:

- Gospel of the Egyptians (mid 2c). Salome asks when death will end; is told "when you women stop having children." Procreation as such is disprized.[12]
- Gospel of Thomas (2c) #61. "Salome said, Who are you, man? You have reclined on my couch and have eaten at my table." Jesus said to her, "I am he who derives his being from him who is undifferentiated. The things of my Father have been given to me." [She said], "I am your disciple."[13]

The intimacy here is that of sharing a meal; "undifferentiated" refers to the lack of distinction between the sexes (and the disapproval of procreation) in Gnostic belief. Wives who leave their husbands to live chastely are common in the later literature.

The disciple Salome was later referred to as a temptress:

- Book of the Resurrection by Bartholomew the Apostle (5c/6c). "Salome who tempted him" is listed among the Women at the Tomb.[14]

This may go back to a too enthusiastic reading of "You have reclined on my couch," in the above passage of the Gospel of Thomas.

---

[9]Here is another instance of second-author fatigue: Matthew reverts to his Mark source.

[10]Bauckham **Salome** describes Salome throughout as Jesus' disciple, entirely suppressing the economic function she has in our earliest witness, Mark. His evidence for Salome as originally Jesus' sister does not convince the present writer. The general tendency is for traditions to increasingly emphasize kinship (Bauckham p246 relies in part on Epiphanius, Panarion 78/9:6, 376, an 04c text which is perhaps quoting the late 2c Hegesippus). Bauckham also relies in part on the genuineness of the Secret Gospel of Mark, which has recently been discredited as a forgery by its supposed discoverer, Morton Smith (see Carlson **Hoax**).

[11]Elliott 669. The Women there mentioned also include those named in Luke 8:3, plus Luke's inventions Mary and Martha, and Leah, whose son Jesus raised at Nain (Lk 7:11).

[12]Elliott 16, quoted by Clement of Alexandria (Elliott 18).

[13]Elliott 143, with adjustments.

[14]Elliott 669.

Salome the Family Companion is said to have been present at Christ's birth:

> • Protevangelium of Jacob (late 2c). The midwife tells Salome of the virgin birth. Salome doubts, but is miraculously convinced.[15]
> • Gospel of Pseudo-Matthew (8c?). *Two* midwives, Zelomi and Salome.[16]
> • History of Joseph the Carpenter (4c/5c). Salome accompanies the Holy Family to Egypt.[17]

Salome the Disciple and Salome the Family Companion are combined in:

> • Homily Attributed to Evodius: Evodius, with Salome and Joanna, and others, lived with Mary after the Passion.

which merely shows the fluidity of the later popular tradition.

------••••-------

Salome as the mother of the Zebedees and patroness of the Jesus movement soon vanished from Christian consciousness. It was as an intimate of Jesus, and secondarily of his mother, that she lived on. Here as elsewhere, later tradition's concentration on the figure of Jesus has led to loss of more pedestrian information which is better preserved in the earlier sources, and a change in the character, and the intensity, of the relationship which these women are imagined to have had with Jesus or his mother.

Thus does the increasingly unworldly figure of Jesus draw all to it, as time goes on. This is a familiar characteristic of all traditions, whether religious or secular.[18]

Works Cited

Harold W Attridge. The Acts of Thomas. Polebridge 2010

Richard Bauckham. Salome the Sister of Jesus, Salome the Disciple of Jesus, and the Secret Gospel of Mark. NovT v33 (1991) 245-275

E Bruce Brooks. Four Gospel Trajectories. Alpha v1 (2017) 15-16

E Bruce Brooks. Paul's Letters to Philippi. Alpha v1 (2017) 112-118

Bernadette J Brooten. Women Leaders in the Ancient Synagogue. Scholars 1982

Stephen C Carlson. Gospel Hoax. Baylor 2005

J K Elliott. The Apocryphal New Testament. Oxford 1993

Mark Goodacre. Fatigue in the Synoptics. NTS v44 (1998) 45-58

Robert H Gundry. Matthew. Eerdmans 1982

Lloyd Lewis. Myths After Lincoln. Readers Club 1941

Alfred Plummer. An Exegetical Commentary on . . . St Matthew. Clarke 1909

[15]Elliott 64. The doubt of Thomas in Jn 20:27-28 is cured by placing a hand in the other's body cavity. For Salome, who doubts Mary's virginity following the birth of Jesus, the cavity is Mary's vagina. On placing her finger in it, Salome exclaims, "Woe for my wickedness and my unbelief, for I have tempted the living God, and behold, my hand falls away from me, consumed by fire!" (Elliott 65). On touching the infant as then directed, her hand is healed.

[16]Elliott 92. This is clearly a development from the preceding, in which Salome has been doubled as two people with identical function and nearly identical names.

[17]Elliott 114.

[18]For a political example, with explicit parallels to the life of Jesus, see Lewis **Myths**.

Mark at Perga

E Bruce Brooks

University of Massachusetts at Amherst

(24 Dec 2013)

Information about the archaeology of Perga was recently summarized by Mark Fairchild.[1] This plus Acts 13, which recounts Mark's failure at Perga, suggests that passages added to Mark's Gospel to adapt it for non-Jews were after all unsuccessful.

Excavations at Perga and vicinity include material up to at least the 3rd century. No synagogue has been found in Perga.[2] The earliest evidence for Jews in Perga is a 3c (?) synagogue dedication inscription at Aphrodisias, 160 miles NW of Perga, which mentions Samuel, an Elder from Perga (ΣΑΜΟΥΗΛ ΠΡΕΣΒΕΥΤΗΣ ΠΕΡΓΕΟΥΣ).[3] That he was an Elder implies a Jewish community; that he helped fund the Aphrodisias synagogue suggests that the Perga Jews were too few to build their own synagogue. If such was the case with the Jews of 3rd century Perga, the Jews of 1st century Perga are unlikely to have been more numerous. There may have been none at all.

> **Ac 13:13**. Now Paul and his company set sail from Paphos and came to Perga in Pamphylia, and John [Mark] departed from them and returned to Jerusalem. [14] But they, passing through from Perga, came to Antioch of Pisidia, and they went into the Synagogue on the Sabbath day and sat down.

It would then seem that Mark quit when he first encountered a non-Jewish audience. Now, there are signs in Mark of attempts to adapt that Gospel to make it intelligible to those without knowledge of the Scriptures[4] or of Jewish customs. Among these is:

> **Mk 7:1**. And there are gathered together unto him the Pharisees and certain of the scribes, who had come from Jerusalem, [2] and had seen that some of his disciples ate their bread with defiled, that is, unwashen, hands.
>
> > [3] For the Pharisees and all Jews, except they wash their hands diligently, eat not, holding the tradition of the elders, [4] and when come from the market, except they bathe, they eat not; and many other things there are, which they have received: washing of cups and pots and brazen vessels).
>
> [5] And the Pharisees and scribes ask him, Why walk not thy disciples according to the tradition of the elders, but eat their bread with defiled hands?

---

[1] Fairchild **Perga**.

[2] Fairchild 55. This is the key fact.

[3] Fairchild 55-57. Samuel is the only 3c Jew who can be firmly connected with Perga.

[4] The dying cry of Jesus in Mk 15:34 is a defeat – *unless* the reader completes the allusion to Psalm 22, which turns it into a transcendent victory. For those unable to complete the allusion, Mark's story is unrelievedly pessimistic; see in detail below.

Alpha v1 (2017)

Not only is 7:3-4 parenthetical (the story resumes smoothly at 7:5), but it assumes *a different audience* than the Scripturally aware one Mark otherwise addresses. These details suggest an interpolation. Mk 7:3-4 occurs in all manuscripts, and is thus not a scribal corruption; it is better assigned to the text's formation period. It would seem to be Mark's attempt to adjust his text to the needs of a new audience.

Another passage (7:19b) may be ascribed to the same impulse: to simplify issues for Gentiles unfamiliar with Jewish references. The context is complex, and contains a shift of subject implying a later addition. Jesus is discussing Pharisee traditions:

Mk 7:13 . . . making void the word of God by your tradition which ye have delivered, and many such like things ye do.

[14] And he called to him the multitude again, and said unto them, Hear me all of you, and understand: [15] There is nothing from without the man, that going into him can defile him; but the things which proceed out of the man are those that defile the man.[5] [17] And when he was entered into the house from the multitude, his disciples asked of him the parable. [18] And he saith unto them, Are ye so without understanding also? Perceive ye not, that whatsoever from without goeth into the man, cannot defile him, [19] because it goeth not into his heart, but into his belly, and goeth out into the draught?

[19b] [This he said], making all meats clean.

[20] And he said, That which proceedeth out of the man, that defileth the man. [21] For from within, out of the heart of men, evil thoughts proceed, fornications, thefts, murders, adulteries, [22] Covetings, wickednesses, deceit, lasciviousness, an evil eye, railing, pride, foolishness; [23] all these evil things proceed from within, and defile the man.

The subject of 7:1-13 is Pharisee purity rules, including food preparation;[6] 7:14-23 rejects food rules and identifies sin as the real defilement.[7] This second step has its own introduction, and should be seen as a later phase in the argument, not composed at the same time as the segment ending at 7:13. To that second step, implicitly voiding the Pharisee food prohibitions, 7:19b offers a clear and explicit statement. It would appear to be a final clarifying addition, like 7:3-4, and intended for the same audience.

This argument depends on the factuality of Acts 13:13. Luke, the presumed author, also claims knowledge of Mark's mother's house in Jerusalem where the Christians gathered, none of which seems suspect. Luke is a creative author, and needs to be watched. It was undoubtedly to Luke's advantage to tell a negative story about Mark, whose Gospel Luke aimed to replace, but the story itself may be true. I here accept it. But this raises a further question, namely, Mark's reason for doing what Acts says he did at Perga. Acts simply says that "he departed from them and returned to Jerusalem," and that Paul later "thought best not to take with them one who had withdrawn from them in Pamphylia, and had not gone with them to the work" (Ac 15:38).

[5]Mk 7:16, here omitted, is considered by critical scholars to be a scribal addition

[6]The lack of continuity between 7:1-13 (washing) and 7:14-20 (permissible food) is manifest; Johnson 133 calls the latter "much more radical."

[7]For the list of sins, which has an outside source, see Brooks **Two** 40.

Motive. Why did Mark quit at Perga? Perhaps because *he preached his Gospel*, and his Gospel was not fully intelligible to Gentiles. For one thing, Mark's Passion narrative is suffused throughout by a sort of background music of Scripture allusions. Consider only the echoes and evocations of Psalm 22:[8]

Mark 15 Text	Psalm 22 Evocations
[22] And they bring him unto the place Golgotha, which is, being interpreted, the Place of a Skull. [23] And they offered him wine mingled with myrrh, but he received it not. [24] And they crucify him, and part his garments among them, casting lots upon them, what each should take. [25] And it was the third hour when they crucified him.	[16b] They pierced my hands and my feet. [18] They part my garments among them, and on my vesture do they cast lots.
... [29] And they that passed by railed on him, wagging their heads and saying, Ha! thou that destroyest the temple and buildest it in three days,	[7] All they that see me laugh me to scorn, they shoot out the lip, they shake the head, saying,
[30] save thyself and come down from the cross. [31] In like manner also the chief priests mocking him among themselves with the scribes, said, He saved others; himself he cannot save. [32] Let the Christ, the King of Israel, come down from the cross, that we may see and believe.	[8a] Commit thyself unto Jehovah, let him deliver him;
... [33] And when the sixth hour was come, there was darkness over the whole land until the ninth hour. [34] And at the ninth hour, Jesus cried with a loud voice, Eloi, Eloi, lama sabachthani? Which is, being interpreted,	[8b] Let him rescue him, seeing he delighteth in him.
My God my God, why hast thou forsaken me?	[1] My God, my God, why hast thou forsaken me?

So far Mark's bleak Crucifixion scene. But his readers, knowing the rest of Psalm 22 by heart, will have realized that it ends, not in despair, but in triumph:

> [23] Ye that fear Jehovah, praise him,
> All the seed of Jacob, glorify him,
> And stand in awe of him, all ye the
> seed of Israel
> [24] For he hath not despised nor
> abhorred the affliction of the afflicted;
> Neither hath he hid his face from him,
> But when he cried unto him, he heard.

---

[8]For a detailed account of Psalm 22 here and in related texts, see O'Brien **Use** 147-154.

Those unable to complete the righthand column will go away with an unrelievedly bleak account of Jesus' end. And knowing nothing of the Temple and its meaning, what will they make of Mark's symbolic representation of Jesus' vindication . . .

> [37] And Jesus uttered a loud cry
> and gave up the ghost. [38] And the
> veil of the Temple was rent in twain,
> from the top to the bottom.

. . . against the Temple authorities, who had been Jesus' enemies from the beginning? Answer: Nothing. The Scriptural music is lost, and the final symbol is inscrutable.

Mark's Gospel is a collaboration between author and audience; it works only for an audience which can smoothly supply the other half of the story as Mark tells it. Those of Perga, unfamiliar with Jewish life and Scripture, would have been baffled.

Conclusion. There is dirt archaeology. And there is text archaeology, whose business here is to note interpolations and detect allusions. What does all that work of noting and detecting tell us? In this case, it tells us that Mark's Gospel was designed for reading[9] by Jews or by Gentiles familiar with Jewish Scripture and customs. Despite Mk 7:3-4, 7:19b, and other last-minute patches (such as translations of Aramaic words) to make it work for a non-Jewish audience, Mark, preaching it at Perga, evidently failed to get it across. The patches were just not enough.

From Perga, Mark returned to Jerusalem (Acts 13:13), and to his mother's house, where his Gospel was once again in Jewish context.[10] If we credit local tradition,[11] Mark and his Gospel later found a home among the Jewish Christians of Alexandria. These at least would have had no trouble with Mark's Scriptural echoes.

Appendix: Last-Minute Additions to Mark

It would be wrong to conclude without noticing other plausible last-minute additions to Mark. Those here given supply information on Jewish ritual matters or translate terms from the Aramaic language. Their number implies a serious effort by Mark to deprovincialize his Gospel for wider use. That Mark's subtle use of Scripture allusions could not be ameliorated by this method does not impugn his good sense in employing the method where he could.

---

[9]Note Mk 13:14, "let him *that readeth* understand." Oral delivery is not excluded, but it would appear that Mark's own attempt to deliver the whole thing orally was not a success.

[10]The maid's name was Rhoda (Ac 12:13); see further Rothschild **Prosopography** 295f.

[11]Which seems to be on the whole sound, apart from an assimilation to the myth of Mark as Peter's interpreter at Rome, and a probably standard martyrdom story; see the short summary in Atiya **History** 25-28, and the longer appreciation in Oden **African**. Mark's association with Alexandria is the background for his appearance as one of twelve in the Assumption of the Virgin (4c), "And Mark, who was still alive, came from Alexandria with the rest, as has been said, from their several countries," and "And Mark also answered and said, As I was finishing the service of the third hour in the city of Alexandria, while I prayed, the Holy Ghost caught me up and brought me to you" (Elliott 702, 703). Nor is the Assumption an African text.

These groups of passages may plausibly be assigned to the final layer of Mark:

Explanations of Jewish customs and beliefs or adaptation to non-Jews:

- 2:27. In effect abolishes Sabbath rules
- 7:3-4. Explains Jewish washing of hands and food-preparation vessels
- 7:19b. A universalizing statement, that all foods are permissible
- 12:18b. Identifies the Sadducees as not believing in resurrection
- 14:12b. Defines the First Day of Unleavened Bread as the time when the Passover lambs are sacrificed

Translations of Aramaic phrases or Semitic words:

- 3:17. Boanerges = "sons of Thunder" [epithet of the Zebedees]
- 5:42. Talitha cumi = "little girl, rise" [word of healing]
- 7:11. Corban = "dedicated [to God]"
- 7:34. Ephphatha = "be opened" [word of healing]
- 14:36. Abba, "father"
- 15:22. Golgotha = "the place of a skull"
- 15:34. Eloi, Eloi, lama sabachthani = "My God, my God, why hast thou forsaken me?" [last words of the crucified Jesus]

Many of the Aramaisms in Mark occur at moments of great tension: words of healing, Jesus' prayer in Gethsemane, and his last utterance on the cross. That is presumably why they were put there in the first place; they are part of the drama which Mark has designed into his work. Mark later tried to preserve the drama by rendering these terms transparent for his new audience.

Not translated are the terms Rabbi (9:5, 11:21, and 14:45) and Rabboni (10:51). From the context it is evident that these are terms of respect used in addressing Jesus, and Mark probably thought them self-evident, even for non-Jewish hearers.[12]

Works Cited

Aziz S Atiya. History of Eastern Christianity. Gorgias 2010

C Clifton Black. John Mark in the Acts of the Apostles; in Thompson et al (ed), Literary Studies in Luke-Acts, Mercer (1998) 101-120

E Bruce Brooks. The Two Ways. Alpha v1 (2017) 39-47

Mark R Fairchild. Why Perga? BAR v39 #6 (2013) 52-59, 84

Sherman E Johnson. The Gospel According to St Mark. Black 1960

Kelli S O'Brien. The Use of Scripture in the Markan Passion Narrative. Clark 2010

Thomas C Oden. The African Memory of Mark: Reassessing Early Church Tradition. InterVarsity 2011

Clare K Rothschild. ἐτυμολογία, *Dramatis Personae*, and the Lukan Invention of an Early Christian Prosopography; in Rothschild et al (ed), The Rise and Expansion of Christianity in the First Three Centuries of the Common Era. Mohr (2013) 279-298

[12]Not content to rely on context, the Gospel of John deals with its first occurrence of the term thus: "Rabbi, which is to say, being interpreted, Teacher" (1:38), though leaving it untranslated on later occurrences (3:2, 3:26, 4:31, 6:25, 9:2, 11:8).

Jerusalem and Paul

E Bruce Brooks

University of Massachusetts at Amherst

(2013)

I here take up some problems connected with Paul's three visits to Jerusalem, plus the ill-fated mission journey of Mark with Paul between the second and third visits, and add a brief note on one of Paul's major opponents: Jacob the Lord's Brother.

1. Paul's Conversion and First Visit to Jerusalem

Paul persecuted the early Christians. As he himself says in Gal 1:13,

> For ye have heard of my manner of life in time past in the Jews' religion, how that beyond measure I persecuted the church of God, and made havoc of it.

Why did Paul persecute the early Christians? His self-descriptions make it clear. Jesus openly flouted the Sabbath (Mk 2:23-24) and argued against purity rules (Mk 7:5f); he recognized only six commandments (Mk 10:19). Jesus was thus a Jewish reformer. Paul was a Jewish conservative, focused on the Law, "being more exceedingly zealous for the traditions of my fathers" (Gal 1:14). Naturally he took offense. As with others whom we shall meet presently, offense for him took the form of arrest and murder.

Why then did he later *join* this hateful movement? Probably because it had changed in the meantime, to include the idea of Jesus' bodily resurrection.[1] This touched Paul's other nerve. As a Pharisee, he believed in the Law, whose exceeding many provisions made sin and death inevitable, but as a Pharisee, he also believed in the resurrection of the dead. The seemingly well-attested resurrection of Jesus resolved this dilemma. For Paul, Jesus' resurrection became the whole content of religion (1 Cor 6:14, "And God both raised the Lord and will raise up us through his power").

When did this Resurrection doctrine appear in Christianity? Its secondary status in Mark does not give us a date. Paul does. "After three years" (Gal 1:18) he went up to Jerusalem to consult Peter, most likely to hear about Peter's vision of Jesus.

Now we come to a sticking point: chronology.[2] What does "after three years" mean? From 1 Cor 9:1-2, we know that Paul was jealous of his Apostolic credentials. It would be like him to date his vision to the same year as Peter's, which was in 30; this was Paul's claimed year of rebirth as a Christian. Then by "three years" he may mean "in the third year of my life as a Christian." This would be 33, give or take a year for inclusive versus exclusive dating. I will adopt the date 33 as a working hypothesis for this first Jerusalem visit of Paul.

---

[1]For the lateness of the Resurrection idea in Mark, see Brooks **Resurrection**.

[2]Moffatt **Introduction** (1911) 62f already lists 23 solutions to the chronology problem.

2. The Food Issue and Paul's Second Visit to Jerusalem[3]

Jewish purity rules kept Jews and Gentiles from sharing meals. As Gentiles joined the Jesus movement, and as commensality grew in ritual importance, this became an issue. Paul, who had abandoned food rules with the rest of the Law, saw no problem. Others did. To resolve the matter, Paul went to Jerusalem, "after the space of fourteen years" (Gal 2:1) If these, again, are Paul's years as a Christian, the year is 44. "I laid before them the gospel which I preach among the Gentiles" (Gal 2:2). There, "Jacob and Cephas and John, they who were reputed to be pillars, gave to me and Barnabas the right hands of fellowship." In Jacob and John [Zebedee] and Cephas [or Peter], we may easily recognize the disciples who regularly accompany Jesus in Mark.[4]

Paul in Gal 2:12 complains that "certain from Jacob" later came to Antioch, demanding observance of the food rules. Why would Jacob give a liberal ruling, and then enforce a conservative one? I believe Beare has found the answer: the two Jacobs are not the same.[5] The liberal Jacob Zebedee had ruled in favor of abrogating the food laws. Jacob the Lord's conservative Brother, who after Jacob Zebedee's death became the chief figure at Jerusalem, sought to countermand the other Jacob's liberal ruling.

If so, we must read Gal 2:9-12 this way:

> **Gal 2:9**. and when they perceived the grace that was given unto me, Jacob [Zebedee] and Cephas and John [Zebedee], they, who were reputed to be pillars, gave to me and Barnabas the right hands of fellowship, that we should go unto the Gentiles, and they unto the circumcision; [10] Only that we should remember the poor, which very thing I was also zealous to do. [11] But when Cephas came to Antioch I resisted him to the face, because he stood condemned. [12] For before certain came from Jacob [the Brother], he ate with the Gentiles, but when they came, he drew back and separated himself, fearing them that were of the circumcision.

The three who extended fellowship to Paul in the year 44 will then have been the Jesus Three: Peter and the Zebedees. In Mark, Peter is the leading figure. But in a seemingly late passage, Mark also notes the Zebedees' desire for leadership in the movement; Jesus accepts their request, but also predicts their death (Mk 10:35-40). This was fulfilled in the killing of Jacob and the escape of Peter, evidently second on the hit list (Ac 12:1-3). Herod died in 44.[6] Then the ruling itself was in early 44. Herod's action was meant to please the Jews (Ac 12:3); they were outraged by the ruling, which negated Judaism as they knew it. The Jewish leadership had tolerated the Jesus movement, but only so far. Jacob Zebedee had overstepped that limit.

---

[3]For a survey of opinions about this crux, see Talbert **Again** 26 n3. Knox **Fourteen** (1936) notes efforts to to reconcile Acts 15 with Galatians 2 (perhaps accomplished by Parker 1967). Knox **Chronology** (1939) 18 lists three datable events in Paul's life: his conversion, trial before Gallio, and imprisonment at Caesarea. I here suggest that the Jer usalem decree is also datable by the death of Jacob Zebedee, followed by that of Herod Antipas I, both in the year 44.

[4]As in the healing of Jairus' daughter (Mk 5:22-43) and the Transfiguration (Mk 9:2-9a).

[5]Suggested with becoming modesty in Beare **Sequence** 305f.

[6]Josephus Ant 19:343-351; Ac 12:19-20.

We are fortunate to have a view of the crisis from the Jewish side. b.Sanhedrin 43a lists five Jesus disciples who deserve to die. Klausner's decoding of the distorted names has been improved by Hirschberg and others; the best reading seems to be:

Mattai = Matthew
Naqai = [Simon] the Zealot, by transposition of letters within Hebrew
Netser = Andrew (following Klausner)
Buni   = Boanerges = John, the one surviving Zebedee (following Klausner)
Todah = Thaddaeus

That is, *the five original disciples of Jesus*, with Matthew having earlier replaced Levi, and Simon the Zealot and Thaddaeus now replacing the dead Jacob Zebedee and the escaped Peter. Then at some earlier point, the First Five had moved from Capernaum to Jerusalem,[7] where they continued as the leaders of the Jesus movement in that city. Sanhedrin 43a tells us that pursuit of the Christian leadership continued after the death of Jacob Zebedee; it reached to his (and Peter's) replacements in the First Five.

Exodus. The situation being thus untenable for the leaders, and presumably also for other liberals, there followed an exodus from Jerusalem (so Acts 8:1b implies), leaving Jesus' conservative Brother, who was acceptable to the Temple authorities, to fill the resulting leadership gap. If, as was argued above, the move of the leadership to Jerusalem was in 32, and the great scattering began in 44, then the term of the leading movement figures in Jerusalem *will have been twelve years*. This agrees with a tradition quoted by Clement of Alexandria as from the Preaching of Peter,[8] and later by Eusebius as from Apollonius,[9] that Jesus himself had commanded the apostles, "after twelve years, go ye out into the world, lest any say, We did not hear."[10]

The notion that Christian missionarizing began "from Jerusalem" is ridiculous. Christian missionarizing began with Jesus. Already in his lifetime, with converts making other converts,[11] it probably reached Rome, Antioch, and Alexandria, not to mention Saul's Tarsus. What seems to have happened in 44 was a later explosion, leading to an effort which in part went beyond the previous geographical limits.

In 44, Jacob Zebedee was killed; Peter escaped. Peter soon appeared in Antioch, there to be faulted by Paul for retreating from the liberal position on food. Later on, there was a Cephas Party at Corinth, another Paul complaint (1 Cor 1:12). Peter's apocrypha center on Rome.[12] His brother Andrew is credited with deeds in Achaia and Macedonia;[13] Jacob Zebedee's brother John, with works in Ephesus and thereabouts.[14] All this is within the probable geographical zone of previous mission expansion.

---

[7]Thus began the Jerusalemizing trend in early Christian history; see Brooks **Four** 28.

[8]Stromateis 6/6:4; ANL v12 p328.

[9]Eusebius 5/18:14.

[10]Translation from James **Apocryphal** 17. For "all must hear," see Mk 13:10.

[11]For the extent of this early "contact missionarizing," the earliest phases of which are apparently unknown to later Apostolic tradition, see Brooks **Kingdom** 90.

[12]The Acts of Peter, James 300f.

[13]The Acts of Andrew, James 337f.

[14]The Acts of John, James 228f.

Now comes something different. Matthew's field of mission activity is Ethiopia,[15] south of the previous limit, Alexandria. Thaddaeus and Bartholomew are associated with Edessa, in eastern Syria,[16] east of the previous limit, Antioch. Thomas went yet further in that same direction.[17] I suggest that *it is this second, wider missionary push*, not Christian missionarizing as such, that "began from Jerusalem" in 44.[18]

Between the Second and Third Visits to Jerusalem

One detail from this period is Paul's missionary journey in Cyprus, Pamphylia, and points north with Barnabas and Barnabas' cousin Mark.[19] This would have been in 46, after Mark had finished his Gospel, adapted it to an expected Gentile audience, and joined Paul in Antioch. Mark's conviction of the importance of the Gentile mission had grown upon him, but ended by being total: Mark has Jesus say in Mk 13:10 that the awaited End would not come until the Gospel had been preached to all nations.[20] His own missionary efforts were then meant to contribute toward hastening that end.

They were not successful. Local tradition has it that Mark ended his career as a respected leader in the old Alpha Christian community of Alexandria. So far Acts I.[21] Acts II adds that Mark's withdrawal from Paul's journey to Cyprus and Pamphylia caused a permanent rift between Paul and Barnabas (who never reappears in Acts II). But this is contradicted by Paul, who speaks of Barnabas as a coworker in 1 Cor 9:6.[22]

The Collection and Paul's Third Visit to Jerusalem

The assistance to "the saints" which Paul had promised during his second visit was presumably supplied shortly afterward, "by the hand of Barnabas and Saul," the two envoys to Jerusalem on that occasion.[23] This would still have been in the year 44, and the sender would have been the Antioch church, an old Christian establishment, one which Paul had not founded, and to which at that time he was himself subject.[24]

---

[15]The Apostolic History of Abdias Book 7 (James 406f).

[16]Letters of Christ and Abgarus (James 476f).

[17]To Parthia, and to the known Parthian kings of the Indus Valley (Attridge **Acts** 12-13).

[18]Simon Zelotes figures as is a child healed by the Child Jesus in the Arabic Infancy Gospel (James 82); he is called from his grave (as is Thaddaeus) to attend the Assumption of the Virgin (Elliott 702). One of two late texts conflated as the Acts of Philip says that Simon was assigned by Jesus to Spain (Bovon 74). An earlier tradition gives this "furthest west" mission to Paul.

[19]See Brooks **Perga**.

[20]For the lateness of this passage in Mark, see Brooks **Time** 74.

[21]Supplemented by Alexandrian tradition, for which see again Brooks **Perga**.

[22]Luke in effect portrays Mark's missionary effort as not only ineffectual, but disruptive.

[23]The two are separated in our Acts. The doublets in Acts I (noted by many; see Dupont **Sources** 33-50) seem to me to deserve further analytical attention. I must defer discussion of the problem of the "we" passages in Acts II, which, supported by personalia in Phm 1:24 and Deutero-Pauline Col 4:14 and 2 Tim 4:11 (perhaps by Timothy; see Brooks **Editors** 123), imply that Luke accompanied Paul on mission. Such eyewitness claims occur also in Mark and John.

[24]Ac 13:1-3 shows the Antioch authorities choosing who shall go on a particular mission.

Later, Paul seems to have had the idea of a second gift, gathered from his own churches and probably aiming at reconciliation with Jerusalem. Despite references in 2 Cor 8 and 9 to "Macedonia," Paul's letters to Thessalonica and Philippi do not mention it. 1 Cor 16:1 mentions the Galatian churches as involved, but the Epistle to the Galatians does not solicit them. Then the idea for a second collection probably occurred to Paul between Galatians and the Corinthian letters, perhaps c56.

That this third visit was perilous, Acts 21-22 makes clear. Its failure, and Paul's arrest and transfer to Rome for final judgement, are known only from Acts, but are probably factual. Luke in Acts II (c88) has little interest in relations between Paul and Jacob's Jerusalem; he wishes to dramatize the rejection of Christians by the later Pharisaic leadership, expressed in the Birkat ha-Minim, and emblematized in Paul's final Rome interview in Ac 28:23-28 and its two precedents in Corinth (Ac 18:5-11) and in Pisidian Antioch (Ac 13:45-49).[25]

Jacob the Brother

Of candidates for the authorship of the Epistle of Jacob, Jacob the Brother is the best known, but this is not a decisive reason for choosing him.[26] Against it is the good Greek of the Epistle, plus its focus on the "Law of Liberty" (Ja 2:12), whose six injunctions[27] can be observed by anyone, in contrast with the law of the Pharisees, whose hundreds of minute prescriptions all have power to damn.

Probably Jesus and his brother Jacob were educated by Pharisees. Consistent with that background is Jesus' opposition to divorce (recalling the Galilean rabbi Shammai) and his joining John the Baptist's hyperpuristic movement. Jesus later abandoned that approach, but in so doing distanced himself from his family, including his brothers.[28] The claim of Jesus' resurrection must have convinced Jacob, who became a movement member in that sense, but without other change in his views; his early legendary image is of a more-than-priestly purity.[29] He was then just the man to lead the Jerusalem Jesus movement back in a conservative direction. His death in 62[30] seems to show that there were hazards from which even that conservatism did not always protect him.

The puristic Jacob had a second life in Gnosticism. The Gospel of Thomas core (gTh 1-12) never mentions Thomas; it ends with Jacob as leader.[31] His presence in the Nag Hammadi texts offers important material for understanding this development.[32]

---

[25]For these passages, see further Brooks **Acts-Luke** 147.

[26]For Jacob of Alphaeus as a likelier candidate, see Brooks **Jacob**.

[27]See again Mk 10:19, where Jesus lists the six. Ja 2:11-12 mentions two of them.

[28]Mk 3:21, 31-35; compare Mk 10:29-30 on the convert's distancing from worldly family.

[29]For a description due to Hegesippus (late 2c), see Eusebius 2/23:4-6.

[30]Josephus Ant 20:200f; the context in Josephus gives the date 62.

[31]Later, Jacob, the mere *brother,* was superseded in that text by Thomas, the *twin brother,* of the Lord. See Brooks **Apostolic** and **Thomas A**.

[32]For a convenient survey of the Nag Hammadi material, see Painter **James** 159-181.

Chronology

30. Crucifixion of Jesus; Paul persecutes the Jesus movement
32. Move of the Jesus movement leadership from Galilee to Jerusalem
32. Appearance of the Resurrection doctrine in Jerusalem, and its dissemination
33. Conversion of Paul; he sees a vision of Jesus in Heaven (2 Cor 12:2-4)
33. Paul visits Jerusalem to compare notes with Peter
34. Paul preaches under the direction of Antioch; proves successful with Gentiles
44. Paul visits Jerusalem to ask ritual latitude for Gentiles; Jacob Zebedee grants it
44. Paul and Barnabas deliver a thank-offering from Antioch to Jerusalem
44. Herod Antipas I, offended by Jacob Zebedee's decision, kills him
44. Peter leaves Jerusalem for Antioch; Matthew briefly succeeds Jacob Zebedee
44. Herod Antipas I dies; Jewish opposition to liberal Jesus followers continues
44-45. Exodus of liberal Jesus movement figures from Jerusalem
45. Mark adapts his Gospel for preaching to Gentiles; goes to Antioch
45. Jacob the Lord's conservative Brother becomes the leader at Jerusalem
46. Jacob the Brother sends envoys to Antioch to countermand liberal ruling
46. Peter, in Antioch, is cowed by Jacob the Brother's envoys; this offends Paul
46. Paul, having lost at Antioch, sets out to preach in Cyprus and beyond
46. Mark accompanies Paul on that mission; gets as far as Perga and returns
56. Paul conceives the idea of a second gift to Jerusalem; begins a collection
57. Paul writes anticipatory letter to Rome; sets out to deliver collection to Jerusalem
58. Paul is arrested in Jerusalem and detained at Caesarea
59-60. Paul is sent under guard from Caesarea to Rome, and executed there
62. Jacob the Brother is killed by the Temple authorities at Jerusalem

Works Cited

Harold W Attridge. The Acts of Thomas. Polebridge 2010

François Bovon and Christopher R Matthews. The Acts of Philip. Baylor 2012

Frank W Beare. The Sequence of Events in Acts 9:15. JBL v62 (1943) 295-306

E Bruce Brooks. Acts-Luke. Alpha v1 (2017) 143-157

E Bruce Brooks. Apostolic Alignments. Alpha v1 (2017) 196-197

E Bruce Brooks. Paul's Editors. Alpha v1 (2017) 121-126

E Bruce Brooks. The Epistle of Jacob. Alpha v1 (2017) 58-70

E Bruce Brooks. Four Gospel Trajectories. Alpha v1 (2017) 15-16

E Bruce Brooks. Mark at Perga. Alpha v1 (2017) 99-103

E Bruce Brooks. Mark's Parables of the Kingdom. Alpha v1 (2017) 89-91

E Bruce Brooks. The Resurrection of Jesus in Mark. Alpha v1 (2017) 81-88

E Bruce Brooks. Thomas A. Alpha v1 (2017) 198-201

E Bruce Brooks. Time Depth in Mark. Alpha v1 (2017) 73-80

Jacques Dupont. The Sources of the Acts. 1960; tr Herder & Herder 1964

Harris Hirschberg. Simon Bariona and the Ebionites. JBL v61 (1942) 171-191

Joseph Klausner. Jesus of Nazareth. Macmillan 1926

John Knox. Fourteen Years Later. JRel v16 (1936) 341-349.

John Knox. The Pauline Chronology. JBL v58 (1939) 15-29

John Painter. Just James. South Carolina 1997

Pierson Parker. Once More, Acts and Galatians. JBL v86 (1967) 175-182

Charles H Talbert. Again: Paul's Visits to Jerusalem. NovT v9 (1967) 26-40

Insidious Agreement

E Bruce Brooks
University of Massachusetts at Amherst
(8 August 2015)

I here wish to call attention to a device of argument for which there is apparently no term in classical rhetoric. Here is a passage from Ecclesiastes 11:9.

> Rejoice, O young man, in thy youth, and let thy heart cheer thee in the days of thy youth, and walk in the ways of thy heart, and in the sight of thine eyes; but know thou, that for all these things God will bring thee into judgement.

This is cited by Fenner (1584) as an example of concessio: granting what will be hurtful to an opponent.[1] What interests me about this passage is not its hurtfulness, but its sidewise drift: it starts in one place (seeming to approve the pleasures of the young), but winds up in another (they will be condemned for enjoying them). The beginning is undermined by the end. The tactic of first establishing agreement with an existing situation, and then preaching something different, is common in the Apostle Paul.

Thessalonians. A compact example of initial praise followed by an exhortation to do better. The praise becomes, retrospectively, an implied censure.

> **1 Thess 4:1**. Finally, then, brethren, we beseech and exhort you in the Lord Jesus, that, as ye received of us how ye ought to walk and to please God, even as ye do walk – that ye abound more and more.

Philippians. That church did not have a theology of the cross; it had an earlier idea of Jesus, centering rather on his obedience to God. To urge obedience to himself, Paul quotes that hymn, but inserts, in passing, a reference to the theology of the cross:

> [Php 2:8] And being found in fashion as man
> > He humbled himself
> > Becoming obedient unto death
> > (and that a cross-death!)[2]

Romans. Paul is addressing Roman Christians who regard Jesus as descended from David. He wants to get them aboard, and then update them theologically.

> **Rom 1:3** . . . who was born of the seed of David according to the flesh, [4] who was declared to be the Son of God with power, according to the Spirit of holiness, by the resurrection from the dead, even Jesus Christ our Lord.

Rom 1:3 invites the Roman Christians to feel that Paul agrees with them about Jesus. But in the next verse, 1:4, he inserts the Resurrection into the appeal. Paul could not care less about Jesus "according to the flesh," that is, what Jesus was in his lifetime. To Paul, the only important fact about Jesus is his death and subsequent resurrection.

---

[1]Sister Miriam Joseph **Arts** 382.
[2]From Hunter **Paul** 41 (based on Lohmeyer's understanding of the hymn).

Corinthians. Sometimes the point of agreement must itself be elaborately established. In 1 Cor, that process occupies four chapters. 1 Cor first takes note of factions at Corinth, with no less than four contending parties:

> **1 Cor 1:12**. Now this I mean, that each of you saith, I am of Paul, and I of Apollos, and I of Cephas, and I of Christ.[3]

Paul begins by eliminating *all* factions, including his own:

> [1:13] Is Christ divided? Was Paul crucified for you? or were ye baptized into the name of Paul?

And from that common position, he proceeds to argue himself back into the picture. After a somewhat wandering continuation, he resumes the theme of equality in Christ:

> [3:21] Wherefore let no man glory in men. For all things are yours, whether Paul, or Apollos, or Cephas, or the world, or life, or death . . . all things are yours, [23] and ye are Christ's, and Christ is God's.

Finally, with the argument now at the level of Christ, we get this distinction:

> [4:14] I write not these things to shame you, but to admonish you as my beloved children. [15] For though ye have ten thousand tutors in Christ, yet not many fathers, for in Christ Jesus I begat you through the Gospel. [16] I beseech you therefore, be ye imitators of me.

Primary respect is due to Paul, not his rivals. He is the *sole point of access* to Christ.

"My beloved children," says Paul at 4:14. We may recall that Paul often speaks of himself, not only as the father, but sometimes even as the mother, of his converts:

> • **1 Thess 2:7**. But we were gentle in the midst of you, as when a nurse cherisheth her own children . . .
> • **Gal 4:19**. My little children, of whom I am again in travail until Christ be formed in you . . .

See again 1 Thess 4:1, above. But note that a mother, however gentle, has sole ownership. It is that position – the focus of indebtedness for the one addressed – toward which all these Pauline devices seem to be maneuvering.

If it were desired to add one more term to the Latin list of rhetorisms, I might favor Obliquitio. Sidewiseness. Unlike the treacherously cryptic oracles of Apollo at Delphi, obliquitio, in its crabwise way, is perfectly clear. It is perfectly clear at both its ends. It is just that those two ends are in different places.

Works Cited

E Bruce Brooks. Mark's Parables of the Kingdom. Alpha v1 (2017) 91-93
E Bruce Brooks. Paul's Letters to Philippi. Alpha v1 (2017) 112-118
E Bruce Brooks. The Two Ways. Alpha v1 (2017) 39-47
A M Hunter. Paul and His Predecessors. 1940; 2ed SCM 1961
Sister Miriam Joseph. Shakespeare's Use of the Arts of Language. Columbia 1947

---

[3] I take the "Christ" faction as the Alpha Christians whose contact with Jesus' teaching went back to pre-Apostolic times. For this term, see Brooks **Two** 39. For pre-Apostolic propagation of the Word, see Brooks **Parables**.

Paul's Letters to Philippi

E Bruce Brooks
University of Massachusetts at Amherst
(5 Oct 2014)

Philippians has often been thought to be a conflation of several letters; the usual recent suggestion (Beare, Reumann) is three. I here propose a four-letter model.

Interpolations

Before turning to the Paul material, we will first need to remove any interpolations. The hymn quoted at 2:6-11 is pre-Pauline;[1] not, as some have proposed, extraneous. I suggest the following as *editorial* additions or amendments to Paul's letter or letters:

- 1:1b. "with the bishops and deacons" implies post-Pauline organization.[2]
- 2:20-23. Excessive praise of Timothy, and implied dispraise of others; neither necessary nor appropriate for the occasion. The obvious beneficiary is Timothy, and this was probably inserted by him as a member of the editorial team.[3]
- 4:22. "All the saints salute you, especially they of Caesar's household." "All the saints" is superfluous after "the brethren that are with me" in 4:21, and "Caesar's household" is probably meant to imply a Roman imprisonment, though an Ephesian origin for the Philippian correspondence is more likely.[4]

Another seeming interruption is:

- 4:2-3. "I exhort Euodia, and I exhort Syntyche, to be of the same mind in the Lord. Yea, I beseech thee, true yokefellow, help these women, for they labored with me in the Gospel, with Clement also, and the rest of my fellow-worker, whose names are in the Book of Life." Not in a million years would this have been sent to the church at Philippi; it is a private, personal note to Paul's representative there, asking him to assist in a sensitive personal matter. A visit from Timothy is envisioned at 2:19, and this was probably sent to him after his arrival. Only he could have provided it to the editorial committee. Timothy is also the likeliest person to have inserted the praise of himself in 2:20-23. All this argues for Timothy's presence on the editorial committee.

So 4:2-3 is better regarded as a letter fragment, and takes its place in this hypothesis alongside the three letters more commonly distinguished. It is thus here proposed that four Pauline elements have been combined to produce what we know as Philippians.

[1]Lohmeyer **Philipper** 90-99; summarized in Hunter **Paul** 40f. Paul in quoting this early hymn has added a half-line to inject his own theology of the cross, lacking in the original.

[2]Moffatt **Introduction** 171, "catholicizing gloss."

[3]One of the original letters was co-signed by Timothy, which makes his contributions to the editing of this letter than much more likely. See further below, and also Brooks **Editors**.

[4]Reumann 14, "An Ephesians provenance explains more . . . than any other theory.".

Discontinuities

The one most often noticed is at 3:2.[5] It does not resemble an epistolary beginning, and must represent a truncated letter. How far from that point can we read without encountering another discontinuity? The answer is the Timothy fragment at 4:2-3. This junction defines a segment consisting of 3:2–4:1. That segment ends thus:

> **Php 4:1**. Wherefore, my brethren beloved and longed for, my joy and my crown, so stand fast in the Lord, my beloved.

This might be a letter nearing its end, but lacking a final greeting. Perhaps one will turn up, and we may for the moment reserve 3:2–4:1 for further consideration.

As the converse of discontinuity, we can look for resumed continuity. The point before the 3:2 bump, 3:1, seems to be resumed at 4:4. The keyword is "rejoice:"

> **Php 3:1**. Finally, my brethren, **rejoice** in the Lord. To write the same things to you, to me indeed is not irksome, but for you it is safe.

> [4:4]. **Rejoice** in the Lord always, and again I will say, **Rejoice**.

Then both 3:2–4:1 and the fragment 4:2-3 have been inserted into something else, something which was broken off at 3:1 and which resumes again at 4:4.

Loose Ends

Taking up that resumption, and reading on past 4:4, we reach:

> **Php 4:8**. Finally, brethren, whatsoever things are true, whatsoever things are honorable, whatsoever things are just, whatsoever things are pure, whatsoever things are lovely, whatsoever things are of good report, if there be any virtue, and if there be any praise, think on these things.[9] The things which ye both learned and received and heard and saw in me, these things do, and the God of peace shall be with you.[6]

. . . and we seem to be at the end of the letter that began at 1:1a. But we already had a "Finally" in 3:1 (above), at which point the 1:1a letter was seemingly in closing mode. Paul would probably not use this device twice in the same letter. We may then keep 4:4-7 as part of the 1a letter, but we will do better to put 4:8-9 elsewhere.

The "whatsoever" part of 4:8 has a parallel at:

> **Php 2:1**. If there is therefore **any** exhortation in Christ, if any consolation of love, if any fellowship of the Spirit, if any tender mercies and compassions, make full my joy, that ye be of the same mind, having the same love, being of one accord, of one mind, [3] doing nothing through faction . . .

and the appeal for unity is another parallel. This further strengthens the likelihood that Php 4:8-9 belongs with another letter than the one which began at Php 1:1a and included 2:1. Then the 1:1a letter does not seem to go further than 4:4-7.

---

[5]Comments include "interrupted" (Lightfoot 69), "as to defy explanation" (Goodspeed, quoted at Beare 3), "abrupt" (Beare 100), "abrupt, harsh imp[perati]v[e]s" (Reumann 467).

[6]Paul had earlier quoted the Philippi Hymn, with which he disagreed theologically, for purposes of asking obedience. 4:8 sat first seems to invite this kind of latitude, but 4:9 corrects it by urging Paul's own Gospel. For this device in Paul, see Brooks **Insidious**.

Another point against putting 4:4-7 and 4:8-9 in the same letter is this repetition:

> Php 4:7. And the peace of God, which passeth all understanding . . .
>
> Php 4:9. . . . and the God of peace shall be with you.

Again, there is nothing unPauline about "God of peace," but once per letter is enough.

Then 4:8-9 must be the conclusion of a different letter. Which one? The note of thanks which begins at 4:10 is more social than sermonic, and this advice to the church does not fit the personal fragment 4:2-3. But the "Dogs" letter at 3:2f is an appeal for unity, and this is also the theme of the letter beginning at 1:1a. Thematic parallels between them are thus not unlikely, and I assign 4:8-9 as the ending of the "Dogs," or better, the Unity letter, which begins at 3:2. In that letter, Paul is not yet in prison, so it probably precedes the Prison letter. The Unity letter thus now consists of segments which were separated in the process of conflation, namely 3:2–4:1 and 4:8-9.

With 4:8-9 so assigned, we come to 4:10-20, which has no beginning. It seems to be a letter of thanks for a gift brought by Epaphroditus, as implied at 2:25 and 2:30. This suggests the following event sequence:

- Letter of counsel from Ephesus (not in prison): 3:2-4:1, 4:8-9
- Paul in prison; Epaphroditus brings aid. Letter of thanks: 4:10-20
- Epaphroditus ill, returns with prison letter: 1:1a, 1:2–2:19, 2:24–3:1, 4:4-7
- Timothy follows, Paul sends him a private directive: 4:2-3

We have only three more verses to consider, 4:21-23, of which we ignore 4:22 as an editorial enhancement. They read:

> **Php 4:21**. Salute every saint in Christ Jesus. The brethren that are with me salute you. [23] The **grace** of the Lord Jesus Christ be with your spirit.

The only letter now left without an ending is the letter of thanks, which begins at 4:10. 4:21 is already in place as continuing that letter. If we leave it there, we have:

> **Php 4:20**. Now unto our God and Father, be the glory for ever and ever. Amen.
> [21] Salute every saint in Christ Jesus. The brethren that are with me salute you.
> [23] The **grace** of the Lord Jesus Christ be with your spirit.

In this arrangement, concluding references to "**grace**" are distributed among different letters, and so are references to "whatsoever things are good," and "the God of peace." It is easier to imagine Paul recurring to these favorite themes in several letters written at about the same time, rather than duplicating some of them within a single letter.

Conflation Strategy for the separation and recombination of the letters is then:

A (Unity)		3:2–4:1	4:8-9
B (Thanks)			4:10-21, 23
C (Prison)	1:1a, 1:2–2:19, 2:24–3:1	4:4-7	
D (Timothy)		4:2-3	

in which the endings of letters A and C are separated and placed further toward the end of the composite letter, the body of A and fragment D are placed between C and its now separated ending, and the letter of thanks (B), with its original ending, is placed last for a happy conclusion. The "polemical" Unity letter, written to oppose Jewish practices, and the Timothy fragment, which exposes a quarrel in the church, being less happy, are retained, but muted by being put in the middle.

The editors then seem to have wished not to leave out any available Paul material, but also to shape the result to better preach Paul to the Christendom of the future. Besides minimizing friction, they wanted the composite letter to speak to that purpose. As a backbone for that message, they wanted a sermon, and the nearest thing available was the Letter from Prison (C). Its opening was retained, and the openings of the other letters were discarded, lest they make the conflation obvious. The conclusions of letters A and C were put nearer the end, to avoid an obvious violation of epistolary closing conventions. The letter of thanks (B), complete with its ending, brought the whole to a close. To the resulting single letter the editors added new material, (1) anticipating the system of bishops and deacons, which probably existed in some places as they worked; (2) supporting the myth (implicitly required by the Pastorals) that Paul had survived his Roman imprisonment to preach elsewhere, and that Philippians itself was written from Rome; and (3) praising Timothy above Paul's other colleagues, this touch being most likely a contribution of Timothy himself, as one of the editorial team.

That is, the process is both strategically and personally intelligible.

So the proposed conflation is possible, but it must also be convincing. The best test of this is to display the proposed four letters, leaving readers to judge for themselves how plausible they are as original, independent letters. The proposed letters follow.

Reconstruction

A. LETTER URGING DOCTRINAL UNITY
An early letter, warning of error. Not sent from prison. Opening omitted.

[3:2] . . . Beware of the dogs, beware of the evil workers, beware of the circumcision: [3] for we are the circumcision, who worship by the Spirit of God, and glory in Christ Jesus, and have no confidence in the flesh: [4] though I myself might have confidence even in the flesh: if any other man thinketh to have confidence in the flesh, I yet more: [5] circumcised the eighth day, of the stock of Israel, of the tribe of Benjamin, a Hebrew of Hebrews; as touching the law, a Pharisee; [6] as touching zeal, persecuting the church; as touching the righteousness which is in the law, found blameless. [7] Howbeit what things were gain to me, these have I counted loss for Christ. [8] Yea verily, and I count all things to be loss for the excellence of the knowledge of Christ Jesus my Lord: for whom I suffered the loss of all things, and do count them but refuse, that I may gain Christ, [3:9] and be found in him, not having a righteousness of mine own, [even] that which is of the law, but that which is through faith in Christ, the righteousness which is from God by faith, [10] that I may know him, and the power of his resurrection, and the fellowship of his sufferings, becoming conformed unto his death; [11] if by any means I may attain unto the resurrection from the dead. [12] Not that I have already obtained, or am already made perfect: but I press on, if so be that I may lay hold on that for which also I was laid hold on by Christ Jesus. [13] Brethren, I count not myself yet to have laid hold: but one thing [I do], forgetting the things which are behind, and stretching forward to the things which are before, [14] I press on toward the goal unto the prize of the high calling of God in Christ Jesus. [15] Let us therefore, as many as are perfect, be thus minded: and if in anything ye are otherwise minded, this also shall God reveal unto you: [16] only, whereunto we have attained, by that same let us walk. [17] Brethren, be ye imitators together of me, and mark them that so walk even as ye have us for an example.

[18] For many walk, of whom I told you often, and now tell you even weeping, [that they are] the enemies of the cross of Christ: [19] whose end is perdition, whose god is the belly, and [whose] glory is in their shame, who mind earthly things. [20] For our citizenship is in heaven; whence also we wait for a Saviour, the Lord Jesus Christ: [21] who shall fashion anew the body of our humiliation, conformed to the body of his glory, according to the working whereby he is able even to subject all things unto himself.

[4:1] Wherefore, my brethren beloved and longed for, my joy and crown, so stand fast in the Lord, my beloved. [8] **Finally**, brethren, whatsoever things are true, **whatsoever** things are honorable, whatsoever things are just, whatsoever things are pure, whatsoever things are lovely, whatsoever things are of good report; if there be any virtue, and if there be any praise, think on these things. [9] The things which ye both learned and received and heard and saw in me, these things do: and the God of **peace** shall be with you.

B. LETTER ACKNOWLEDGING A GIFT FROM PHILIPPI
Sent from prison on receipt of a gift brought by Epaphroditus. Opening omitted.

[4:10] . . . But I rejoice in the Lord greatly, that now at length ye have revived your thought for me; wherein ye did indeed take thought, but ye lacked opportunity. [11] Not that I speak in respect of want: for I have learned, in whatsoever state I am, therein to be content. [12] I know how to be abased, and I know also how to abound: in everything and in all things have I learned the secret both to be filled and to be hungry, both to abound and to be in want. [13] I can do all things in him that strengtheneth me. [14]. Howbeit ye did well that ye had fellowship with my affliction. [15] And ye yourselves also know, ye Philippians, that in the beginning of the gospel, when I departed from Macedonia, no church had fellowship with me in the matter of giving and receiving but ye only; [16] for even in Thessalonica ye sent once and again unto my need. [17] Not that I seek for the gift; but I seek for the fruit that increaseth to your account. [18] But I have all things, and abound: I am filled, having received from Epaphroditus the things [that came] from you, an odor of a sweet smell, a sacrifice acceptable, well-pleasing to God. [19] And my God shall supply every need of yours according to his riches in glory in Christ Jesus. [20] Now unto our God and Father [be] the glory for ever and ever. Amen. [21] Salute every saint in Christ Jesus. The brethren that are with me salute you. [23] The **grace** of the Lord Jesus Christ be with your spirit.

C. SERMON SENT FROM PRISON TO PHILIPPI
Carried by Epaphroditus, returning to Philippi after his recovery. Opening included.

[1:1a] Paul and Timothy, servants of Christ Jesus, to all the saints in Christ Jesus that are at Philippi, [2] Grace to you and peace from God our Father and the Lord Jesus Christ. [3] I thank my God upon all my remembrance of you, [4] always in every supplication of mine on behalf of you all making my supplication with joy, [5] for your fellowship in furtherance of the gospel from the first day until now; [6] being confident of this very thing, that he who began a good work in you will perfect it until the day of Jesus Christ: [7] even as it is right for me to be thus minded on behalf of you all, because I have you in my heart, inasmuch as, both in my bonds and in the defense and confirmation of the gospel, ye all are partakers with me of **grace**. [8] For God is my witness, how I long after you all in the tender mercies of Christ Jesus. [9] And this I pray, that your love may abound yet more and more in knowledge and all discernment; [10] so that ye may approve the things that are excellent; that ye may be sincere and void of offence unto the day of Christ; [11] being filled with the fruits of righteousness, which are through Jesus Christ, unto the glory and praise of God.

[12] Now I would have you know, brethren, that the things [which happened] unto me have fallen out rather unto the progress of the gospel; [13] so that my bonds became manifest in Christ throughout the whole praetorian guard, and to all the rest; [14] and that most of the brethren in the Lord, being confident through my bonds, are more abundantly bold to speak the word of God without fear. [15] Some indeed preach Christ even of envy and strife; and some also of good will: [16] the one [do it] of love, knowing that I am set for the defense of the gospel; [17] but the other proclaim Christ of faction, not sincerely, thinking to raise up affliction for me in my bonds. [18] What then? Only that in every way, whether in pretense or in truth, Christ is proclaimed; and therein I rejoice, yea, and will rejoice. [19] For I know that this shall turn out to my salvation, through your supplication and the supply of the Spirit of Jesus Christ, [20] according to my earnest expectation and hope, that in nothing shall I be put to shame, but [that] with all boldness, as always, [so] now also Christ shall be magnified in my body, whether by life, or by death. [21] For to me to live is Christ, and to die is gain. [22] But if to live in the flesh, – [if] this shall bring fruit from my work, then what I shall choose I know not. [23] But I am in a strait betwixt the two, having the desire to depart and be with Christ; for it is very far better: [24] yet to abide in the flesh is more needful for your sake. [25] And having this confidence, I know that I shall abide, yea, and abide with you all, for your progress and joy in the faith; [26] that your glorying may abound in Christ Jesus in me through my presence with you again. [27] Only let your manner of life be worthy of the gospel of Christ: that, whether I come and see you or be absent, I may hear of your state, that ye stand fast in one spirit, with one soul striving for the faith of the gospel; [28] and in nothing affrighted by the adversaries: which is for them an evident token of perdition, but of your salvation, and that from God; [29] because to you it hath been granted in the behalf of Christ, not only to believe on him, but also to suffer in his behalf: [30] having the same conflict which ye saw in me, and now hear to be in me. [**2:1**] If there is therefore **any** exhortation in Christ, if any consolation of love, if **any** fellowship of the Spirit, if **any** tender mercies and compassions, [2] make full my joy, that ye be of the same mind, having the same love, being of one accord, of one mind; [3] [doing] nothing through faction or through vainglory, but in lowliness of mind each counting other better than himself; [4] not looking each of you to his own things, but each of you also to the things of others.

[2:5] Have this mind in you, which was also in Christ Jesus:

[6] who, existing in the form of God,
counted not the being on an equality with God
a thing to be grasped,

[7] but emptied himself,
taking the form of a servant,
being made in the likeness of men;

[8] and being found in fashion as a man,
he humbled himself,
becoming obedient [even] unto death, [yea, the death of the cross!]

[9] Wherefore also God highly exalted him,
and gave unto him the name
which is above every name;

[10] that in the name of Jesus
every knee should bow,
of [things] in heaven and [things] on earth and [things] under the earth,

[11] and that every tongue should confess
that Jesus Christ is Lord,
to the glory of God the Father.

[12] So then, my beloved, even as ye have always obeyed, not as in my presence only, but now much more in my absence, work out your own salvation with fear and trembling; [13] for it is God who worketh in you both to will and to work, for his good pleasure. [14] Do all things without murmurings and questionings: [15] that ye may become blameless and harmless, children of God without blemish in the midst of a crooked and perverse generation, among whom ye are seen as lights in the world, [16] holding forth the word of life; that I may have whereof to glory in the day of Christ, that I did not run in vain neither labor in vain. [17] Yea, and if I am offered upon the sacrifice and service of your faith, I joy, and rejoice with you all: [18] and in the same manner do ye also joy, and rejoice with me. [19] But I hope in the Lord Jesus to send Timothy shortly unto you, that I also may be of good comfort, when I know your state. [25] But I counted it necessary to send to you Epaphroditus, my brother and fellow-worker and fellow-soldier, and your messenger and minister to my need; [26] since he longed after you all, and was sore troubled, because ye had heard that he was sick: [27] for indeed he was sick nigh unto death: but God had mercy on him; and not on him only, but on me also, that I might not have sorrow upon sorrow. [28] I have sent him therefore the more diligently, that, when ye see him again, ye may rejoice, and that I may be the less sorrowful. [29a] Receive him therefore in the Lord with all joy; [30] because for the work of Christ he came nigh unto death, hazarding his life to supply that which was lacking in your service toward me.

[3:1] **Finally**, my brethren, rejoice in the Lord. To write the same things to you, to me indeed is not irksome, but for you it is safe. [4:4] Rejoice in the Lord always: again I will say, Rejoice. [5] Let your forbearance be known unto all men. The Lord is at hand. [6] In nothing be anxious; but in everything, by prayer and supplication with thanksgiving, let your requests be made known unto God. [7] And the **peace** of God, which passeth all understanding, shall guard your hearts and your thoughts in Christ Jesus.

D. FRAGMENT OF A PERSONAL NOTE
Sent to Timothy at Philippi. His visit was anticipated in the previous letter at 2:19

[4:2] I exhort Euodia, and I exhort Syntyche, to be of the same mind in the Lord. [3] Yea, I beseech thee also, true yokefellow, help these women, for they labored with me in the gospel, with Clement also, and the rest of my fellow-workers, whose names are in the Book of Life.

--------·-··-·--------

Works Cited

F W Beare. Philippians. Harper 1959

E Bruce Brooks. Insidious Agreement. Alpha v1 (2017) 110-111

E Bruce Brooks. Paul's Editors. Alpha v1 (2017) 121-126

E Bruce Brooks. The Resurrection of Jesus in Mark. Alpha v1 (2017) 81-88

P J Harrison. Paulines and Pastorals. Villiers 1964

Morna Hooker. The Letter to the Philippians [NIB v7]. Abingdon (2000) 467-549

A M Hunter. Paul and His Predecessors. 1940; 2ed SCM 1961

J B Lightfoot. St Paul's Epistle to the Philippians. 1868; Macmillan 1908

Ernst Lohmeyer. Der Brief an die Philipper. 1930; (ed Schmauch) Vandenhoeck 1953

John Reumann. Philippians. Yale 2008

Walter Schmithals. Paul and the Gnostics, 1965; tr Abingdon (1972) 65-122

E F Scott. Philippians [IB v11]. Abingdon (1955) 1-129

The Post-Apostolic Transition

Paul's Editors

E Bruce Brooks

University of Massachusetts at Amherst

GPG (8 June 2013); Alpha (20 Jan 2015)

Interpolations so far identified in the epistles of Paul appear in all manuscripts, and thus belong to the *formation period* of these texts; they were probably added when the letters were edited for wider circulation.[1] The likely editors are those who cosign a letter: Sosthenes (1 Cor), Timothy (2 Cor and Php), Timothy and Silvanus (1 Thess), or go on very sensitive missions: Timothy (1 Cor 4:17, Php 2:19, 1 Thess 3:2) and Titus (2 Cor 8:23, 12:18); along with Paul's probable operations manager, Onesimus. I here consider the possibility that they are also the authors of the Deutero-Paulines.

Onesimus

Philemon is not a church letter, and properly has no place in the Pauline corpus. It must have been included at someone's urging, and only Onesimus, its beneficiary, is likely to have even have known of it (he was its bearer).[2] As head of an operation which he ran from the front lines, Paul badly needed an office manager. Paul promises to make good any peculation, in order to secure Onesimus's service for himself.

Paul's assistants were ideally placed to find posts in the post-Apostolic period. Onesimus himself became Bishop of Ephesus.[3] Writes Ignatius of Antioch in c114:

> **Ign Eph 1:3**. seeing that in God's name I have received your whole multitude in the person of Onesimus, whose love passeth utterance and who is moreover your Bishop – and I pray that ye may love him . . . for blessed is He that granted unto you according to your deserving to have such a Bishop.

Later, Ignatius alludes to several passages in Philemon. The request for Burrhus:

> **Ign Eph 2:1**. Now concerning my fellow servant Burrhus, your deacon by the will of God, who is blessed in all things, I beg that he may stay longer, for your honor and for that of the Bishop . . .

echoes Paul's request (Phm 13) that Philemon be allowed to stay with him. And

> **Ign Eph 3:1**. I do not command you as if I were someone great, for though I am a prisoner for the Name, I am not yet perfect in Jesus Christ . . . I have taken it upon me to exhort you . . .

puts Ignatius in Paul's position (Phm 8-9), a prisoner at Ephesus.[4]

---

[1] I have in mind especially the recent work of William O Walker Jr.

[2] I here largely agree with the point of Knox **Philemon** 82.

[3] It has been objected that there could be any number of people named Onesimus. But Onesimus "Useful" is a slave name. How many slaves have the makings of a Bishop?

[4] I agree with Knox **Philemon** (further parallels at 85-87) that these gracious echoes are decisive for the identity of the Bishop and the slave.

Onesimus was probably at least 25 when he ran away from his master in c55, and some 60 years later, he will have been in his mid-eighties; a not impossible longevity. But if a slave did indeed become a Bishop, what was his path to that dignity?

The authentic letters of Paul are agreed to be seven,[5] symbolizing completeness.[6] But 1 and 2 Cor are to the same church, and even counting Philemon as a church letter (Phm 2b, probably editorial), that makes only six *churches*. It was thus necessary to compose a seventh church letter, to complete the ideal number and introduce the rest. Goodspeed, considering Colossians genuine, thought that this was Ephesians.[7] But Colossians is *not* genuine, and is itself the best candidate. Who wrote it? Its opening (Col 1:3-4) mimics that of Philemon (4-5) and a long passage on slaves (Col 3:22-4:1) implies personal interest.[8] Then Onesimus is the probable author of Colossians, and also of Ephesians, which has the same labored style in Greek.[9] Ephesians is an update of Colossians, though it is also aware of other Pauline writings.[10]

What would have prompted an Ephesians update? Perhaps Onesimus' entry into his responsibilities as Bishop, when he took a wider view, not only of Paul's heritage, but of the issues then facing Christianity.[11] If so, then we have this sequence:

(1) Phm [by Paul, concerning Onesimus] > Col > Eph [both by Onesimus]

Timothy

That Timothy was among Paul's editors is likely, given his position of trust under Paul. One indication of that trust is Paul's intention to send him on a delicate mission to the Philippians ("I hope in the Lord Jesus to send Timothy to you soon," Php 2:19). I have suggested that the clearly private note preserved as Php 4:2-3 was addressed to Timothy as he undertook that errand.[12] It asks Timothy to compose the differences between two women, Euodia and Syntyche. It could not have been sent to the church, only to Timothy privately. Then it was not recovered from any archive at Philippi, and can only have been provided to the editors by its recipient: Timothy.

The gratuitous praise of Timothy in Php 2:20-22 ("For I have no man like-minded, who will care truly for your state, for they all seek their own, not the things of Jesus Christ. But ye know the proof of him, that, as child serveth a father, he served with me in furtherance of the Gospel") may well have been inserted by Timothy himself.

---

[5]By those whose opinions I consider sound. For a detailed overview, see Collins **Letters**.

[6]The seven baskets taken up at the Feeding of Four Thousand (Mk 8:18-21) symbolize provision for all the nations (Israel alone is symbolized by the twelve baskets at the Feeding of Five Thousand, Mk 6:34-44). Compare the 70 (or 72) nations of the world in Genesis 10.

[7]Goodspeed **Meaning** 5-6.

[8]The Colossians "domestic code," 3:18-4:1, is interruptive (Belz 46-48), yet characteristic. Then Colossians, once written, was open to self-improvement during the editorial process.

[9]Lincoln xlviii, "long sentences, frequent relative constructions, genitive constructions."

[10]Besides the Paulines proper, Ephesians also has contacts with the Pastorals; Ware passim.

[11]Beare **Ephesians** 604, "Ephesians . . . is an attempt to formulate a philosophy of religion which is at the same time a philosophy of history, out of Pauline materials"

[12]See Brooks **Philippi** 112.

If so, he was not long content with it. One of the Pastorals, 2 Timothy, contains further praise of Timothy, which is not germane to the ostensible purpose of the letter:

2 Tim 1:5. having been reminded of the unfeigned faith that is in thee, which dwelt first in thy grandmother Lois, and thy mother Eunice, and, I am persuaded, in thee also.

This would make Timothy a third generation Christian, a credential superior to that of Paul himself. Paul's speaking of Timothy as his "child in the Lord" (1 Cor 4:17) suggests that Timothy had been converted by Paul: a less grand status. This statement:

2 Tim 1:6. For which cause I put thee in remembrance that thou stir up the gift of God, which is in thee through the laying on of my hands.

implies commissioning (as that of Paul, in Acts 13:3), but not necessarily conversion. Again, the dispraise of colleagues in Timothy's interpolation Php 2:20-22 is given far more elaborate scope in 2 Timothy. Paul is assumed to be speaking:

2 Tim 4:10. For Demas forsook me, having loved this present world, and went to Thessalonica; Crescens to Galatia, Titus to Dalmatia. Only Luke is with me.

2 Tim 4:16. At my first defense no one took my part, but all forsook me.

Note that Demas gets much better treatment in what I have called the Onesimus strand:

Phm 23. Epaphras, my fellow prisoner in Christ Jesus, sends greetings to you. [24] And so to Mark, Aristarchus, Demas, and Luke, my fellow workers.

Col 4:14. Luke, the beloved physician, and Demas greet you.

The Luke connection is problematic; it suffices here to notice who mentions it.

All that Demas is accused of in 2 Tim is aspiring to be important to some church. Titus and 1 Tim show two of Paul's lieutenants being put in charge of churches, perhaps reflecting the shift from the old visiting apostle system to local management.

Harrison's case for genuine Paul fragments in the Pastorals deserves to be judged on the longest and most dramatic of them: Paul's farewell from prison in 2 Timothy. But his reconstruction (**Paulines** 117f) has to be reassembled from scattered material (2 Tim 1:16-17, 3:10-11, 4:1-3, 4:5b, 4:6-9, 4:16-19, 4:20b-21a). There is no reason for a conflated letter to be broken into so many pieces. Did Timothy perhaps remember how a fragment of his own letter had been worked into the conflated Philippians?

And is it a forgery? One detail of that supposed letter suggests a motive:

2 Tim 1:16-17. The Lord grant mercy unto the house of Onesiphorus, for he oft refreshed me, and was not ashamed of my chain; but when he was in Rome, he sought me diligently, and found me (the Lord grant unto him to find mercy of the Lord in that day); and in how many things he ministered at Ephesus, thou knowest very well.

"Onesiphorus" here is probably a variant for Onesimus. Timothy continues in nominal colleagueship to Onesimus, while making *himself* the recipient of Paul's last message. The implication is evident: *it is not Onesimus, but Timothy, who is Paul's true heir.* If so, we may sum up Timothy's deutero-Pauline connection in this way:

(2) Php [by Paul, with an interpolation by Timothy] > 2 Tim [by Timothy]

And we have now isolated a second strand of post-Pauline tradition.

Titus

Easton suggests,[13] and Murphy-O'Connor confirms,[14] that Titus and 1 Tim are distinct from 2 Tim. For Titus, we must then seek a different author than Timothy, perhaps Titus himself, the beneficiary of that Epistle (it gave him authority in Crete). Can we link any editorial additions in the authentic epistles with anything in Titus?

Consider the interpolated 1 Cor 7:17-24,[15] which interrupts Paul's advice on marriage to suggest that all should remain socially as they are, whether slave or free, a precept justified by, and linked with, the atoning death of Christ. Compare:

1 Cor 7:20b. Wast thou called being a bondservant? Care not for it.

Tit 2:9a. Servants *to be in subjection* to their own masters . . .

1 Cor 7:23. Ye were bought with a price; become not bondservants of men.

Tit 2:14. Who gave himself for us . . .

The similarity is obvious. And the first pair (1 Cor 7:20b and Tit 2:9a) might be read as critical of the freed slave Onesimus. So especially might this next phrase:

Tit 2: 9b. . . . not gainsaying, [10] not purloining

inasmuch as the real-life Onesimus had gotten into financial trouble with Philemon, which Paul, in asking for Onesimus' freedom, had guaranteed to repay (Phm 19).

Given the strong similarities between Titus and 1 Tim, it is most likely that one author wrote both of them. That Titus should advertise himself as worthy of trust in Crete is reasonable, but why should he write 1 Timothy, which at both its beginning and its end asks Timothy to correct matters in a doctrinally disorderly Ephesus?

1 Tim 1:3. As I exhorted thee to tarry at Ephesus when I was going into Macedonia, that thou mightest charge certain men not to teach a different doctrine, [4] neither to give heed to fables and endless genealogies, which minister questionings . . . [5:20] O Timothy, guard that which is committed unto thee, turning away from the profane babblings and oppositions of the knowledge which is falsely so called, [21] which some professing have erred concerning the faith.

This might address elements in Colossians (here considered as being by Onesimus) which have been widely noted in the commentaries as potentially Gnostic in character; the key word in this quote is "knowledge falsely so called." To dispute the doctrinal soundness of Onesimus is to challenge his position in Ephesus, where his influence as Paul's resident manager would have been greatest. One common element in the Pastorals seems to be opposition to Onesimus, which is detectable in Timothy (2 Tim), and is perhaps more overt in Titus (Titus and 1 Tim).

If so, then in terms of editorial additions followed by independent deutero-Paulines, we would have:

(3) 1 Cor 7:17-24 [interpolated by Titus] > Titus and 1 Tim [both by Titus]

[13]Easton **Pastoral** 17f

[14]Murphy-O'Connor **2 Timothy** 418.

[15]As evidence for its interpolation, note 1 Cor 7:17b "and so ordain I in all the churches," a claim of universality which suits the likely agenda of the collected letters.

Silvanus

That Silvanus might have written 2 Thessalonians is a natural thought, since he cosigned the original 1 Thessalonians.[16] 2 Thess is much concerned about doctrine, and doctrine of a recognizably Alpha sort. The phrase "obey" the Gospel (1:8, 3:14) implies a Gospel of commandments, such as the six listed by Jesus in Mk 10:19. The Atonement figures in all three of the Pastorals, but is nowhere visible in 2 Thess.[17] Finally, 2 Thess revives the coming of Christ at the end of the world, as first predicted in Mk 13. In these details, the author of 2 Thess seems close to Mark, with whom Silvanus' origin in Jerusalem (Ac 15:22f) might in any case associate him.

2 Thess goes beyond any other deutero-Pauline in not only offering to *correct* something in a genuine epistle, but in *questioning the genuineness* of a genuine epistle. Paul in Phm 19 insists that he is writing in his own hand, as though to create a legally sound document, and in Gal 6:11 he comments on the largeness of his handwriting. In 2 Thess, these hints are picked up in this way:

> **2 Thess 2:2**. That ye be not quickly shaken from your mind, nor yet be troubled, either by spirit or by word, or by epistle as from us . . . [3:17] The salutation of me, Paul, with mine own hand, which is the token in every epistle: so I write.

This is an effort to replace earlier teachings with later ones. We then have:

> (4) 1 Thess [co-signed by Silvanus] > 2 Thess [written by Silvanus]

Sosthenes

Sosthenes, the co-sender of 1 Corinthians, appears this way in Acts:

> **Ac 18:17a**. And they [the Jews who had accused Paul before Gallio in Corinth] all laid hands on Sosthenes, the ruler of the synagogue, and beat him before the judgement-seat.

He is then a Corinthian; a local ally of Paul. In co-signing 1 Cor, he probably helped to secure that letter's acceptance in Corinth, and probably agreed with its reproof of factionalism. We might associate him with the interpolated 1 Cor 13,[18] whose message is that mutual regard is preferable to doctrinal or other squabbles. Then:

> (5) 1 Cor [co-signed by Sosthenes] > 1 Cor 13 [interpolated by Sosthenes]

Apollos

In 1 Cor 1:12 he is the leader of a faction at Corinth. At the end of 1 Cor (16:12), Paul answers a question about when Apollos might come. That this question is asked of Paul implies a degree of practical cooperation; that he cannot answer definitively implies some independence on Apollos' part. He seems to be a colleague at a distance, and thus is not a strong candidate for Paul's editorial team.

---

[16]Since 1909; see the survey in Best **Thessalonians** 50-52.

[17]Its brief appearance in the early 1 Thess 5:10 "who died for us, that, whether we wake or sleep, we should live together with him" is subject to doubt as an interpolation.

[18]For that passage (more exactly 1 Cor 12:31b–14:1a), see Walker **Interpolations** 147-165.

Apollos in Acts is from Alexandria; an Alpha Christian "mighty in the scriptures" (Ac 18:24) but needing re-instruction before he is theologically sound (Ac 18:26). This matches what can be inferred from Hebrews as to the author of Hebrews.[19] Then:

(6) [An independent role as of 1 Cor] > Hebrews [written by Apollos]

Conclusion

All told, there is reason to think that the interpolations in Paul's genuine letters were added on one occasion by his editors; that the editors were those who had been his chief colleagues during his lifetime; that they were neither unanimous about doctrine or without personal ambition, and that once the editorial task was done, and the letters had been published, they continued to write new epistles which adjusted Paul's message and kept his name before the public; providing, according to their several lights, for an emergent Christianity which still had to be guided on its way.

Works Cited

Harold W Attridge. Hebrews [Hermeneia]. Fortress 1989
Francis W Beare. The Epistle to the Colossians [IB v11]. Abingdon 1955
Francis W Beare. The Epistle to the Ephesians [IB v10). Abingdon 1953
Lisa Marie Belz. The Rhetoric of Gender in the Household of God. PhD Loyola 2013
Ernest Best. The First and Second Epistles to the Thessalonians. Harper 1972
E Bruce Brooks. The Two Ways. Alpha v1 (2017) 39-47
E Bruce Brooks. Paul's Letters to Philippi. Alpha v1 (2017) 112-118
F F Bruce. The Pauline Circle. Eerdmans 1985
Raymond F Collins. I & II Timothy and Titus. Westminster 2002
Raymond F Collins. Letters That Paul Did Not Write. Michael Glazier 1980
Burton Scott Easton. The Pastoral Epistles. Scribner 1947.
Edgar J Goodspeed. The Meaning of Ephesians. Chicago 1933
P N Harrison. Paulines and Pastorals. Villiers 1964
Glenn S Holland. The Teaching You Received From Us. Pub Date
B N Kaye. Acts' Portrait of Silas. NovT v21 #1 (Jan 1979) 13-26
John Knox. Philemon Among the Letters of Paul. 1935; 2ed Collins 1960
J B Lightfoot. St Paul's Epistle to the Philippians. Macmillan 1908
J B Lightfoot and J R Harmer. Apostolic Fathers. Macmillan 1891
Andrew T Lincoln. Ephesians. Zondervan 1990
John Muddiman. The Epistle to the Ephesians. Hendrickson 2001
Jerome Murphy-O'Connor. 2 Timothy Contrasted with 1 Timothy and Titus. RB v98 (1991) 403-418
Petr Pokorny. Colossians. 1987; tr Hendrickson 1991
E G Selwyn. The First Epistle of St Peter. Macmillan 1946
William O Walker Jr. Interpolations in the Pauline Letters. Sheffield 2001
James P Ware. Synopsis of the Pauline Letters in Greek and English. Baker 2010

[19]First noted by Luther. Attridge **Hebrews** 4 is reluctant to accept the identification, but surely Onesimus' combination of traits and talents must have been rare.

The Companions of Paul in Acts

Glenn S Holland

Allegheny College

(18 March 2016)

The Acts of the Apostles portrays the companions of Paul in different ways and in greater or lesser detail. The portrayal of his companions contributes to a particular presentation of Paul as the figure that comes to dominate the second half of the book.

Barnabas

Barnabas is the chief companion of Paul in Acts. He first appears as one of those who exhibit the enthusiasm Acts presents as typical of the earliest Jesus communities:

> **Ac 4:32**. Now the whole group of those who believed were of one heart and soul, and no one claimed private ownership of any possessions, but everything they owned was held in common . . . [34] There was not a needy person among them, for as many as owned lands or houses sold them and brought the proceeds of what was sold. [35] They laid it at the apostles' feet, and it was distributed to each as any had need. [36] There was a Levite, a native of Cyprus, Joseph, to whom the apostles gave the name Barnabas (which means "son of encouragement"). [37] He sold a field that belonged to him, then brought the money, and laid it at the apostles' feet.

Barnabas provides not only a particularly notable example of generosity towards the community, but also a striking contrast to the scheming Ananias and Sapphira, whose story immediately follows (Ac 5:1-11).

It is Barnabas – not only a Levite, but an exemplary follower of Jesus in Jerusalem – who acts as an intermediary between the newly-converted Paul and the other disciples in his native city:

> **Ac 9:26**. When he [Saul] had come to Jerusalem, he attempted to join the disciples, and they were all afraid of him, for they did not believe that he was a disciple. [27] But Barnabas took him, brought him to the apostles, and described for them how on the road he had seen the Lord, who had spoken to him, and how in Damascus he had spoken boldly in the name of Jesus.

Barnabas' earlier financial generosity is paralleled here by a generosity of spirit, as he offers himself as Saul's patron and benefactor, someone who will vouch for him to the Jesus community in Jerusalem.

The collaboration between Barnabas and Saul as fellow apostles begins in Acts 11, when leaders in the church in Jerusalem hear of preliminary missionary activity in Antioch in Syria, and send Barnabas there to investigate (11:22). He encourages the new believers, "for he was a good man, full of the Holy Spirit and of faith" (11:24a). Barnabas then goes on to Tarsus to recruit Saul for the work in Antioch, where they stay for a year (11:25-26).

Barnabas and Saul then return to Judea with a monetary gift from Antioch, after a prophet from Jerusalem, Agabus, predicts a widespread famine (11:28-30). After that mission is completed, Barnabas and Saul return from Jerusalem, bringing John Mark with them (11:24).[1] But in the next verse (13:1), Barnabas is listed first among the five "prophets and teachers" at Antioch, with Saul appearing last. As a result of prompting by the Holy Spirit, Barnabas and Saul are commissioned by the congregation in Antioch to travel to Salamis. There "they proclaimed the word of God in the synagogues of the Jews" (13:2-5a). John Mark goes along "to assist them" (13:5b).

In Acts 13:13 the group is referred to as "Paul and his companions." Saul earlier took the lead for the first time (and was redesignated "Paul") during the conflict with the magician Bar-Jesus (Elymas) in the court of the proconsul Sergius Paulus (13:7-12). Now the group travels from Paphos to Pisidian Antioch. John Mark, however, returns to Jerusalem instead (13:13b). In Pisidian Antioch, the elders of the synagogue ask whether any of Paul's group have "any word of exhortation for the people" (13:15b). But it is Paul alone who "stood up and with a gesture began to speak" at length (13:16b-41). Although the shift to Paul's primacy is subtle, the leadership has at this point passed from Barnabas to Paul.

There are several other instances in the next two chapters where both Paul and Barnabas are asked to speak, and both apparently do so (13:42-43, 46). Notably, "both Paul and Barnabas spoke out boldly, saying, It was necessary that the word of God should be spoken first to you [Jews]. Since you reject it and judge yourselves to be unworthy of eternal life, we are not turning to the Gentiles" (13:46). This statement outlines a missionary strategy (first Jews, then Gentiles) which Acts subsequently shows Paul pursuing in Corinth (18:5-6) and in Rome (28:25-28).[2] But most often Paul alone is the one who speaks. This point is emphasized in Acts' account of a mircle in Lystra, when it is Paul who heals a crippled man with a command (14:8-10). As a result, the people hail both Barnabas and Paul as gods in human guise (14:11), but notably, "Barnabas they called Zeus, and Paul they called Hermes, because he was the chief speaker" (14:12). These divine names may be meant to indicate a physical distinction: Barnabas the more physically impressive, Paul less so.[3] Paul and Barnabas together reprimand the crowd (14:14-18). But when "Jews came from Antioch and Iconium and won over the crowds" (14:19a), it is only Paul who is stoned and left for dead (14:19b-20). Leter, it is both Paul and Barnabas who "spoke the word" in Perga, and reported on their mission once back in Antioch (14:26-27).

In Antioch, the "circumcision party" arrives and disputes with Paul and Barnabas (15:1-2a), leading to "Paul and Barnabas and some of the others" being appointed "to discuss this question with the apostle and the elders" (notably, not the same group) in Jerusalem (15:2b).

---

[1] Substituting, as many do, "from" for "to."

[2] For another way in which these three passages may be related, see Brooks **Acts-Luke** 149f.

[3] Consider the hints of Paul's unimpressive physical appearance in 2 Cor 10:10, or the description in the Acts of Paul and Tecla 3:5 (see Meeks **Writings** 212).

Once there, the party "reported all that God had done with them (15:4), with Barnabas and Paul doing so again at the meeting called to resolve the issue (15:12). The issue is in fact resolved immediately afterwards by a degree from James/Jacob (15:21). The resolution is to be conveyed to Antioch by Paul and Barnabas, but they are to be accompanied by two representatives of the Jerusalem congregation, Judas Bar-Sabbas and Silas (15:22), who also carry a letter reproduced in Acts 15:23-29.

Paul and Barnabas subsequently remain in Antioch (15:35), but Paul proposes returning to the various cities where they have established congregations (15:36). Barnabas wishes to take John Mark (15:37), "but Paul decided not to take with them one who had deserted them in Pamphylia and had not accompanied them in the work" (15:38). This leads to a "disagreement [that] became so sharp that they parted company; Barnabas took Mark with him and sailed away to Cyprus. But Paul chose Silas and set out, the believers commending him to the grace of the Lord" (15:39-40). And that is the last we hear of Barnabas in Acts.

John Mark

He is first introduced in the story of Peter's escape from prison (12:1-17), when Peter goes "to the house of Mary, the mother of John whose other name was Mark, where many had gathered and were praying" (12:12). When Barnabas and Saul return to Antioch from Jerusalem, they take John Mark with them (12:25) and he assists Barnabas and Saul during their missionary journey to Salamis (13:5). But John Mark returns to Jerusalem from Paphos, instead of continuing to Antioch of Pisidia with Paul and Barnabas (13:13b). Paul and Barnabas part company, and "Barnabas took Mark with him and sailed away to Cyprus" (15:39b) and out of the story.

Silas

The name first appears in Acts 15:22 as one of the two emissaries from Jerusalem sent to Antioch with Barnabas and Paul (15:27), though it is not clear whether this is meant to be the same Silas who later travels with Paul. Silas is one of two "prophets" who encourage the faithful in Antioch (15:32). Paul takes Silas with him, in lieu of Barnabas himself, on the trip to the cities where he and Barnabas had established congregations (15:40). Compared with Barnabas, Silas is more an assistant than a partner; still, as with Barnabas, what happens to Paul also happens to Silas. "They seized Paul and Silas and dragged them into the marketplace" (16:19b); "About midnight Paul and Silas were praying and singing hymns to God" (16:25); "The jailer . . . fell down trembling before Paul and Silas" (16:29); "After Paul and Silas had passed through Amphipolis and Apollonia" (17:1), "Some of them were persuaded and joined Paul and Silas" (17:4a); "While they were seareching for Paul and Silas to bring them out to the assembly" (17:5b); "That very night the believers sent Paul and Silas off to Beroea" (17:10). But when Paul leaves Thessalonica, Silas stays behind with Timothy, and is thereafter associated exclusively with him and only secondarily with Paul (17:14, 17:15b, 18:5a).

Since Judas and Silas are sent back to Jerusalem in Acts 15:33, the reappearance of Silas at 15:40 may represent a later intention of the author of Acts.

Timothy

He first appears with a full introduction:

Ac 16:1. Paul went on also to Derbe and to Lystra, where there was a disciple named Timothy, the son of a Jewish woman who was a believer, but his father was a Greek. [2] He was well spoken of by the believers in Lystra and Iconium. [3] Paul wanted Timothy to accompany him, and he took him and had him circumcised because of the Jews who were in those places, for they all knew his father was a Greek.

Timothy later joins Paul while Paul is already being assisted by Silas (15:40), and both are later "left behind" when Paul leaves Thessalonica (17:14-15). Together they join him in Corinth, where "Paul was occupied with proclaiming the Word, testifying to the Jews that the Messiah was Jesus" (18:5b). Timothy is also sent with Erastus to Macedonia, perhaps to prepare Paul's intended journey to Jerusalem (19:21), while Paul himself remains in Asia (19:22). Timothy is again associated with Macedonia when he goes there with a coterie of associates to await Paul at Troas (20:3-5). This is not a mission errand, and Timothy's role is not enhanced by his association with it.

Erastus

In Acts, only at 19:21, abovementioned. He was undoubtedly a real person, at one point serving as an official in Corinth,[4] but his promotion to mission associate in Acts is without support elsewhere.

The seven companions of Paul listed in Acts 20:4 are Sopater, Aristarchus, Secundus, Gaius, Timothy, Tychicus, and Trophimus. Neither Sopater nor Secundus appears anywhere else in the New Testament. Four of the other five appear in Acts:

Aristarchus and Gaius

Aristarchus first appears in 19:29 with Gaius, as a "travel companion" of Paul, who gets caught up in a riot in Ephesus. The two are also companions when Paul goes to Macedonia (20:4), and again when Paul sails for Italy (27:2). These are not mission associates They appear otherwise only in the personalia (always dubious) of Paul's genuine letters or in the deutero-Paulines. Gaius is probably not the one mentioned in 1 Cor 1:14 ("I thank God that I baptized none of you except Crispus and Gaius").

Trophimus and Tychicus

They appear in Acts only in the list of companions in Acts 20:4. They are absent in Paul's genuine letters, and appear otherwise only in the deutero-Paulines. In Acts, they can be said to be companions, but not mission associates.

Luke

He is not directly mentioned in Acts, but the "we" passages invite the inference that Luke in those passages is recounting his own service as a companion of Paul.

---

[4]For Erastus, with evidence from archaeology, see Harrison **Paulines** 100-105.

Overview

Luke and Acts present Jerusalem as the center of the Jesus movement, as the place where it began (Lk 24:46-49, Acts 2) and as the seat of its authority (Acts 15:1-19). Of the various companions of Paul, three – Barnabas, John Mark, and Silas – are identified with Jerusalem (4:36, 12:12, 15:22). The others are identified with the Diaspora: Timothy is from Lystra (16:1), and the other companions are associated in some way with Macedonia or with Paul's travels there.

Barnabas is presented as exemplary in every respect. He is a model of generosity towards the Jesus community in Jerusalem, he acts as Saul's benefactor and patron, and he recruits Saul for his first missionary journey, commissioned as an apostle by the community in Anioch. He is an equal partner to Paul, the "Zeus" to his "Hermes," until they split over whether to include John Mark in a second journey, after his earlier desertion. Barnabas' willingness to give John Mark a second chance is commendable, even if Paul's objections are also understandable. Though the two apostles go their separate ways, neither Barnabas nor Paul is shouldered with the blame for the split.

Of the other companions of Paul, Silas' role in Acts is similar to that of Barnabas, although on a smaller scale. Silas is Barnabas' replacement after Paul and Barnabas separate (15:40). Although subordinate to Paul as an assistant, Silas takes an equal share in Paul's adventures in Philippi (16:11-40), Thessalonica (17:1-9), and Beroea (17:10-14a). But after he stays behind with Timothy when Paul departs for Athens (17:14b-15), Silas does not again appear as Paul's partner, although Silas and Timothy are later reuinted with him in Athens (18:5). Paul thereafter travels with a series of companions, but none are as closely associated with him as either Barnabas or Silas had been. Nor do any of the other companions of Paul – with the exception of John Mark – have any discernible personalities.

What sets John Mark apart is his decision to leave Barnabas and Paul at Paphos and return to Jerusalem (13:13b). We are not told why he does so, but he is from Jerusalem, where his mother Mary also lives (12:12). Whether John Mark was culpable or not (the reference to "the one who had deserted them [τὸν ἀποστάντα ἀπ᾽ αὐτων] implies culpability, at least in Paul's eyes), he had forfeited the right to join a triumphant return to the cities where the missionary work – work he did not share in – had been done. Mark instead joins Barnabas as a companion in his missionary journey to Cyprus (15:39), an account of which Acts neglects to include.

Acts 15 is in many was the center of the book, at least in regards to Paul's work as an apostle, which consumes the remainder of the history. In Acts 15 Paul separates from Barnabas, cutting Paul's ties to Antioch as the source of his apostolic authority.[5] From this point on, Paul acts as the undisputed head of his missionary work, the apostle to the Gentiles, without partners but with various companions who assist him in his work. If none of them are as fully developed as Barnabas (who himself remains a somewhat underdeveloped figure), this only allows Paul, the star of the second half of Acts, to shine all the brighter.

---

[5]Lüdemann **Acts** 169, "The parting is necessary at this point because from now on there is no longer any room in the Pauline mission for a representative of the Antiochene community."

Comment
E Bruce Brooks, 2016

There are striking differences between the Acts picture of Paul's companions and the impression we get from Paul himself. These may bear on the agenda of Acts.

Barnabas. In Acts, Barnabas vanishes after 15:39, implying that the rift between him and Paul over John Mark was permanent, but Paul mentions Barnabas as a fellow worker, and as one familiar to the Corinthians, as late as 1 Cor 9:6. Acts has thus exaggerated the split, which in any case Paul himself never mentions.

John Mark is the only companion negatively portrayed in Acts. As the likely author of the Gospel which Luke (the presumptive author of Acts) sought to replace, a negative report of him might be meant to advance the cause of Luke's own Gospel.

Silas is most often equated with the Silvanus who twice appears in Paul's genuine letters (2 Cor 1:19 and, as co-author, in 1 Thess 1:1). Silas or Silvanus in Acts has a distinctly lower status than co-authorship, and Acts has thus subtly downgraded him.

Timothy is the associate most often mentioned in Paul's own letters.[6] So also in the Pastorals (1 and 2 Tim) and as a co-sender of the deutero-Pauline 2 Thess (1:1). But as Glenn notes, his function in Acts is sometimes merely that of an arranger.

Erastus is mentioned in the perhaps dubious personalia of Romans 16; his only other mention outside Acts is in 2 Tim 4:20 ("Erastus remained at Corinth"). His promotion to companion status in Acts does little more than lower that of Timothy, with whom he is associated in Erastus' minor errand to Macedonia.

Luke. Paul is the star of what I have called Acts II, but who of all his companions is most faithful? Surely the "we" persona of Acts, whom we are invited to infer is Luke himself. He accompanies Paul along the seacoast from Macedonia around to Caesarea and into the lion's mouth at Jerusalem; he is with Paul thereafter, witnessing his miracles en route and then (it is to be inferred) his preaching in Rome. In this view, the deutero-Paulines (and the personalia of the otherwise genuine Phm 24) concur. "Only Luke is with me" says 2 Tim 4:11. "Luke the beloved physician" coos Col 4:14. If Luke is in fact trying to insinuate himself into the Paul picture which is is drawing, he would seem to be getting massive support from the deutero-Paulines.

What all this would look like, if and when it should be untangled, who can say? Meanwhile, it might be fruitful to regard Acts II as just one more deutero-Pauline text. A text with an agenda; a text with something to prove – including, about its author.

Works Cited

E Bruce Brooks. Acts-Luke. Alpha v1 (2017) 143-157
E Bruce Brooks. Mark at Perga. Alpha v1 (2017) 99-103
P N Harrison. Paulines and Pastorals. Villiers 1964
Gerd Lüdemann. Early Christianity According to the Traditions in Acts. Fortress 1989
Wayne A Meeks et al (ed). The Writings of St Paul. Norton 2007

[6] 1 Cor 4:17, 16:10; 2 Cor 1:1, 1:19; Php 1:1, 2:19, 2:22; 1 Thess 1:1, 3:2, 3:6; Phm 1

Matthew's Parable of the Two Sons

Robert H Gundry

Westmont College

(Authorized 7 Oct 2014)

EDITORS' NOTE: Pages 421-424 of Gundry's **Matthew** (Eerdmans 1982) are here adapted, with the permission of the author and the publisher, to make them more readily available to our readers as a study in creative adaptation.

Mt 21:28-32 (Luke 7:29-30). The parable of the two sons is unique to Matthew and starts a series of three parables in the Gospel (see also 21:33-46 [the Parable of the Wicked Tenants] and 22:1-14 [the Parable of the Marriage Feast][1]). Not even the second and third parables, though they are paralleled, appear side by side in Mark or Luke. Each of the three deals with the Jewish leaders' rejection of Jesus. The plural number of "parables" in Mk 12:1, combined with Mark's providing only one parable on that occasion, led Matthew to gather three parables together.

The parallelism that typifies Matthew's style is evident in the parable of the two sons. "And approaching the first, he said, Son, go work today in the vineyard" (v28c) corresponds to "And approaching the other, he said likewise" (v30a). "And answering, he [the son] said" appears both in v29a and v30b. "I will not" (v29b) antithetically parallels "I will, Sir" (v30c). "But changing his mind, he later went away [to work]" (v29c) contrasts with "and he did not go away [to work]" (v30d). "Who of the two did the will of the father?" (v31a) echoes "But what do you think? A man had two sons" (v28ab). "They say, The first" (v31b) matches "Jesus says to them, Truly I say to you that the publicans and the prostitutes go into the Kingdom of God before you" (v31c). "For John came to you in [the] way of righteousness, and you did not believe him" (v32ab) antithetically parallels "but the publicans and the prostitutes believed him, and you, seeing, did not even change your minds later so as to believe him" (v32cd).

This sketch of parallelistic structure rests on a text-critical judgement in favor of the reading supported by S* C K W and others (see the UBS). This reading has in its favor the probability that the asking of the other son depends on the refusal of the first son. Furthermore, with this reading the first son turns out to be the last and the other, or last, son turns out to be first in accord with Jesus' statement to this effect and with Matthew's special interest in it (see 19:30 and 20:1-16). Support for the reading comes also from Matthew's fondness for ἑτέρῳ (5, 1), as opposed to un-Matthean δευτέρῳ. The latter goes with the variant reading, which may have arisen out of later application of the parable to Jews and Gentiles. That application demanded a reversal in the order of the sons to agree with the historical order of Jewish disobedience followed by Gentiles' repentance. See further Metzger ad loc.

---

[1] [Paralleled respectively in Mk 12:1-12 || Lk 20:9-19 and in Lk 14:16-24 – The Editors].

Diction. Alongside highly literary parallelism, Matthew's special diction abounds:

τί δὲ ὑμῖν δοκεῖ (4,2), ἄνθρωπος (35,17; see comment on 13:24 concerrning its general frequency in Matthew, and on 18:23-25 concerning Matthew's special use of it in parables); δύο (bis – 19,4; almost always concerning pairs of people, here concerning τέκνα; cf other unparalleled occurrences of τέκνα in 2:18, 18:25, 27:25); προσελθών (bis – 38,6); πρώτῳ/ος (2,5-6); ὕπαγε (5,6 – esp as an imperative); σήμερον (4,3); ἐργάζου (6,7 for ἐργ-) . . . Furthermore, the publicans' and prostitutes' entering the Kingdom of God looks like the uniquely Matthean formulae in 5:20, 7:21, 19:17.

The Prodigal Son. Apparently Matthew composed this parable (1) as a counterpart to the parable of the prodigal son and his elder brother, Lk 15:11-32, (2) in reminiscence of the distinctive parable of the laborers in the vineyard, Mt 20:1-6, and (3) with reference to John the Baptist in the debate over Jesus' authority, Mt 21:23-27. Since the Jewish leaders who challenged that authority lacked faith, προάγουσιν surely indicates their exclusive displacement, not merely their later entrance into the kingdom. The expression gives us an example of meiosis. The present tense of the verb probably implies entrance into the current form of the kingdom (cf Lk 16:16). In v32 the parable finally leads up to a revision of the tradition behind Lk 7:29-30, which Matthew replaced with 11:12-14 (cf Lk 16:16) in a discussion about John the Baptist (see 11:7-19 together with Lk 7:24-35). All in all, behind Matthew's composition and editing lies the purpose of highlighting the Jewish leaders' guilt.

We may detect echoes of Mt 20:1-16 at a number of points: the use of the root ἐργ- for the motif of work; the locale of the work in a vineyard; the use of ὑπάγω in the command to go to the vineyard; the use of ἀπέρχομαι in describing the going and not going; the division of the parable into chronological stages; the summarizing use of ὡσαύτως to qualify the action of getting workers into the vineyard; the identification of the owner with κύριος; the lack of a polite address on the part of the rebellious; and the reversal of first and last. The reminiscence of Mt 20:1-16 also anticipates the immediately following parable of the vineyard in Mt 21:33-46. Believing and not believing John the Baptist stem from the people's regarding John as a prophet and the chief priests' and elders' unbelief in John, just mentioned in vv 25-26. This assimilation to the preceding context leads Matthew to replace being baptized by John and not being baptized by John (so Luke 7:29-30) with believing and not believing John (v32). "For John came" (c32) echoes Mt 11:18 exactly (contrast the somewhat different wording in Lk 7:33). πρὸς ὑμᾶς harks back to προσελθὼν τῷ πρώτῳ / ἑτέρῳ in the parable proper. The contextual address to the chief priests and elders of the people determines the change of the third person plural (so Lk 7:29-30) to the second person plural. The several uses of ὁδός since the beginning of Jesus' ascent to Jerusalem (see 20:L17, 30; 21, 8 [bis], 19) combine with ἐδικαίωσαν "they acknowledged [God's] righteousness" (Luke 7:29) to make Matthew write ἐν ὁδῷ δικαιοσύνης, which corresponds and refers to his portrayal of the Baptist as a preacher of righteousness. "The way of righteousness" appears also in Prov 8:20; 12:28; 16:31; 2 Pet 2:21; Jub 23:26; 25:15; 1 Enoch 92:3; 99:10; Barn 1:3, 5:4.

Typically, then, Matthew is borrowing a widely used expression from the OT. The borrowing will be confirmed by his inserting in v41 a further allusion to Ps 1:3, which concerns the way of the righteous (see Ps 1:6). The publicans come from Lk 7:29-30, but we read "the harlots" instead of the associated phrase "all the people." Probably the latter phrase owes something to Luke's redaction and rests on the crowd in the tradition (see Lk 7:24 and compare the concordance, sv λαός with Aland's synopsis). Matthew's previous and distinctive association of the people with the antagonistic elders (v23) would have forestalled a favorable reference to the people here. The rejection of God's will in Lk 7:30 matches the behavior of the chief priests and the elders, who are represented by the disobedient son, remarkably well (though the term βουλήν "will" may come from Luke's hand).

God. We might ask why Matthew writes about "the kingdom of God" instead of his usual "kingdom of heaven," if he bears responsibility for composing the parable and its interpretation. The answer lies in the contextual need for the personal emphasis in God's name. Just as in Mt 12:28 the contextual references to Satan's kingdom and God's Spirit called for retention of "God" with "kingdom," so also here the contextual figure of the father, whose vineyard represents the kingdom, calls for use of the divine name (compare the vl in 6:33 with 6:32). Compositional use of "the kingdom of God," then, poses no greater problem than retention of "the kingdom of God" in traditional material. In other ways too, Matthew shows he is not limited to "the kingdom of heaven." He writes of the Father's kingdom (6:10, 13:43, 26:29), the kingdom of the Son of Man (13:41, 16:28; compare 20:21), the kingdom without qualification but in association with the gospel, righteousness, Jews ("sons of the kingdom"), the Word, and the disciples (4:23; 6:33 vl; 8:12; 9:35; 13:19, 38; 24:14; 25:34), as well as of God's kingdom (6:33 vl; 12:28; 19:24; 21:31, 43). Often these expressions are peculiar to his gospel. Therefore, it should not surprise us that in his own composition he uses "the kingdom of God" instead of "the kingdom of heaven."

In sum, Matthew composes the parable as an illustration of the dominical saying we find in Lk 7:29-30. Earlier, he reserved that saying for inclusion in the present passage. Both his composing the parable and his reserving the saying have the purpose of emphasizing the Jewish leaders' guilt. Like the first son, the publicans and prostitutes repented at the preaching of John the Baptist after exhibiting carelessness toward the law. Like the other son, the Jewish leaders refused John's message despite their claimed allegiance to the law. The last line of v32 goes beyond the parable in noting that the Jewish leaders added guilt upon guilt by failing to change their minds even when given a second chance – probably a reference to Jesus' ministry. This progression beyond the parable assimilates the ministries of Jesus and John both in the shifting of believing publicans and prostitutes from Jesus to John and in the making of Jesus' ministry a renewal of the opportunity granted in John's ministry. Indeed, putting John "on the way of righteousness" has already brought him alongside Jesus the Teacher of Righteousness (see esp Mt 5:17-48). That such assimilation typifies Matthew's theology sets the seal to composition by him.

The Urban Food Supply and the Lord's Prayer

Randall C Webber

Wayside Christian Mission, Louisville Kentucky

20 July 2014

The Lord's Prayer has been seen as a series of eschatological petitions. I here consider the uncertain urban food supply in the contemporaneous Mediterranean as an alternate explanation of the "daily bread" line of the Prayer, and by implication, of the whole of the Prayer.

The Eschatological Interpretation

Johannes Weiss in 1892 considered that the petition "may your kingdom come" set the tone for the following petitions.[1] Rudolf Bultmann considered the eschatological character of the prayer, particularly its first three petitions, a foregone conclusion, and argued that Jesus took for granted that the deity's regime was to benefit the Jewish people.[2] Others further articulated this eschatological perspective.[3] Joachim Jeremias was the foremost proponent of the eschatological perspective after WW2. He looked at the two petitions regarding subsistence and forgiveness, interpreting the first as a reference to bread for tomorrow, in the sense of the Great Tomorrow, and the second as a plea for forgiveness at the final reckoning.[4] This interpretation of the subsistence petition, in particular, depended on Jeremias' proposal for an underlying Aramaic original; that hypothetical version included the entirety of the Lucan petitions, though with a preference for Matthean terminology in some instances.[5]

The various statements of the eschatological view carried the seeds of their own instability. Weiss, for example, considered the request for the sanctification of the deity's name a reverent liturgical introductory formula.[6] Bultmann noted the mundane references to physical life and forgiveness in the fourth and fifth petitions.[7] Jeremias' interpretation of the subsistence petition in light of the Great Tomorrow is inconsistent with the terminology of the three sources in which the Prayer appears.[8] Finally, the textual history of the prayer suggests that to the compiler of Matthew or his source is due the credit for the eschatological dimensions of the longer version of the Prayer.

[1] Weiss **Proclamation** 73.

[2] Bultmann **Word** 42-43.

[3] For a summary, see Gibson **Eschatological** 96.

[4] Jeremias **Prayer** 24-25.

[5] For this reconstruction, see Jeremias **Prayer** 15.

[6] Weiss **Proclamation** 73 n29.

[7] Bultmann **Word** 181.

[8] Hultgren **Bread Petition** 47.

The Text of the Lord's Prayer

The history of text transmission is largely one of harmonizing the shorter Lucan version to its longer Matthean counterpart; Matthew's version includes the Lucan petitions in their entirety. The Didache uses the Matthean version, attributing it explicitly to "the Gospel," and adding only a final benediction. In light of this history, it would be more difficult to argue for the Lucan version as an abridgement than to argue for the Matthean/Didache version as an expansion.[9]

More importantly for the question of eschatological vs mundane perspective, the Matthean expansion exhibits a consistent redactional principle. In each case, it adds a reference to metaphysical dualism to interpret a petition from the Lucan version. A translation of the Matthean version with the Lucan petitions (Matthean wording) in standard type and the additions italicized illustrates the application of this principle:

> *Our* Father, *the one in Heaven,*
> May your name be sanctified.
> May your regime come.
> *May your will be done, as in Heaven, so also on earth.*
> Give us today our subsistence ration,
> And forgive our debts as we have forgiven our debtors.
> Do not lead us into the test,
> *But release us from the Evil One.*

The petition for the Deity's will to be done interprets the plea for his regime to come by implying a contrast between the Deity's rule in Heaven with conditions on earth. Likewise, the final Matthean petition contrasts the father at the top of the Heavenly bureaucracy with the Evil One, his fiendish counterpart. This secondary, dualistic overlay raises the question of the Prayer's frame of reference apart from the overlay. We next turn to this question.

The Lord's Prayer: A Mundane Perspective

Jeffrey Gibson proposed a non-eschatological focus for the Lord's Prayer. He characterized the Prayer as a plea for "divine provision for guarding the disciples from going over to the side of "this generation.""[10] In other words, he considered the Prayer a request for protection against apostasy such as that which characterized the Israelites during the Exodus. This characterization is compatible with Hultgren's understanding of the subsistence petition as a reference to bread such as the manna provided during the Exodus (Ex 16:4, 15; Ps 78:24, 105:40).[11]

The writings which include the Prayer utilize the Scriptural corpus from which the manna tradition is derived, but this does not exhaust the mundane perspective on the food supply situation. In fact, the unpredictability of the urban food supply throughout classical antiquity provides an additional perspective on a problem which most likely occurred with some regularity for the compilers and audiences of the Gospels.

[9]Jeremias **Prayer** 12-14.

[10]Gibson **Matthew** 104.

[11]Hultgren **Bread Petition** 48-50.

In most parts of the Mediterranean basin, the success of a harvest was dependent on favorable weather conditions, which might or might not obtain in a given year in a particular location. Aristotle noted the variability in rainfall throughout the region: "sometimes drought or rain is widespread and covers a large area of country; sometimes it is only local."[12] This suggests that food abundance and food shortage were localized, with the situation in a given area varying from one harvest to the next.

Peter Guernsey calculated the probability of crop failure in Attica. By his estimate, the wheat crop might be expected to fail in 28%, barley in 5·5%, and dry legumes in 71% of the harvests.[13] Other parts of the Mediterranean give evidence of comparably high failure rates. Guernsey concluded that food shortage, defined as "a short-term reduction in the amount of available foodstuffs, indicated by rising prices, popular discontent, hunger . . . was common."[14] The Apocalypse illustrates the familiarity of John's urban audiences with food shortages and with the differing failure rates for wheat and barley. The inflation of grain prices to a denarius (about a day's wage) for one measure of wheat or three measures of barley (Rev 6:6) is one of the curses delivered by the Four Riders. In this scenario, subsistence for an individual or a small family required a worker's entire wage, and left nothing for other expenses.

When food shortages occur frequently, the ability to manage the resulting crises is an asset. The Lord's Prayer sits within a tradition that recognized the necessity of managing the food supply. The Pentateuch included a tradition regarding Joseph's prediction of and preparation for a seven-year regional famine (Gen 41). In that account, Joseph established a policy of storing excess grain from abundant years; during lean years, he alleviated the effects of famine by selling the excess grain.

Similar arrangements prevailed throughout the Greco-Roman world. A monument memorializing Augustus' accomplishments praises his grain supply management:

> I did not decline at a time of the greatest scarcity of grain the charge of the grain supply, which I so administered that, within a few days, I freed the entire people, at my own expense, from the fear and danger in which they were . . .
>
> When consul for the thirteenth time, I gave sixty denarii apiece to the plebs who were then receiving public grain; these were a little more than two hundred thousand persons.[15]

Augustus was one of many notables to receive the title *pater patriae*. He had managed the grain supply so as to minimize unrest among the lower classes. His grain supply management is unusual only for its scale: he had used existing political structures to implement his subsistence measures. The patronage system, which was pervasive in the Mediterranean, let the well-to-do enhance their prestige by being benefactors to economically vulnerable dependents. The clients, in turn, could rely on handouts from their patron for subsistence.[16]

---

[12]Aristotle **Meteorologica** 2:4.

[13]Guernsey **Famine** 10.

[14]Guernsey **Famine** 6.

[15]Res Gestae Divi Augusti 1:5, 3:15, tr Shipley 353, 369-371.

[16]Webber **Analysis** 143-148.

The Urban Environment of the Lord's Prayer

Roman society took the shape of a steep social pyramid. A few rulers sat atop the pyramid, followed by indigenous elite and then by retainers who served their interests. The other 95% of the population included rural peasants, artisans, and the urban poor. Of these groups, the urban poor were more vulnerable economically than were the peasants, who had direct recourse to the land.[17] This gave the cities high densities of impoverished populations and thus ample potential for unrest.

Food shortages affected persons at all levels of society. With crop failure rates such as those Guernsey calculated, the urban poor might often be unable to afford sufficient food to feed their families. Wealthy civic benefactors could spend large sums to provide grain in order to minimize the unrest that widespread hunger might create. Alternatively, they might make themselves the objects of unrest by hoarding grain to sell at a high price during periods of shortage. Peasants, who worked small plots of land and paid most of their produce to the landowners, were slightly better off than the urban poor, but still remained insecure.

The subsistence petition of the Lord's Prayer fits well within a context in which urban food insecurity is the normal condition. This petition is simply a supplication to the divine benefactor to provide an adequate food supply. The Amidah echoes this sentiment in its ninth petition. Some Roman plebeians apparently considered Augustus their benefactor, for his measures to stabilize their food supply. The communities that recited the Lord's Prayer a few generations later, and those that used the Amidah, considered their deity their ultimate benefactor.

The Lord's Prayer takes the form of a series of requests from a dependent (client) to a benefactor (patron). The form of the address ("father") is not necessarily a familiar, juvenile term. The simple Lucan form could be viewed in such a light. However, the opposite perspective is more likely. The father was seen as a patriarch and head of household, in accordance with a tradition cited both by Plato (Laws 680B) and by his student Aristotle Pol 1/1:7.[18] The Matthean version actually points in this direction by formalizing the address to the deity. Thus the Lord's Prayer conceptualizes the deity not only as a public benefactor but also as a provincial counterpart of a Roman *paterfamilias*.

The last two Lucan petitions also fit within the context of urban food insecurity. Forgiveness, the renunciation of vengeance in dealings with a social inferior, requires a benefactor to behave with restraint when his responsibility for the food supply places him in control of a dependent's life and health. This petition has an inexact counterpart in the sixth petition of the Amidah. In the Lucan version (11:4ab), the Prayer requests forgiveness from the deity on the grounds that the Christian community already has adopted that principle. Likewise, the petition that the deity not lead the communities into the test (11:4c) functions quite logically as a plea to be spared the tests of food shortage, privation, and the ensuing unrest.

---

[17]Lenski **Power** 266-279.

[18]*Contra* Jeremias **Prayer** 19-20.

Comment
E Bruce Brooks

The above proposal can be further supported at several points.

First, in the propagation of the Christian message, there does seem to have been a shift from rural to urban. Jesus, for sufficient reason, had shunned the cities. His veiled Parables of the Kingdom (especially Mk 4:3-9) envision contact propagation, some converts being notably more successful at this than others (whence the "sixtyfold" and "hundredfold," which are inexplicable in terms of more organized preaching). The instructions to the Apostles (Mk 6:10-11, from the 30's) envision a town-to-town model of first visits. Jacob (from the 40's) addresses economically mixed, and thus probably more urban, communities. Paul in the 50's (his early letters, if any, are lost) communicates exclusively with urban centers. Doubtless there was always a mixture, but it is reasonable to infer that by the time Luke came along (late 60's and early 70's) the Christians were predominantly urban.

Second, that the Lukan Prayer is prior to the Matthean has the support of many.[19] Both may have Aramaic originals. If so, the same relationship apparently obtains: retrotranslation into Aramaic suggests that Luke's version is in a standard Aramaic meter, attested from the 05c to the hymns of the Syrian church father Ephraem, while the Matthean form, with its liturgical additions, is more individual.[20] Like another early prayer, the Aramaic ejaculation Maranatha ("Come, Lord"),[21] the Lord's Prayer seems to look toward a soon return of Jesus at the Last Days.[22] The Prayer fits into this context as a request for day-to-day maintenance in the short meantime, and a hope that the speaker's acts of forgiveness will move God to a like forgiveness at the end.

We may thus put the Matthean adaptation behind us. I would then ask: If Luke's version is earlier, what is its origin? Luke himself (Lk 11:1, "Lord, teach us to pray, even as John also taught his disciples") credits the influence of the fixed prayers of the Baptist movement, whose fixed prayers are numerous,[23] though there is no Mandaean parallel to the Lukan Prayer. There were also the fixed prayers already in use. Perhaps, noting all this, someone went to the Gospel of Mark and asked, What prayers of Jesus. pr what advice about prayer can we follow, to make a real prayer out of this?

[19]eg Kilpatrick **Sources** 21, Montefiore **Synoptic** 2/472, Gundry **Matthew** 104-110. That some credit the existence of a "Q" does not affect their sense of the directionality.

[20]Lohmeyer **Prayer** 27-29, compare the reconstruction in Fitzmyer **Luke** 2/901. Lohmeyer himself declines to infer directionality between the two Aramaic forms.

[21]Didache 10:6 [on the Eucharist], "May **grace** come, and may **this world pass away! Maranatha! Amen!** 1 Cor 11:26 [describing the Eucharist], For as often as ye eat this bread and drink this cup, ye proclaim the Lord's death **till he come**. 1 Cor 16:22-23 [the end of the Epistle], "If any man loveth not the Lord, let him be anathema. **Maranatha!** Rev 22:20-21 (the end of the text], "He who testifieth to these things saith, Yea, **I come quickly. Amen**; **Come, Lord Jesus!** The **grace** of the Lord be with the saints. **Amen!**

[22]The delay of this Return is the subject of some of the most agonized passages in the NT.

[23]See Drower **Prayerbook**, which includes hundreds of fixed prayers. That Luke knew the Baptists is suggested by the parallels between his respectful treatment of the Announcement to Zacharias (Lk 1:14-17) and the Mandaean Book of John 18.

The answer might have looked like the following:

Mark	Luke
14:36. Abba, Father,	11:2b. Father,
	11:2c. Hallowed be thy name.
Maranatha ("Come, Lord")[24]	11:2d. Thy Kingdom come.
	11:3. Give us day by day our daily bread.
11:25. And whensoever ye stand praying, forgive, if ye have aught against any one, that your Father also who is in Heaven may forgive you your trespasses.	11:4a. And forgive us our sins, for we ourselves also forgive every one that is indebted to us.
14:38. Watch and pray, that ye enter not into temptation.	11:4b. And bring us not into temptation.

That leaves just two elements in the Lukan Prayer unaccounted for: 11:2b and 11:3.

One of them (Lk 11:2b) is standard Jewish reverence for God, common in the OT. It might also be supplied from the Amidah or daily synagogue prayers, in this way:

Amidah	Luke
3. Thou art holy, and thy name is holy.[25]	11:2c. Hallowed be thy name.

The other, the "daily bread," is much discussed in the literature. In back of any such idea must lie the manna in the wilderness, the miraculous provision by God which was only good for one day:

Exod 16:15b. It is the bread which Jehovah hath given you to eat. [16] This is the thing which Jehovah hath commanded: Gather ye of it every man according to his eating, an omer a head, according to the number of your persons, shall ye take it, every man for them that are in his tent. [17] And the children of Israel did so, and gathered some more, some less. [18] And when they measured it with an omer, he that gathered much had nothing over, and he that gathered little had no lack; they gathered every man according to his eating. [19] And Moses said unto them, Let no man leave of it till the morning . . . [21a] And. And they gathered it morning by morning, every man according to his eating.

What changed this central cultural memory to a present necessity may have been the economic situation of the early Christians. They had been told to divest themselves of everything, in expectation of greater rewards in the imminent End, when Jesus would come again. Thus Mark's Jesus, speaking to the rich young man:

Mk 10:21. And Jesus looking on him, loved him, and said unto him, One thing thou lackest: go, sell whatsoever thou hast and give to the poor, and thou shalt have treasure in Heaven, and come, follow me.

This is emphasized by the interpolated Mk 10:23-31, but the policy of total divestment is clear enough from this passage alone. As is separation from family in Mk 3:31-35, another early practice which led to mutual dependence in the early churches.

[24]Already established in frequent use, and certainly to be included.

[25]Lohmeyer 302, translated from the modern version reflected in Singer.

The communities addressed by the Epistle of Jacob reached a point when the rich left the group, incurring violent enmity from the writer, and leaving the group without wealthy members for its support.[26] Such a situation was envisioned by Luke as stable at first (Ac 2:44-47), but later involving curses and death for the rich who withheld their contributions (Ac 4:32-5:11), and complaints about unequal sharing (Ac 6:1-3).

Luke in his Sermon on the Plain rationalized this situation as a theology of poverty, in which *possessions now* imply *rewards now*, but preclude any rewards in future:

Lk 6:20b. Blessed are ye poor, for yours in the Kingdom of Heaven. [21] Blessed are ye that hunger now, for ye shall be filled . . .

Lk 6:24. But woe unto you that are rich, for ye have received your consolation. [25] Woe unto you, ye that are full now, for ye shall hunger.

Of relevance for Luke's assembling of the Lord's Prayer, his Sermon also says:

Lk 6:36. Be ye merciful, even as your Father is merciful (cf Lk 1:4a).

The community was living in a state of holiness, but also of poverty. Staying alive from day to day was a concern. It may have been this situation that led to the prayer for daily, if temporary, sustenance. Poverty in Luke is not a disability to be relieved, but a qualification to be prized. On this reading, nothing in Luke's Prayer seems to contradict the eschatological perception of the early Jesus groups.

Works Cited

E Bruce Brooks. The Epistle of Jacob. Alpha v1 (2017) 58-70

E Bruce Brooks. Mark's Parables of the Kingdom. Alpha v1 (2017) 89-91

Rudolf K Bultmann. Jesus and the Word. 1926; tr Scribner 1934, 1958

E S Drower. The Canonical Prayerbook of the Mandaeans. Brill 1959

Joseph A Fitzmyer. Luke. 2v Doubleday 1970, 1985

Jeffrey B Gibson. Matthew 6:9-13 / Luke 11:2-4: An Eschatological Prayer? Biblical Theology Bulletin v31 #3 (2001) 96-105

Peter Guernsey. Famine and Food Supply in the Graeco-Roman World. Cambridge 1988

Robert H Gundry. Matthew. Eerdmans 1982

Arland J Hultgren. The Bread Petition of the Lord's Prayer. Anglican Theological Review Supplement Series 11 (March 1990)

Joachim Jeremias. The Lord's Prayer. 1962; tr Fortress 1964

G D Kilpatrick. The Origins of the Gospel According to Matthew. Oxford 1946

H D P Lee (tr). Meteorologica [Loeb]. Harvard 1987

Gerhard E Lenski. Power and Privilege. North Carolina 1984

Ernst Lohmeyer. The Lord's Prayer. 1952; Collins 1965

C G Montefiore. The Synoptic Gospels. 1909; 2ed 2v Macmillan 1927

Frederick W Shipley (tr). Res Gestae Divi Augusti [Loeb]. Harvard 1979

S Singer. The Authorized Daily Prayer Book. 9ed Eyre & Spottiswoode 1912

Randall C Webber. An Analysis of Power in the Jerusalem Church of Acts. UMI 1989

Johannes Weiss. Jesus' Proclamation of the Kingdom of God. 1892: tr Fortress 1971

[26]Brooks **Jacob** 58-60.

Acts-Luke

E Bruce Brooks

University of Massachusetts at Amherst

(7 Feb 2011)

Fitzmyer (**Luke** 1/309f) found that the Lukan Birth Narrative (Lk 1-2) was not original, and that Luke's text had originally begun with the synchronisms of Lk 3:1. Though not further developed by Fitzmyer, this conclusion logically requires that Luke *was formed in two compositional stages*: one (my Luke A) which began with Lk 3:1, and a later one (Luke B) which also included Lk 1-2. I here explore that possibility.

Then Luke is not one text, but at least two, and occupies not one, but at least two, points on the Synoptic diagram. *This one fact revolutionizes all Synoptic calculations.* If for example Luke A precedes, and Luke B follows, Matthew, then bidirectionality in the common Lk/Mt material does not require the hypothesis of an outside source. It can instead be seen as the natural result of borrowing in both directions. Indications of growth in Acts lead in the end to a Luke A/B/C three-stage text-formation model. The plausibility of that model can be tested. What happens if from the long Lukan "travel narrative" (9:51–18:14), passages with Mt > Lk directionality are removed, leaving behind a presumptively original Luke A text? Does that text remain jumbled, no more coherent than the present one? Or does it have a more consecutive character? One part of the answer to that question is taken up at the end of this essay.

How Many Lukes?

The Birth Narrative is probably the most conspicuous addition to an earlier Luke, but it is not the only one. Consider these three passages.

The Nazareth Episode, Lk 4:16-30, comes at the start of Jesus' Galilean ministry, not later, as in Mark.[1] Fitzmyer 1/71 says that it "presents in capsule form the theme of fulfilment and symbolizes the rejection that will mark the ministry as a whole." Just so; that is surely why Luke moved it. Now consider the demand of the Nazarenes, "whatsoever we have heard done at Capernaum, do also here in thine own country" (Lk 4:23). But at that point in Luke, Jesus *has not yet been to Capernaum*. If this line were in Mark, and was overlooked when Luke took it from Mark and put it earlier in his own text, all would be well. *But it is not in Mark.* So Luke can only have added it. But when? Did he add it as a gratuitous absurdity, when he took the story from Mark and put it in a *pre-Capernaum* position? Or as a dramatic enhancement, when the Nazareth episode was still in the Markan *post-Capernaum* position in his own text?

---

[1]In Mark 6:1-6 it follows the Healing of Jairus' Daughter and precedes the Sending of the Twelve. The corresponding position in Luke would be between Lk 8:56 (the end of the Healing of Jairus' Daughter) and 9:1 (the beginning of the Sending of the Twelve).

I prefer the less ridiculous option: that in Luke A the Nazareth episode occupied its Markan position and was enhanced by the "Capernaum" demand, and that Luke B later relocated it, for the reason Fitzmyer gives, not noticing that, *in that new position,* the previously added Capernaum line now created a narrative inconcinnity.

The Call of Peter. In Lk 4:38, Jesus "rose up from the synagogue, and entered the house of Simon. And Simon's wife's mother was holden with a great fever." Fine, but at this point in Luke's story, *we have not yet met Simon.* This problem does not arise in Mark, where Jesus first calls Simon (and Andrew, and the two Zebedees, who instantly follow him) and *then* preaches in the Capernaum synagogue. It arises because in Luke, the Call has been moved to a spot after the Capernaum Preaching (Lk 5:1-11), where, as Fitzmyer says, "it acquires a more psychologically plausible position, depicting disciples attracted to Jesus after a certain amount of ministry and preaching by him." Just so. Not only have the Four heard Jesus' Capernaum sermon, they have seen the Miraculous Catch of Fish, so emblematic of a fruitful lifetime in the preaching of the Word.. So when the Lukan Jesus says to Simon, "Fear not, from henceforth thou shalt catch men," the prediction is magnificently orchestrated.

But was the social abruptness of Lk 4:38 part of Luke's first design, or is it a consequence of his having later moved the story from a Markan position, where it involved no confusion in the order of events? The likelier option is to regard this flaw as an authorially overlooked detail rather than an intentional literary effect. I conclude that in Luke A no such flaw existed, and that, at the cost of an unintended absurdity, the Call of Peter was later moved to its present position.

The Call of the Seventy, Lk 10:1-12, follows Jesus' entry into a Samaritan village which refused to admit him (Jesus declines to call down fire on them, 9:55, and they simply go "to another village"). A few persons offer to follow him. Then Jesus "appointed seventy others, and sent them two by two before his face into every city and place *where he was about to come.*" Their seeming dispatch into Samaria is soon contradicted, since during the rest of the journey Jesus meets Jews but no Samaritans. As he draws nigh to Jerusalem via Jericho (19:1), we realize that, in geographical fact, Jesus has been following the lowland or Jordan route to Jerusalem.[2]

Is this confusion intentional? Or is it the result of adding a Samaritan beginning to an original Jordan journey? I find no basis for the first option, and adopt the second: Jesus in Luke traveled by the Jordan, and the Samaritan beginning was added later. That "Samaritans" stand for "Gentiles" has been suggested by few, but the Seventy may plausibly be understood as emblematic of a mission to all nations.[3]

Can all three of these instances be explained by the minimal Luke A/B hypothesis? Or must we posit something more complicated? To find out, I now turn to Acts.

---

[2]Creed 139, "It is implied at 9:52 that he followed the route through Samaria. But at 18:35, 19:1 he passes through Jericho. This is not consistent with a direct journey through Samaria."

[3]The allusion is to the 70 (or 72) nations of Genesis 10. See Enslin **Samaritans** 279f.

Acts I and II

In Acts, I note the signs of a break between Acts 15:35 and 15:36.

Language. Bernhard Weiss in 1886 noted the Semitic character of the first half of Acts; Torrey in 1916 proposed that it was a translation from Aramaic.[4] For an Aramaic original I can imagine no plausible scenario. I agree with those who regard the style difference as due to Luke's intentional use of a Septuagintal style, to give a high and solemn tone to a narrative guided at many points by God, who (or whose angels) inspires, or advises, or releases individuals from prison, or transports them to places favorable for a brief missionary encounter, and generally directs the course of events. For such a history, an elevated tone and a Biblical style would be highly appropriate. This tone, I suggest, is what Luke has provided in this part of Acts.

Narrative Continuity. There is a also a drastic inconcinnity after Acts 15:35:

> **Ac 15:32**. And **Judas and Silas**, being themselves also prophets, exhorted the brethren with many words and confirmed them. [33] And after they had spent some time, they **were dismissed in peace** from the brethren unto those who had **sent them forth**. [35] But Paul and Barnabas tarried in Antioch, teaching and preaching the Word of the Lord, with many others also.

> **Ac 15:36**. And after some days Paul said unto Barnabas, "Let us return now and visit the brethren in every city wherein we proclaimed the word of the Lord, [and see] how they are." [37] And Barnabas was minded to take with them John also, who was called Mark. [38] But Paul thought not good to take with them him who withdrew from them in Pamphylia, and went not with them to the work. [39] And there arose a sharp contention, so that they parted asunder one from the other, and Barnabas took Mark with him and sailed away unto Cyprus, [40] But **Paul chose Silas** and went forth . . .

How does Silas, who we have been told in Ac 15:32-33 went back with Judas to Jerusalem, come to be in Antioch in Ac 15:40? The text provides no answer.

This is not something to be labeled as an "aporia" and lightly passed by. It is a gross contradiction – so gross that the later scribes go to great lengths to mitigate it. Ephraemi Rescriptus (5c) and some later manuscripts insert a rationalizing verse:

> **Ac *15:34**. But it seemed good unto Silas **to abide there**.

The improvement was further improved in Codex Bezae, which added to *15:34 the clause "and Judas returned alone." These patches solve the problem *for their readers*. But the original text lacked them. Ac 15:36 is not the sort of thing an author is likely to write on the same day as 15:33; it suggests a later reopening of the story. Then an original conclusion at Ac 15:35 was later overridden by a continuation at Ac 15:36f, in which Paul and Barnabas set out to visit the churches.

---

[4]Weiss **Lehrbuch** 569-584, Torrey **Composition** 40; compare Cadbury **Making** 224. For other suggestions that Acts breaks at 15:35 (Dieu 1920), see Dupont **Sources** 25, 29. Probably relevant is the fact is that Scriptural citations in Acts II are far fewer than those in Acts I (Torrey **Composition** 57). Independently, and from a rhetorical point of view, Kennedy **New** finds that Ac 1:1-15:35 "seems to be a compositional unit and could be read as a complete work" (p127). That Acts 15:35 was the original ending of Acts is the proposal of the present study.

Message. The two segments defined by these considerations also differ in content. In Acts I, Peter and Paul are virtually assimilated to each other.[5] Peter, not Paul, first preaches to Gentiles.[6] Both preach with success to mixed audiences. Both preach from OT prophecy. There are no differences of doctrine; no trace of the faith/works issue.[7] The circumcision controversy is adjudicated at Jerusalem in a way agreeable to all: "When they had read it, they rejoiced for the consolation" (Ac 15:31). Acts I ends on this note of amity between Jewish and Gentile Christians.

In Acts II, the landscape is utterly different. Peter is gone,[8] and only Paul remains. Except for one at Athens, Paul's speeches are in his own defense. In them, Paul is not preaching the Gospel, but pleading for Christianity as harmless to Rome. Amity in Acts II is achieved not between Jewish and Gentile believers, but between official Rome and Christianity. Remarkably, the Jewish-Gentile amity of Acts I is replaced by Jewish-Christian hostility. Acts ends with rejection of Christianity by the Jews of Rome. Paul, after preaching to the Jews for an entire day, finds them utterly obdurate:

> **Ac 28:25**. And when they agreed not among themselves, they departed, after that Paul had spoken one word: Well spake the Holy Spirit through Isaiah the prophet unto your fathers, [26] saying:
>> Go thou unto this people and say,
>> By hearing ye shall hear, and shall in no wise understand,
>> And seeing ye shall see, and shall in no wise perceive,
>> [27] For this people's heart is waxed gross
>> And their ears are dull of hearing / And their eyes they have closed,
>> Lest haply they should perceive with their eyes,
>> And hear with their ears, and understand with their heart,
>> And should turn again, and I should heal them.
>
> [28] Be it known therefore unto you, *that this salvation of God is sent unto the Gentiles; they will also hear*. [30] And he abode two whole years . . .

As far as this passage is concerned, the break is final.[9]

---

[5] For the parallels, see Rackham **Acts** xlvii-xlviii.

[6] The piece establishing this is Peter's Conversion of Cornelius, Ac 10. It is noteworthy, in view of the forensic apologia of which Acts II in large part consists, that the first Gentile to be converted in Acts is a Roman; compare the Lukan story of the Centurion's Boy, Lk 7:2-10. Not blaming Rome for the death of Jesus was part of Christian strategy from the beginning, as witness the hesitations of Pilate, already in the Markan Crucifixion story (Mk 15:6-15).

[7] That is, the Atonement doctrine (Brooks **Jacob** 111-112). Two passages in Mark imply that doctrine (Mk 10:45, 14:24); *Luke repeats neither*. Paul in Acts preaches from the OT, and never mentions the Atonement, or any other version of theologia crucis (his remark at Ac 20:28 is personal, addressed to an Ephesian colleague; not public). This strange lack has been observed (Vielhauer 45, "Nothing is said of the saving significance of the cross of Christ;" Moule 171, "There is in Acts almost as complete an absence of any explicitly *redemptive* interpretation of the death of Christ as in Luke's Gospel," but these observations have not been followed up. What they lead to is that Luke knew the Atonement doctrine *but opposed it*; he excised it both from his Gospel and from his history of Christianity.

[8] His exit line is Ac 12:17c, which thus ends the account of his escape from jail and report at the house of John Mark's mother: "And he departed, and went to another place."

[9] Doubted by Soards **Speeches** 206. But in linear art, the final message *is the message*.

The break at Rome has a precedent in Corinth (Ac 18:5-11), whose key line is:

Ac 18:6. And when they opposed themselves and blasphemed, he shook out his raiment and said unto them, Your blood be upon your own heads; I am clean; *from henceforth I will go to the Gentiles.*

A still earlier scene, at Pisidian Antioch in Acts I, seems to violate the contrast between Jewish/Gentile amity in Acts I and Jewish/Christian severance in Acts II. Upon inspection, however, the Ac 13 "severance" passage appears to be intrusive:

Ac 13:44. And the next Sabbath almost the whole city was gathered together to hear the word of God.

[45] But when the Jews saw the multitudes, they were filled with jealousy, and contradicted the things which were spoken by Paul, and blasphemed. [46] And Paul and Barnabas spake out boldly, and said, It was necessary that the word of God should first be spoken to you. Seeing ye thrust it from you, and judge yourselves unworthy of eternal life, lo, we turn to the Gentiles. [47] For so hath the Lord commanded us, saying, "I have set thee for a light of the Gentiles, / that thou shouldest be for salvation unto the uttermost part of the earth." [48] And as the Gentiles heard this, they were glad, and glorified the word of God, and as many as were ordained to eternal life believed. [49] And the word of the Lord was spread abroad throughout all the region.

[50] But the Jews urged on the devout women of honorable estate, and the chief men of the city, and stirred up a persecution against Paul and Barnabas and cast them out of their borders. [51] But they shook off the dust of their feet against them, and came unto Iconium. [52] And the disciples were filled with joy and with the Holy Spirit.

This passage as it stands gives two accounts of the same incident. In outline:

A. An audience gathers [44].
  B. *But* when the Jews saw the many present, they were *jealous* [45]
  C. Paul rejects the Jews in favor of the Gentiles [46-47]
  D. The Gentiles *rejoice*; the Word is spread widely [48-49]
  B. *But* the Jews urged others to stir up opposition [50]
  C. Paul and Barnabas leave, rejecting the city [51]
  D. They go on to Iconium. The disciples *rejoice* [52]

The duplicating of initial *but* (δὲ, 13:45 and 50) is typical of interpolations.[10] The phrase "filled with jealousy" (ἐπλήσθησαν ζήλου) occurs also in Ac 5:17, but there it suits the Sadducees. The spreading of the Word is a typical conclusion to an Acts unit (compare 2:41-43 and 6:7, both mentioning the Word), but 13:48-49 *does not end* the Pisidian Antioch unit; rather, it creates a conflict with the other ending in 13:50-52. Then the original Pisidian Antioch scene (recounting Jewish opposition rather than Christian/Jewish severance) belongs to Acts I, and Ac 13:45-49 was later added to harmonize all of Acts along the thematic lines of Acts II.[11]

Acts I is thematically consistent, and so is Acts II. This, with the other evidence, supports the conclusion that Acts I and Acts II are distinguishable texts.

---

[10]For this trait of interpolated passages, see Walker **Evidence** 19.

[11]For Ac 13:45f (Acts II) and Lk 4:25f (Luke C, Neirynck **Luke 4:16-30** 374), see p167.

Acts and Luke

The minimal Luke hypothesis is Luke A/B. We now have Acts I/II. It would be convenient if they matched up as Luke A + Acts I followed by Luke B + Acts II. But the Gentile Mission emphasis in Acts I and the Sending of the Seventy in Luke B suggest instead that Luke B and Acts I represent the same text-formation phase, thus:

Luke A	Luke B
	Acts I	Acts II

Was there then a Luke C, corresponding to Acts II? Seemingly so: several passages in Luke sound the "Gentiles Only" motif of Acts II. Here are five instances.[12]

A Nazareth Addition, Lk 4:25-30. Jesus' reading from Isaiah (Lk 4:17-21) is a public self-identification ("Today hath this scripture been fulfilled in your ears," 4:21). To proclaim that self-identification was the probable point of relocating this passage to the beginning of the Galilean ministry, and that detail may be ascribed to Luke B. But then comes a quite different statement by Jesus. It reads as follows:

> **Lk 4:24**. And he said, Verily I say unto you, No prophet is acceptable in his own country.
>
> [25] But of a truth I say unto you, There were many widows in Israel in the days of Elijah, when the heaven was shut up three years and six months, when there came a great famine over all the land; [26] and unto none of them was Elijah sent, but only to Zarephath, in the land of Sidon, unto a woman that was a widow. [27] And there were many lepers in Israel in the time of Elisha the prophet, and none of them was cleansed, but only Naaman the Syrian. [28] And they were all filled with wrath in the synagogue, as they heard these things, [29] and they rose up, and cast him forth out of the city, and led him unto the brow of the hill whereon the city was built, that they might throw him down headlong. [30] But he passing through the midst of them went his way.

Jesus' "Gentiles Only" message, presaging rejection of Israel by God, is met by the Nazarenes' rejection of Jesus, who try to kill him. The addition belongs to Luke C.

A Feast Addition, Lk 14:24. The Feast parable, Lk 14:15-24, has a parallel in Matthew (Mt 22:1-10), Both parables end with the servants gathering enough people to fill the wedding hall (Mt 22:10, Lk 14:23]. But beyond that last point of similarity, there is a further line in the Lukan version which is not matched in Matthew, a final comment of the host, as though drawing a general moral: "[24] *For I say unto you, that none of those men that were bidden shall taste of my supper*." Here is the note of exclusion: only the last-called [the Gentiles], and *none of the first-called* [the Jews], shall find felicity. This addition to the Feast parable probably belongs to Luke C.

A Lazarus Addition, Lk 16:27-31. The basic Lazarus story (Lk 16:19-26) contains the archetypical Lukan poverty message: the rich man has already had his day; whereas in the next world, poor Lazarus will enjoy felicity.

---

[12]On the present hypothesis, Goulder's suggestion (Tuckett **Beatitudes** 212) that Lk 6:22f reflects the (c85) Birkat ha-Minim could be construed as a Luke C addition. But that Beatitude has its parallel in the derivative Matthean Beatitudes, and thus must have stood in Luke A.

So far Luke A. But the final paragraph goes further:

> Lk 16:27. And he said, I pray thee therefore, father, that thou wouldest send him to my father's house, [28] for I have five brethren, that he may testify unto them, lest they also come into this place of torment. [29] But Abraham saith, They have Moses and the prophets, let them hear them. [30] And he said, Nay, father Abraham, but if one go to them from the dead, they will repent. [31] And he said unto him, If they hear not Moses and the prophets, neither will they be persuaded, if one rise from the dead.

This directly expresses the hopelessness of preaching Christ Risen to those who "have Moses and the prophets;" namely, the Jews. Only Gentiles are open to that persuasion. This final paragraph may thus be seen as belonging typologically to Luke C.

The Good Samaritan, Lk 10:29-37, shows a priest and a Levite conspicuously refusing to give aid to a wounded man, whereas a Samaritan . . . well, let Luke tell it:

> [33] But a certain Samaritan, as he journeyed, came where he was, and when he saw him, he was moved with compassion, [34] and came to him, and bound up his wounds, pouring on oil and wine, and he set him on his own beast, and brought him to an inn, and took care of him. [35] And on the morrow he took out two shillings and gave them to the host, and said, Take care of him, and whatsoever thou spendest more, I, when I come back again, will repay thee.

The point of the story is not the kindness of the Samaritan, but the *refusal of kindness by the Jews*. As Jesus puts it, "Which of these three, thinkest thou, proved neighbor to him that fell among the robbers?" The entire parable thus belongs to Luke C.

The Ten Lepers, Lk 17:11-19, shows ten healed, but only one, a Samaritan, returning to give thanks. Jesus summarizes that situation this way: "[17b] Were not the ten cleansed? But where are the nine? [18] Were none found that returned to give glory to God, save this stranger (ἀλλογενὴς)? [19] And he said unto him, Arise and go thy way, thy faith hath made thee whole."

Only the stranger gives glory to God, and only he has truly received the gift of Jesus. The entire parable thus belongs to Luke C.

Conclusion: The author of Acts II has placed harmonizing material (the Pisidian Antioch interpolation) in Acts I, and he has also placed these harmonizing passages in his Gospel. All of them should be attributed to the time when Acts II was composed, as an extension to Acts I. We thus cannot avoid positing a Luke C. The final lineup is:

Luke A	Luke B	Luke C
	Acts I	Acts II

This concludes the argument for the Luke A/B/C model.

Again Luke B. Does the secondarity of the Lukan Birth Narrative, with which we began, find support elsewhere in Luke and Acts? It does. The element of miracle in the Birth Narrative is also evident in the Miraculous Catch of Fish (Lk 5:1-11). Separately, the pronounced Semitic character of its language (so strong that it has been thought to be based on a Hebrew original; Montefiore 2/364) agrees with the also notably Semitic character of Acts I, and justifies aligning Acts I with Luke B.

Then these *individual* features combine to give a consistent *collective* impression, not of a unitary Luke-Acts, but of Luke and Acts developing in the same direction.

The Luke/Acts Join

The A/B/C theory implies that Acts was not begun at the same time as Luke A; rather, the first part of Acts, my Acts I, was added to the Gospel at the Luke B stage. Is there further evidence that this was the case? There is. It consists in the mismatch between the scene which ends the Gospel and the one which begins Acts.

As Enslin **Ascension** 72 first noticed, and as Epp **Ascension** 224 later agreed, the Ascension of Jesus as a separate event *occurs only in Acts*. In Luke, the last moments of the risen Jesus on earth read like this:

> **Lk 24:50**. And he led them out until [they were] over against Bethany, and he lifted up his hands and *blessed them*. [51] And it came to pass, *while he blessed them*, he parted from them, and was carried up into Heaven.

Jesus simply vanishes *in the middle of a blessing*, without fanfare, much as he had earlier vanished, again after a blessing, from the Emmaus Two in Lk 24:31, thus:

> **Lk 24:30**. And it came to pass, when he had sat down with them to meat, he took the bread and *blessed*, and breaking it he gave it to them. [31] And their eyes were opened, and they knew him, and he vanished out of their sight.

These sudden vanishings are how the risen Jesus parts from his disciples in Luke.

Acts, in striking contrast, envisions a protracted period in which Jesus instructs his disciples, and describes a separate Ascension event with many details not in Luke A:

> **Ac 1:2** . . . until the day in which he was received up, after that he had given commandment through the Holy Spirit unto the apostles whom he had chosen, [3] to whom he also showed himself alive after his passion by **many** proofs, appearing unto them by the space of **forty days**, and speaking **the things concerning the Kingdom of God**. [4] And being assembled together with them, he charged them not to depart from Jerusalem . . . [9] And when he had said these things, as they were looking, he was taken up, and **a cloud received him out of their sight**. [10] And while they were looking steadily into Heaven as he went, behold, **two men** stood by them in white apparel, [11] who also said, Ye men of Galilee, why stand ye looking into Heaven? This Jesus, who was received up from you into Heaven **shall so come in like manner** as ye beheld him going into Heaven. [12] Then they returned unto Jerusalem . . .

Forty days of teaching, two angelic figures who predict the Return – all this is new.

The Acts account is not a more detailed but compatible version of the Luke account. *It is a different account*, and the difference implies discontinuity. These two, again, are not the kind of thing that the same author would write on the same day. Nor are they the kind of narrative inconcinnity that occurred when the author resumed his story of Christianity at Ac 15:36. The Acts Ascension looks more like something which has been mythically expanded in the meantime. The evident passage of time adds further emphasis to the differences already noted between Luke A (without Acts) and Luke B (with appended Acts I). Luke B and Acts I are not authorial afterthoughts; *they are later revisitings and extensions of territory previously covered*.

Then the Gospel was *not originally envisioned* as continuing in Acts. The Gospel was originally the whole story. With Fitzmyer (1/3), and with Parsons/Pervo (60-64), Acts should be seen as a *later sequel* to Luke, not as the second part of a single work.

Supporters of the unity of Luke and Acts have argued that Luke anticipates Acts; Barrett (**Third** 1453f) cites 41 places where this seems to be the case. And Luke *does* anticipate Acts. The only question is *whether those anticipations are original.* Several of Barrett's 41 passages have been construed above as secondary in Luke. The passage on which Barrett most relies, howver, is his #41, at the end of Luke. I here quote it, giving the four relevant Acts passages in brackets. I suggest that two of these four Acts-relevant Luke passages [indented] are later interpolations, which, if excised, leave behind a plausible conclusion for the original Luke:

Lk 24:46. And he said unto them, Thus it is written, that the Christ should suffer, and rise again from the dead the third day,
[47] and that repentance and remission of sins should be preached in his name unto all the nations, beginning from Jerusalem. [Ac 1:4-8]
[48] Ye are witnesses of these things.
[49] And behold, I send forth the promise of my Father upon you, but tarry ye in the city, until ye are clothed with power from on high. [Ac 2:1-4]
[50] And he led them out until they were over against Bethany, and he lifted up his hands, and blessed them. [51] And it came to pass while he blessed them, he parted from them, and was carried up to heaven. [Ac 1-9-11]
[52] And they worshipped him, and returned to Jerusalem with great joy,
[53] and were continually in the Temple praising God. [Ac 1:12-14]

The excised passages work like this. (1) The disciples in 24:48 are witnesses of the risen Christ (24:46), *but not of "preaching to all nations"* (24:47), an event which has not yet occurred; 24:46 and 24:48 tell a consistent story which 24:47 complicates. Thus Lk 24:47 is indeed an anticipation of Acts, but it is best seen an interpolation.[13] (2) Ac 1:8 repeats the promise of Lk 24:49, and shows it being fulfilled. Lk 24:49 is thus indeed an Acts anticipation, but it is not essential to the Gospel narrative.

As for Lk 24:50-51, I have argued above that it is not a *prediction*, but a *different version*, of the Ascension. Note that Ac 1:12-14 does not show the apostles praying in the Temple, but in an "upper room;" it does not realize, but conflicts with, Lk 24:53. Then the two truly predictive verses, 24:47 and 49, can be seen as later additions to an originally unpredictive, but literarily satisfactory, conclusion to the Gospel.

In terms of text formation, we may note that the planting of anticipations of Acts in Luke A, in the Luke B / Acts I phase, is entirely analogous to the planting of the Pisidian Antioch precedent for Acts II in Acts I, in the Luke C phase. Both bespeak an author concerned, not only to update his narrative in the light of recent ideas or events, but to maintain consistency over the whole of the resulting extended text. Luke's Gospel turns out to be continually under Luke's concerned authorial eye.[14]

[13]In addition to its anticipation of the beginning of Acts, Lk 24:47 (Luke B) has a close verbal link to the Conversion of Cornelius (Ac 10:34f, Acts I); see Neirynck **Luke 4:16-30** 379.

[14]These evidences of retouching the earlier layers of both the Gospel and Acts so as to maintain consistency between them, unavoidably implies that the author of Acts, including its second segment, Acts II, *still maintained control over the Gospel*, and was capable of making harmonizing additions to it. This refutes any theory which assumes an Acts separate from, and datable apart from, the Gospel. The Gospel and Acts, throughout their compositional history, must have remained under the same authorship or (what is equivalent) the same sponsorship.

Bidirectionality in Luke and Matthew

Now comes the crux. The argument so far helps to show how Luke worked as an author. But these findings also bear on the Synoptic Problem, defined as drawing lines between the points on the Synoptic Chart which represent Mark, Matthew, and Luke. The present proposal is that *Luke occupies not one, but three* positions on that chart.

What is the directionality of the Mt/Lk common material? Goulder (2/679f) argues for Mt > Lk by showing how Luke has messed up an original Matthew parable:

The Parable of the Talents, Mt 25:14-20 > Lk 19:11-27, which Goulder characterizes as "an unhappy blend of inconsequence and absurdity:"

> **Lk 19:12-13**. "The 'man' of Matthew's parable he makes a noble, and sends him to a 'far country' . . . to receive a kingdom and return . . . Given the scale on which Matthew thinks, with money laid out by the talent, nobles and kingdoms would not be out of place, but Luke has an aversion from big business, and he reduces the investments to a [mina] apiece, 100 denarii . . ."
>
> **Lk 19:20**. "By v20, Luke has forgotten that he had ten servants, and in place of 'the third' writes 'the other.'"[15]
>
> **Lk 19:21**. "Matthew's master is accused fairly of taking the return from the land without working for it; Luke's master is accused unfairly of taking (profit) from (investments) he had not made . . . Luke is not at home with business." [Conclusion]. "Luke . . has superimposed the kingship theme on the Matthean Talents, an uneasy combination."

This would seem to be decisive as to the directionality **Mt > Lk B**. The problem is that other examples *point no less clearly in the other direction.* As witness:

The Parable of the Feast (Mt 22:1-14 < Lk 14:16-24). Many of the absurdities[16] are due to Mt 22:6-7 (where the King's troops attack the murderous guests, destroy them, and burn their – and his own! – city). Omitting this as a possible interpolation predicting the destruction of Jerusalem by Titus in 70, we have left these differences:

> **Mt 22:1**. Luke's "man," presumably a rich man but not otherwise empowered, becomes a king: narratively superfluous but typically Matthean.
>
> **Mt 22:2**. Luke's "banquet" similarly becomes "a marriage feast for his son," an occasion less likely to be declinable by the king's leading citizens.
>
> **Mt 22:11-14**. Not in Luke: The king sees that a guest picked up by his servants lacks a wedding garment (as is natural, given the suddenness of the invitation) and has him bound and thrown into the outer darkness, "where man will weep and gnash their teeth" (a favorite Mattheanism; 8× in Matthew vs 1× in Luke). Love of punishment is a Matthean trait.

Harnack, who sees Matthew as original in almost all the Mt/Lk common material, nevertheless says, of these and several other points, "There is no need of many words to prove that here St Matthew is almost everywhere secondary" (**Sayings** 121). Then Luke is here original, and in contrast to the above example, we have **Lk A > Mt**.

---

[15]For this example of a second author's failure to sustain a change made in a source text, see Goodacre **Fatigue** 55.

[16]Hilariously dealt with in Beare **Matthew** 431-437.

Bidirectionality of the Mt/Lk common material is a main support of the Q theory. But as above noted, the Luke A/B/C model accounts for the bidirectionality without the need to posit an outside text like Q. It will also explain the Minor Agreements, which Q does not, and the Birth Narratives, which Q cannot. The case for Luke A/B/C is thus promising. Further evidence would be a plausible reconstruction of Luke A. That is not practical here,[17] but as a sample, I will reconstruct the first part of the Travel Narrative; the part containing the enigmatic[18] story of Mary and Martha.

A Test of the Model: Lk 9:51-11:32

The story of Mary and Martha occurs early in the long passage Lk 9:51–18:14, known as Luke's "Special Section" or "Travel Narrative," though the material consists of sayings of Jesus and takes little narrative account of the land that Jesus traverses.

The Lk 9:51-11:32 inventory is as follows (Matthean parallels are at right):

Lk	Mt
9:51-56. Refusal of the Samaritan villages to receive Jesus [C]	
9:57-58. A man offers to follow; Jesus dissuades him	8:19-20
9:59-60. A man asks to bury his father; Jesus refuses	8:21-22
9:61-62. A man asks to say farewell; Jesus refuses	
10:1-12. Appointment of the Seventy[19] [C]	
10:13-16. Woes to the Galilean churches	11:21-23, 10:40
10:17-20. Return of the Seventy [C]	
10:21. Wisdom revealed unto babes	11:25-26
10:22. "All things have been delivered unto me"	11:27
10:23-24. "Blessed are your eyes"	13:16-17
10:25-28. The Lawyer's question about inheriting eternal life[20]	
10:29-37. The Good Samaritan [C]	
10:38-42. Mary and Martha	
11:1-4. The Lord's Prayer	6:9-13
11:5-8. The Friend at Midnight	
11:9-13. Ask and the Father will give you good gifts	7:7-11
11:14-23. Casting out a demon; the Beelzebul controversy	12:22-30
11:24-26. Return of the evil spirit	12:43-45
11:27-28. Praise of Jesus' mother rebuked by Jesus	
11:29-32. An evil generation	12:38-40, 42, 41

The demonic series (11:14-26) and the criticism of the age (11:29-32) differ in tone from the material around them and are more at home in Mt 12:22-45 and 12:38-42. Removing them leaves the unique Lukan reproof of a woman who would venerate Jesus' physical mother;[21] Jesus instead directs attention to the family of the faithful.

---

[17]For further work along this line, see Brooks **Steward** and Brooks **Way**.

[18]"[No interpretation] is fully satisfactory" (Nolland 2/601); "ambiguous" (Bovon 2/67).

[19]Draws on the Sending of the Twelve, but Matthew has no parallel to the Seventy as such.

[20]This is a Lukan relocated passage; the Matthean and Markan parallels are at another place.

[21]Such veneration appears in the Birth Narrative, Lk 1-2. But Lk 1-2 *is not original to Luke* (p130 above) and belongs to Luke B. Then Lk 11:27-28 is clearly earlier, and must be Luke A.

Eliminating these, and passages earlier identified as Luke B or C,[22] we get:

Lk	Mt
9:51a. Introduction: Departing for Jerusalem	
9:57-58. A man offers to follow; Jesus dissuades him	
9:59-60. A man asks to bury his father; Jesus refuses	8:19-20
9:61-62. A man asks to say farewell; Jesus refuses	8:21-22
10:13-16. Woes to the Galilean churches	11:21-23, 10:40
10:21. Wisdom revealed unto babes	11:25-26
10:22. "All things have been delivered unto me"	11:27
10:23-24. "Blessed are your eyes"	13:16-17
10:38-42. Mary and Martha	
11:1-4. The Lord's Prayer	6:9-13
11:5-8. The Friend at Midnight	
11:9-13. Ask and the Father will give you good gifts	7:7-11
11:27-28. Praise of Jesus' mother rebuked by Jesus	

Consider first Lk 10:13-16, 21, 22, and 23-:24, which become consecutive once the Seventy passage Lk 10:17-20 [C] is removed. All have Matthean parallels:

Lk 10:13-16	Mt 11:21-23, 10:40	Woes to the Galilean churches
Lk 10:21	Mt 11:25-26	Wisdom revealed unto babes
Lk 10:22	Mt 11:27	"All things have been delivered unto me"
Lk 10:23-24	Mt 13:16-17	"Blessed are your eyes"

Mt 13:16-17 stands out from the other Matthean parallels. In its own context:

Lk 8:9-10	Mt 13:10-15	Explanation of teaching in parables
Lk 10:23-24	Mt 13:16-17	"Blessed are your eyes"
Lk 8:11-15	Mt 13:18-23	Explanation of the Sower Parable

the Mt 13 group *is* consecutive: (1) the people cannot understand; (2) the disciples can understand; (3) an esoteric explanation. In Luke, on the other hand, the wise disciples ("blessed are your eyes") are suddenly called children ("unto babes"). The more consistent context may be the original, If so, then Mt 13:18-23 > Lk (B) 8:11-15.

Going back to Lk 10:13-16, I note that the cursing of the Galilean churches is more in character for legalistic Matthew than for gentle Luke. The Matthean context is:

Lk 7:31-35	Mt 11:16-19	Criticism of the present generation
Lk 10:13-15	Mt 11:20-24	Woes on the Galilean churches
Lk 10:21-22	Mt 11:25-26	Wisdom revealed unto babes

These Mt criticisms seem consecutive: woes on the "senior" Galilean tradition imply praise of the "junior" or Jerusalem tradition. Then the Matthean order may be original, and if so, the directionality is Mt 11:16-26 > Lk (B) 7:31-35, 10:13-15, and 10:21-22.

For the Lord's Prayer, I agree with those who find the Matthean form secondary.[23]

---

[22]See above. The Lawyer's Question (Mt 10:25-28), has obviously been moved in Luke to precede the Good Samaritan, which gives Jesus' answer to the lawyer's second question.

[23]For example, Fitzmyer 2/897. Harnack 64, "All the other clauses found in St Matthew are either accretions which attached themselves . . . during the process of transformation into a solemn congregational prayer . . . or they were added by Matthew himself."

Eliminating passages which seem to be original in Mt, and thus secondary in Lk, gives us, for the probable original content of this part of Lk A, the following passages:

9:51a. Introduction: Departing for Jerusalem
9:57-62. A man offer to follow; Jesus dissuades him
9:59-60. A man asks to bury his father; Jesus refuses
9:61-62. A man asks to say farewell; Jesus refuses
10:38-42. May and Martha
11:1-4. The Lord's Prayer
11:5-8. The Friend at Midnight
11:9-13. Ask and the Father will give you good gifts
11:27-28. Praise of Jesus' mother is rebuked

In this proposed Luke A material, we may now discern a definite formal pattern:

[1. Total Dedication to the Way]
9:51a. Introduction: Departing for Jerusalem
┌9:57-62. A man offers to follow; Jesus dissuades him
 9:59-60. A man asks to bury his father; Jesus refuses
└9:61-62. A man asks to say farewell; Jesus refuses
10:38-42. **Mary and Martha** [against domestic distractions]
[2. Prayer as Companion Along the Way]
┌11:1-4. **The Lord's Prayer**
11:5-8. The Friend at Midnight [prayer will be answered]
└11:9-13. Ask and the Father will give you good gifts
11:27-28. Praise of Jesus' mother rebuked [against sentimental distraction]

The pattern consists of two thematic sections, one on dedication and one on prayer. Each consists of a triplet of statements or illustrations, here followed by a concluding piece which applies the lesson of the triplet to women. The Mary and Martha story, as here restored, concludes the group on the need for dedication. As the man who would take leave of his family is rebuked for hesitation, so Martha, "cumbered about much serving," is rebuked for her priorities. "Mary hath chosen the good part."[24] Reliance on the Heavenly Father in 11:9-13 is contrasted with misguided adoration of Jesus' earthly mother in 11:27-28. In both, "Jesus" directs attention to higher things. An unclear connection[25] is thus clarified[26] by removing intervening later material.[27] The final passages in both groups can be seen to address erring women.

I find this pattern convincing, and offer it as a correct reading of this part of Luke's "Special Section." In view of this result, I propose to call the section Luke's "Sermon on the Way," intending "Way" as both a sermon delivered on the way to Jerusalem, and as expounding the Way: the dedication and hope which characterize discipleship.

---

[24]For the many interpretations of the commentators, see Nolland 2/601.

[25]Fitzmyer 2/926 on Lk 11:27-28, "it is hard to see why Luke has put this episode here."

[26]Creed 162 calls Lk 11:27-28 a "variant" of the Mk 3:19b-21 and 31-35 passage where Jesus rejects his birth family. It is rather a doublet (the counterpart occurs at Lk 8:19-21): not rejection of Jesus' family, but Luke's reproof of the *popular enthusiasm* for Jesus' family, and especially his mother, which probably provided part of the push behind the divinization of Jesus himself in the 1st century (for the textual results, see Brooks **Four** 27).

[27]For the logic of Luke B's placement of this later material, see Brooks **Way** 194-196.

Matthew's Predilection for Twos

Matthew's predilection for twos is obvious.[28] It is evident in the above passage, where Lukan triplets (chiding followers; assurances about prayer) become duplets in Matthew. Here is another example of Matthew's duplet way with Luke's triplets:

    Lk 15:3-7   The Lost Sheep   [Mt 18:12-14]
    Lk 15:8-10   The Lost Coin   [not in Mt]
    Lk 15:11-32   The Lost ["Prodigal"] Son

Matthew is less interested in women than is Luke, so his omission of the Woman with the Lost Coin parable is in character. As for the Lost Son parable, its extreme poverty may have repelled the high-budget Matthew. But he *has* included it, greatly rewritten, as the Parable of Two Sons (Mt 21:28-32),[29] with the clear directionality **Lk A > Mt**. This is then a further example of a Lukan triplet transformed into a Matthean duplet. It is also a further example of the directionality Lk > Mt.

Formal Order and Formal Violation

If Luke's Sermon had such a nicely calculated form (it will inevitably be asked), why would he then spoil that form by his later additions? Such questions recur in the study of ancient texts. The proprietors of the Analects, the home text of the Confucian school of Lŭ, arranged their sayings of Confucius in pairs and grouped the pairs under four topics, resulting in 24-sayings chapters.[30] They later added sayings which violated that arrangement. One can only say that a writer's reason for adding later material is, at that moment, more urgent than any consideration of previous formal arrangements or original narrative coherence. The attention of the writer is directed elsewhere.

Has Horace spoiled his beautifully arranged Carmina, with their peroration at 3:30, by adding further material in his 4th book? Formally, yes. But who would sacrifice Quem tu Melpomene (4:3) to preserve the finality of Exegi monumentum (3:30)?

Envoi

I believe that it has been shown that the bidirectionality of the common Mt/Lk material can be accounted for without the need for an outside source. Besides Q itself, the chief theory which this proposal replaces is the Farrer-Goulder Hypothesis (FGH), after a proposal of Austin Farrer (1955) as later realized by Michael Goulder (1989). In view of the contribution of Morton Enslin to both aspects of the present argument, and if these things are to be given names at all, I should like the model here proposed to be known as the Enslin-Brooks Hypothesis (EBH).[31]

---

[28]Taking Zechariah 9:9 literally, Matthew sends Jesus into Jerusalem on *two* animals (21:7). He also recasts Mark's one Gerasene Demoniac as *two* [Gadarene] Demoniacs (Mt 8:28-34), and Mark's one blind man as *two* blind men (Mt 20:29-34). There are several other instances.

[29]See Gundry **Matthew** 421-424 or Gundry **Parable**.

[30]For details, see Brooks **Analects**.

[31]I am reminded by Stephen Carlson that Ropes (**Synoptic**, 1934) preceded Enslin ("**Luke**," 1938; **Matthew**, 1967) in recording doubts about Q. Considering that the present model deals, as it must, with more than Q, I think I will let the above suggestion stand.

Works Cited

C K Barrett. The Third Gospel as a Preface to Acts? in F van Segbroeck et al (ed), The Four Gospels 1992, 2v Peeters (1992) 2/1451-1466

Francis W Beare. The Gospel According to Matthew. Harper 1981

François Bovon. Luke. 3v Fortress 2002, 2013, 2012

E Bruce Brooks. The Epistle of Jacob. Alpha v1 (2107) 58-70

E Bruce Brooks. Four Gospel Trajectories. Alpha v1 (2017) 15-16

E Bruce Brooks. Luke's Sermon on the Way. Alpha v1 (2017) 167-179

E Bruce Brooks. Luke's Parable of the Canny Steward. Alpha v1 (2017) 158-166

E Bruce and A Taeko Brooks. The Original Analects. Columbia 1998

Henry J Cadbury. The Making of Luke-Acts. 3ed 1958; SPCK 1968

John Martin Creed. The Gospel According to St Luke. Macmillan 1930

Jacques Dupont. The Sources of the Acts. 1960; Herder 1964

Morton S Enslin. The Ascension Story. JBL v47 (1928) 60-73

Morton S Enslin. Luke and Matthew. JQR v57 (1967) 178-191

Morton S Enslin. "Luke" and Paul. JAOS v58 (1938) 81-91

Morton S Enslin. Luke and the Samaritans. HTR v36 #4 (1943) 277-297

Eldon Jay Epp. The Ascension in the Textual Tradition of Luke-Acts. 1981; in Perspectives on New Testament Textual Criticism, Brill (2005) 211-225

A M Farrer. On Dispensing with Q; in D E Nineham, Studies in the Gospels, Oxford (1955) 55-86

Joseph A Fitzmyer. The Gospel According to Luke. 2v Doubleday 1970, 1985

Mark Goodacre. Fatigue in the Synoptics. NTS v44 (1998) 45-58

Michael Goulder. Luke: A New Paradigm. 2v Sheffield 1989

Robert H Gundry. Matthew. Eerdmans 1982

Robert H Gundry. Matthew's Parable of the Two Sons. Alpha v1 (2013) 152-154

Adolph von Harnack. The Sayings of Jesus. 1907; tr Williams & Norgate 1908

George A Kennedy. New Testament Interpretation Through Rhetorical Criticism. North Carolina 1956

Leander E Keck and J Louis Martyn (ed). Studies in Luke-Acts. Abingdon 1966

C G Montefiore. The Synoptic Gospels. 2ed 2v Macmillan 1927

C D Moule. The Christology of Acts; in Keck **Studies** 159-185

Frans Neirynck. Luke 4:16-30 and the Unity of Luke-Acts; in Verheyden **Unity** 357-395

John Nolland. Luke. 3v Word 1989, 1993, 1993

Mikeal Parsons and Richard Pervo. Rethinking the Unity of Luke and Acts. Fortress 1993

R B Rackham. The Acts of the Apostles. Methuen 1901

James Hardy Ropes. The Synoptic Gospels. Harvard 1934

Marion L Soards. The Speeches in Acts. Westminster 1994

Charles C Torrey. The Composition and Date of Acts. Harvard 1916

C M Tuckett and M D Goulder. The Beatitudes. NovT v25 (1983) 193-216

Joseph Verheyden (ed). The Unity of Luke-Acts. Peeters 1999

Philipp Vielhauer. On the "Paulinism" of Acts. 1950; in Keck **Studies** 33-50

William O Walker Jr. Evidence for Interpolation in Paul. Alpha v1 (2017) 17-22

William O Walker Jr. Interpolations in the Pauline Letters. Sheffield 2001

Bernhard Weiss. Lehrbuch der Enleitung in das Neue Testament. Hertz 1886

Luke's Parable of the Canny Steward

E Bruce Brooks

University of Massachusetts at Amherst

SEECR / University of North Carolina (31 Oct 2014)

In the light of the Luke A/B/C formation model introduced in a previous study,[1] I here consider what is usually called the Parable of the Unjust Steward (Lk 16:1-8), its context in Lk 15-16, and a possible, and less inscrutable, Chinese antecedent.

Text. The Parable may be notably difficult,[2] but its *message* is nonetheless obvious (be wise about the *next* world, just as worldlings are wise about *this* world, Lk 16:8b). There follow several comments on the parable: Lk 16:9, 10-12, and 13.[3] The text goes:

> **Lk 16:1**. And he said also unto the disciples, There was a certain rich man who had a steward, and the same was accused unto him that he was wasting his goods. [2] And he called him and said unto him, What is this that I hear of thee? Render the account of thy stewardship; for thou canst be no longer steward. [3] And the steward said within himself, What shall I do, seeing that my lord taketh away the stewardship from me? I have not strength to dig; to beg I am ashamed. [4] I am resolved what to do, that, when I am put out of the stewardship, they may receive me into their houses. [5] And calling to him each one of his lord's debtors, he said to the first, How much owest thou unto my lord? [6] And he said, A hundred measures of oil. And he said unto him, Take thy bond, and sit down quickly and write fifty. [7] Then said he to another, And how much owest thou? And he said, A hundred measures of wheat. He saith unto him, Take thy bond, and write fourscore. [8a] And his lord commended the unrighteous steward because he had done wisely; [8b] for the sons of this world are for their own generation wiser than the sons of the light.
>
> [9] And I say unto you, Make to yourselves friends by means of the mammon of unrighteousness, that, when it shall fail, they may receive you into the eternal tabernacles.
>
> [10] He that is faithful in a very little is faithful also in much, and he that is unrighteous in a very little is unrighteous also in much. [11] If therefore ye have not been faithful in the unrighteous mammon, who will commit to your trust the true riches? [12] And if ye have not been faithful in that which is another's, who will give you that which is your own?
>
> [13] No servant can serve two masters: for either he will hate the one and love the other, or else he will hold to one and despise the other. Ye cannot serve God and Mammon.

I will start with the interpretations (Lk 16:9-13), and then take up the parable itself.

---

[1]Brooks **Acts-Luke**. The model is Luke A > Matthew > Luke B / Acts I > Luke C / Acts II.

[2]Snodgrass 401 "notoriously difficult;" Hultgren 147 "most puzzling of all."

[3]Dodd 30, "We can almost see here notes for three separate sermons on the parable as text." Just so. Similar comments may be found at Jeremias 108 and Fitzmyer 2/1104f.

Luke's Interpretations

These are curiously many:

Lk 16:1-8. Parable and Internal Summary	[Unique to Lk]
Lk 16:9. Second Summary	[Unique to Lk]
Lk 16:10-12. Faithful in Mammon	~ Lk 19:11-27 [Parable of the Minae]
Lk 16:13. God vs Mammon	= Mt 6:24 [Sermon on the Mount]

The summary internal to the story, Lk 16:8b, fits it well enough: use the present to prepare for the future. Then follow three other explanations.[4] (1) 16:9 looks like an attempt to restate this in more familiar Lukan terms: sacrifice worldly possessions to the future Kingdom. It advises making friends by mammon. (2) 16:10-12 urges being "faithful in the *unrighteous mammon*" to deserve a higher trust; (3) 16:13 *deplores* mammon. 16:9 treats mammon expediently, whereas the last two treat it negatively. The last two have contacts elsewhere, and those contacts deserve a closer look.

The Parable of the Minae (Lk 19:11-27). This is secondary to the simpler Matthean Parable of the Talents, and is thus Luke B.[5] It follows that Lk 16:10-12, which uses a similar argument to explain the Steward parable, is also Luke B.

God and Mammon. Mt 6:24 in its Sermon on the Mount context is:

Mt 6:22. The lamp of the body is the eye: If therefore thine eye be single, thy whole body shall be full of light. [23] But if thine eye be evil, thy whole body shall be full of darkness. If therefore the light that is in thee be darkness, how great is the darkness!

[24] No man can serve two masters, for either he will hate the one and love the other, or else he will hold to one, and despise the other. Ye cannot serve God and Mammon.

[25] Therefore I say unto you, Be not anxious for your life, what ye shall eat, or what ye shall drink, nor for your body, what ye shall put on . . .

The dualism of 6:24 (two masters) makes a pair with that of 6:23 (light and darkness). Mt 6:25 links to 6:24 ("therefore"). There is reasonable thematic continuity.[6] Davies and Allison (1/641) note that Mt 6:24 is verbally identical with Lk 16:13, except for:

Mt 6:24 οὐδεί	"no one"
Lk 16:13 οὐδεί οἰκέτης	"no house servant"

There is no other Synoptic occurrence of οἰκέτης, but it does occur in Acts I (10:7, the conversion of Cornelius), and thus, by present hypothesis, in the same text stratum as Luke B.[7] The most likely inference is that both Lk 16:10-12 and Lk 16:13 are secondary in Luke. Then their relevance for understanding the Parable is zero. They are apparently an attempt by Luke B to clarify the Parable as it had stood in Luke A.

---

[4]For the utility of separating them from the parable proper, see Fitzmyer **Luke** 2/1104f.

[5]For a hilarious overview of the way Luke B has confused and spoiled this Matthean parable, see Goulder **Luke** 2/679f, summarized at Brooks **Acts-Luke** 173.

[6]Which is not to say that they need be purely Matthean. In agreement with those who see a Lk > Mt directionality in the Beatitudes, I will argue in a future study that Luke's Sermon on the Plain, *as a whole*, is ancestral to Matthew's agglomerative Sermon on the Mount.

[7]The other NT occurrences of οἰκέτης are: Rom 14:4, Lk 16:13, Ac 10:7, 1 Pet 2:18.

Luke 15-16

Here is an outline of Lk 15-16, with passages assigned to Luke B or C indented:

Lk   Mt

15:1-2. Pharisees criticize Jesus' eating with sinners
15:3-7. The Lost Sheep
15:8-10. The Lost Coin
15:11-32. **The Lost Son**
16:1-8. **The Canny Steward**
16:9. First explanation of above
    16:10-12. Second explanation of above [**B**]   ~ Lk 19:11-27, Mt
    16:13. Third explanation of above [**B**]   Mt 6:24
16:14-15. Wealth-loving Pharisees rebuked
16:16-18. On Law and Divorce   Mt 11:12-13, 5:18, 5:32
16:19-31. **The Rich Man and Lazarus**
    16:27-31. Extension: The brothers will not repent [**C**][8]

The "Lost" parables (Sheep, Coin, Son) are clearly a group. Gundry has argued that Mt 21:28-32, the Parable of the Two Sons, is Matthew's remake of Luke's Lost Son.[9] Then the Lost Son *must have been in Luke A*. So, most likely, must the group of three.

Lk 16:9, Luke A's way of explaining the Steward parable, can be grouped with the Parable itself. Lk 16:14-15, a reproof of the Pharisees "who loved money," links the money parable of the Steward and the wealth parable of Lazarus. So does Luke's 16:9, "that they may receive you into the eternal tabernacles," since the Lazarus parable (Luke A) shows Lazarus being so received. But the legal details in Lk 16:16-18 lack thematic consistency, and their Matthean connections suggest borrowing by Luke B.[10] For the rest, the continuity in Luke appears to be good, and we then have in Luke A:

    15:1-2. Introduction: Pharisees criticize Jesus' eating with sinners
    ⌐15:1-7. The Lost Sheep
     15:8-10. The Lost Coin
    └15:11-32. **The Lost Son**
    ⌐16:1-9. **The Canny Steward**, with Luke A's explanation
     16:10-12. Second explanation of Steward [**B**]   ~ Lk 19:11-27 < Mt
     16:13. Third explanation of Steward [**B**]   < Mt 6:24
     16:14-15. Wealth-loving Pharisees rebuked
     16:16-18. On Law and Divorce [**B**]   < Mt 11:12-13, 5:18, 5:32[11]
    └16:19-26. **The Rich Man and Lazarus**
    16:27-31. Extension: The brothers will not repent [**C**][6]

What exactly is the problem with the Steward Parable? Probably it is the master's approval of the steward's wrongdoing that baffles commentators, ancient and modern.

This brings me to a story which has a similar outline, but lacks that difficulty.

---

[8]For this Lazarus extension as a Luke C addition, see Brooks **Acts-Luke** 135-136.

[9]Gundry **Matthew** 5, 466f; see now also Gundry **Parable**, Brooks **Acts-Luke** 177.

[10]For the logic of Luke B's placement of this later material, see Brooks **Way** 162-164.

[11]Two of these divorce passages (Mt 5:18, 5:32), and Mt 6:24 (mentioned above) are from the Sermon on the Mount. So even in this area, the Lk/Mt relationship remains bidirectional.

Jàn-gwó Tsv̀ 154 (133)

The Jàn-gwó Tsv̀ 戰國策 is a collection of 497 stories,[12] assembled under that title in c022 by the Hàn bibliographer Lyóu Syàng from six named sources, none of which survives or can be equated with the material found at the c0168 Mǎwángdwēi tomb.[13] Much of the JGT (including the exploits of the interstate persuader Sū Chín, who never existed) is evidently of early Hàn date (02c), but some stories seem to be earlier, or not to relate to the favorite Hàn idea of interstate intrigue at all.

This story centers on the Chí magnate Tyén Wv́n, the Lord of Mv̀ng-cháng, who as a minister in the capital maintained a private army of thousands of swordsmen. He also had a fief: Sywē, located elsewhere. Fv́ng Sywæn on joining Tyén Wv́n described his skills as "nothing," but then complained of his niggardly treatment by Tyén Wv́n, and was given food and equipment like the rest,[14] plus support for his mother.[15] Then:

> Later, the Lord of Mv̀ng-cháng sent out a note, asking of his followers, "Who has experience in keeping accounts, and can collect what is due me in Sywē?" Fv́ng Sywæn wrote back, "I can." The Lord of Mv̀ng-cháng wondered at this, and said, "Who is this?" His assistants said, "It's the one who was singing, Long Sword, let's go home." The Lord of Mv̀ng-cháng laughed, and said, "So our guest has some abilities after all. But I have ignored him, and not yet given him an audience." He invited and received him, and apologized, saying, "I am wearied with affairs, and beset by worries, and have accordingly grown stupid. Being swamped by state business, I have incurred guilt with Your Honor. Does Your Honor not only not take offense, but intends to collect what is due me in Sywē?" Fv́ng Sywæn said, "I should like to do so." He readied his carriage, put his attire in order, loaded the debt tallies, and set forth. As he left, he said, "When the debts are collected, what shall I buy with them before returning?" The Lord of Mv̀ng-cháng said, "Whatever you see that my house has little of."
>
> He hastened to Sywē, and had the officers summon all the people who owed debts to come and match the tallies.[16] When all the tallies had been matched, he arose and feigned an order that the debts were to be considered a gift to the people. He burned the tallies, and the people acclaimed the Lord and wished him a myriad years of life.
>
> Driving without stop he reached Chí, and in early morning sought audience. The Lord of Mv̀ng-cháng wondered at his speed; he dressed and received him, saying, "Are the debts all collected? How have you come so quickly?" He said, "They are all collected." [He said], "What did you buy to bring back?"

---

[12]Or so; different editions differ slightly. The 12c Bàu edition (the basis for the Crump translation) seeks to recover a pre-Lyóu Syàng arrangement. The Yáu edition (also 12c, the basis for the HK concordance) is close to Lyóu Syàng. I here cite JGT stories by Crump (Bàu) number, with the HK (Yáu) number in parentheses.

[13]For the Mǎwángdwēi JGT, see Blanford **Studies**.

[14]This identifies a topos: the retainer who seems to lack ability but comes through in a crisis

[15]Gratitude for care of a mother is a recurring motif in these stories. By the time we reach this part in the story, we know that a dramatic service to Tyén Wv́n will be its climax.

[16]Lender and debtor each had half a broken tally; the halves were matched on settling up.

Fv́ng Sywǣn said, The Lord had said, Whatever you see that my house has little of. As your subject reckons it, the Lord's palace is full of rarities and valuables, dogs and horses teem in his stables, and beauties fill his apartments. The only thing the Lord's house has little of is loyalty.[17] He has ventured to buy loyalty for the Lord." The Lord of Mv̀ng-cháng said, "How does one buy loyalty?" He said, "The lord possesses this insignificant little Sywē, but he does not love its people as his children, and values them only as so much profit. Your subject has ventured to feign an order from the Lord that the debts were to be considered a gift to the people, and burned the tallies. The people acclaimed the Lord, and wished him a myriad years of life. This is how your servant has bought loyalty for the Lord." The Lord of Mv̀ng-cháng was displeased, and said, "Very well. Let Your Honor now take his rest."

A full year later, the King of Chí said to the Lord of Mv̀ng-cháng, This Lonely One[18] does not dare to make the former King's ministers his ministers." The Lord of Mv̀ng-cháng [being dismissed] then went to his country in Sywē. He was still a hundred leagues short of arriving, when the people, supporting their aged and carrying their young, went out to meet him on the highway. The Lord of Mv̀ng-cháng turned and said to Fv́ng Sywǣn, "That Your Honor has bought loyalty for me, today I see it."

There follows an afterstory in which Fv́ng Sywǣn prepares additional safeguards for the Lord of Mv̀ng-cháng. This takes us into the area of international intrigue which characterizes the later Jàn-gwó Tsv̀ stories, and is most probably a Hàn elaboration. The story up to that point might be summarized as follows:

- Magnate disprizes his seemingly useless retainer.
- Retainer gets assignment, forgives debts owed to magnate *in the magnate's interest*
- Magnate is at first displeased, but *later* praises retainer's foresight

With a little garbling, of the sort natural in tavern encounters between Silk Road merchants from different places,[19] we might without difficulty get something like this:

- Magnate distrusts his regular manager.
- Manager, still in office, forgives debts owed to magnate *in his own interest*
- Magnate *at once* praises manager's foresight

And the elements which have perplexed centuries of commentators are in place. No transcripts are available, but I suggest that Lk 16:1-8 is something like that garbled version, and that 16:9 is Luke A's first attempt to adapt it to themes familiar elsewhere in his teachings: themes of disregard for money and profit.

---

[17]Yì 義, a kindness that evokes obligation ("loyalty") in return; sometimes equal to "duty" (compare δικαιοσύνη). The cornerstone of a particular kind of Chinese political philosophy.

[18]Conventional self-designation for a hereditary ruler, whose father has necessarily died. This ruler is the successor to the one who had previously favored the Lord of Mv̀ng-cháng.

[19]Bactria. "There's this tortoise, see, and there's this fast runner, see, and the tortoise has a head start, and the fast runner sets out to catch him. Will he make it?" Other guy says, "Sure." First guy says, "No. Look here: first he has to cover half the distance, then half of that . . ." Other guy says, "Gotta be something wrong with that." But he can't figure out exactly what. Back home, he tries it on his friends, and soon it has entered the higher Chinese culture as the paradox of secability. For this "Achilles" paradox and others, see Brooks **Alexandrian**.

Once Again Luke

How did this garbled story *get* to Luke? Given Luke's sympathy with the poor, his own church, which in the opinion of some was in the vicinity of Antioch, cannot have been affluent. But Antioch was on one of the great east-west trade routes. One need not be a merchant to pick up, at some remove, stories told and puzzles exchanged between merchants in the taverns.[20] Like Achilles and the Tortoise,[21] the Story of the Forgiven Debts, where seeming loss is turned to advantage, is just paradoxical enough to have circulated among a secondary audience. I here suggest that someone, perhaps Luke's church leader's brother-in-law, was part of that secondary audience.

The moral of the story in Lk 16:8b is perfectly reasonable, in terms of the Christian concern to sacrifice everything for the future Kingdom. I suspect that the story, as told by someone in Luke's church, reached Luke in something like this form. Luke A, the original Luke, added 16:9 when he included the tale in his Gospel, to link it with the Lazarus parable which, *at that time*, concluded that section of his Sermon on the Way.

Later, Luke B,[22] being influenced by Matthew, added two further passages, one culled from Matthew and the other echoing the point of a borrowed Matthew parable, which seemed to him to further explain the still enigmatic Parable of the Steward. Nothing gets rid of the garbling in the story as it came to Luke A, but the efforts of Luke B to make the story work better as a Christian parable may now be clearer.

Codicil: Luke 17:1-18:14

My previous paper ended with a reconstruction of Lk 9:51-11:1, the first part of Luke's Sermon on the Way. This paper has included an analysis of Lk 15:1-16:31, toward the end of that sermon. Not to waste the textual opportunity, it may be useful to attempt a reconstruction of the rest of the final portion, Lk 17:1-18:14.

First, the two concluding parables, 18:1-8 (God will listen to prayer) and 18:9-14 (be not self-righteous), with their unique introductions explaining why Jesus *told* the parables, are evidently finishing gestures; they articulate themes evident in the parts of the Sermon previously reconstructed.[23] I will take them as a pair unto themselves, a formally distinct conclusion to a Sermon otherwise based on groups of three.

---

[20]In what medium did these stories pass from one culture to another? The usual guess is, in writing, but oral contact is much more likely. Cultures in contact and interested in trading with each other tend to develop a trade language, containing only a few hundred words but capable of expressing everything that trading partners need to say. A well-known example is Chinook Jargon, a trade language of the Pacific Northwest, with a wordstock drawn from Chinook, Chehalis, English, and French. For an etymological lexicon, see Shaw **Chinook**.

[21]For the 04c west-to-east transmission of scraps of Greek lore, apparently involving oral intermediation between texts at both ends, see Brooks **Alexandrian**.

[22]Either the same person as Luke A but with somewhat different views, partly derived from having seen Matthew, or a different person who was very good at replicating Luke A's style. It is not necessary to decide this question for purposes of the present paper.

[23]In Aesopic terms, they feature promythium and epimythium; the moral is given at both beginning and end. See Phaedrus 1/13, the Fox and The Crow (Perry 207, also 221), a retelling in literary Latin from the reign of Tiberius: contemporary with Jesus and earlier than Luke.

Luke's three "Lost" parables (Sheep, Coin, Prodigal son; Lk 15:1-32)[24] seem to be a self-contained triplet, perhaps rebuking the feelings of old converts who resented the fuss made over new converts. This concludes the analysis of Lk 15, and we may pick up the previous analysis at 16:1 with the Canny Steward parable. Passages attributable to Luke B or C are so marked; any Matthew parallels are listed at the right margin:

	Lk	Mt
16:1-9. **The Canny Steward**, with Luke A's explanation		
16:10-12 [Later added explanation][**B**]		
16:13 [Later added explanation][**B**]		
16:14-15. Wealth-loving Pharisees rebuked		
16:16. The Law was until John		11:12
16:17. Not a jot will pass from the Law		5:18
16:18. Divorcing a wife makes her an adulteress		5:32
16:19-26. **The Rich Man and Lazarus**		
16:27-31 Extension: The brothers will not repent [**C**]		
17:1-2. Woe to those by whom temptations come [relocated in Luke A]		
17:3. If a brother sins, rebuke him		18:5
17:4. Forgive him seven times		18:21-22
17:5-6. If you had faith [thematically interruptive]		17:20
17:7-10. The servant must do more than is required		
17:11-19. **The Ten Lepers** [**C**]		
17:20-21. Encouragement: The Kingdom is in the midst of you		

Lk 16:1-9 is linked to Lazarus (16:19f) by the poverty theme. Lk 16:14-15 again strikes that note; the intervening 16:10-13 are intrusive.[25] As Fitzmyer notes, 17:5-6 comes in "abruptly." Perhaps the "sea" in which tempters are drowned in 17:1 gave Luke B a hook to hang the "sea" into which the tree of 17:6 is moved. Lk 17:7-10 resumes the theme of 17:4, one must do more than is required. Lk 17:11-19 features one of Luke C's characteristic Samaritans. Lk 17:20-21, a general encouragement, may be accepted as concluding this segment of the Luke A material.

Then comes the apocalyptic and thematically extraneous 17:22-37:

	Lk	Mt
17:22. You will desire to see the Son of Man		
17:23-24. The return of the Son of Man will be conspicuous		24:26-27
17:25. But first he must suffer many things		
17:26-27. As in the days of Noah		24:37-39
17:28-30. Or of Lot, so it will be		
17:31-32. Let those flee who can; remember Lot's wife		
17:33. Who seeks to gain his life will lose it		10:39
17:34-36. Some will escape and some will not		24:40-41
17:37. Where the body is, there will the eagles be		24:28

[24]For this group, which occupies all of Lk 15, see Brooks **Acts-Luke** 147.

[25]Fitzmyer 2/1114, "has almost nothing to do with [v1-15];" Nolland 2/814, "no intrinsic unity;" Bovon 2/465, "Interpreters have a hard time understanding why the Gospel writer put this saying [16:16] in this spot."

Lk 17:22-37 is extraneous because this Sermon is not theological, it is not a treatise on Jesus; it is instead all about the *believer* in Jesus. Luke B here seems to have drawn on Matthew (for Noah, see Mt 24:37-39), and continued with his own Scriptural extension (the parallel of Lot). None of this material belongs in Luke A.

This gives the following reconstruction of the Luke A original. It consists of two triplets, the second ending with a final word of encouragement:

[The Dangers of Wealth]
⌐16:1-9. **The Canny Steward**, with Luke A's explanation
16:14-15. Wealth-loving Pharisees rebuked
└16:19-26. **The Rich Man and Lazarus**

[Sin and Forgiveness]
⌐17:1-2. Woe to those by whom temptations come
17:3-4. Need for repeated forgiveness of a brother
└17:7-10. The servant must do more than is required
17:20-21. Encouragement: The Kingdom is in the midst of you

The theology of this is interesting. Lk 17:7-10 tells us that conventional piety, which consists in the avoidance of crime (compare Lazarus' rich man, who has not exactly broken any laws, but winds up in Hell all the same) is not enough; one must *do something* to register as virtuous. Duty (like, not killing people) is a given; one must go *beyond* one's duty to get into the heavenly account book.[26] One must appear on the active side of that ledger. This strenuous advice makes all the more welcome what seems to be the concluding word of encouragement in 17:20-21.

We are almost there. The message is of Christian hope and Christian striving. How will Luke bring all this to a conclusion?

[Exit Portal: Two Concluding Parables]
18:1-5. **The Unjust Judge**
18:6-8. Moral: God listens to prayer
18:9-13. **Pharisee and Publican**
18:14. Moral: The humble, who have renounced all, will be exalted

These have a common context in the act of prayer. They also recapitulate the main themes of the preceding Sermon. First, despite any appearances to the contrary, God listens to prayer and will see believers through perils and sufferings. Second, those who humble themselves now will be exalted at the end. Both counsel humility and persistence in prayer. They assure believers that humility and prayer in time of trouble will take them safe to the end of the journey.

Not only is the meaning of each of these two final Parables announced in its narrative opening, it is underlined by Jesus himself (18:6-8 and 18:14, respectively). Luke is taking no chances that his main lessons will be overlooked by his audience.

Do we not see here the practiced preacher, illustrating his message at some length, but then summarizing the heart of it at the end?

---

[26]For the theology of Luke, which turns out to be entirely a matter of transactional ethics, see his Sermon on the Plain, Luke 6:20-49, easily the least read passage in the New Testament..

Here is the end of the Sermon, Lk 15:1-18:4, as so far reconstructed:

[Joy at Recovering a Sinner]

15:1-2. Introduction: Pharisees criticize Jesus' eating with sinners
⌐15:3-7. The Lost Sheep
 15:8-10. The Lost Coin
└15:11-32. **The Lost Son**

[The Dangers of Wealth]

⌐16:1-9. **The Canny Steward**, with Luke A's explanation
 16:14-15. Wealth-loving Pharisees rebuked
└16:19-26. **The Rich Man and Lazarus**

[Sin and Forgiveness]

⌐17:1-2. Woe to those by whom temptations come
 17:3-4. Need for repeated forgiveness of a brother
└17:7-10. The servant must do more than is required
 17:20-21. Encouragement: The Kingdom is in the midst of you

[Exit Portal: Two Concluding Parables in Aesopic Form]

⌐18:1-5. **The Unjust Judge**
└18:6-8. Moral: God listens to prayer
⌐18:9-13. **Pharisee and Publican**
└18:4. Moral: The humble, who have renounced all, will be exalted

For the middle of the Sermon, and for a final overview of the Sermon in its entirety, see Brooks **Way**, the third study in this series.

Works Cited

Yumiko Fukushima Blanford. Studies of the "Zhanguo zonghengjia shu." UMI 1989

E Bruce Brooks. Acts-Luke. Alpha v1 (2017) 143-157

E Bruce Brooks. Alexandrian Motifs in Chinese Texts. SPP #96 (1999)

E Bruce Brooks. Luke's Sermon on the Way. Alpha v1 (2017) 167-179

J I Crump. Chan-kuo Ts'e. 1970, 2ed Michigan 1996

J I Crump Jr. Intrigues. Michigan 1964

W D Davies and Dale C Allison Jr. The Gospel According to Saint Matthew. 3v Clark 1988, 1991, 1997

C H Dodd. The Parables of the Kingdom. 3ed Scribner 1936

Burton Scott Easton. Luke 17:20-21, An Exegetical Study. AJT v16 #2 (1912) 276-283

Joseph A Fitzmyer. The Gospel According to Luke. 2v Doubleday 1970, 1985

Michael D Goulder. Luke: A New Paradigm. 2v Sheffield 1989

Robert H Gundry. Matthew. Eerdmans 1982

Robert H Gundry. Matthew's Parable of the Two Sons. Alpha v1 (2017) 133-135

Arland Hultgren. The Parables of Jesus. Eerdmans 2000

Joachim Jeremias. The Parables of Jesus. 8ed 1970; 2rev Scribner 1972

Ben Edwin Perry. Babrius and Phaedrus [Loeb]. Havard 1965

B E Perry. The Origin of the Epimythium. TPAPA v71 (1940) 391-5419

George C Shaw. The Chinook Jargon and How to Use It. 1909; Isha 2013

Klyne R Snodgrass. Stories with Intent. Eerdmans 2008

Luke's Sermon on the Way

E Bruce Brooks
University of Massachusetts at Amherst
(7 Feb 2011)

In this study,[1] I will attempt to reconstruct the middle portion (Lk 11:29–14:35) of Luke's Sermon on the Way (Lk 9:51–18:14). The Synoptic theory underlying the reconstruction is this sequence of texts:

Luke A > Matthew > Luke B and Acts I > Luke C and Acts II

I reconstruct Luke A by excising: (1) lines taken from Matthew by Luke B; (2) Gentile mission material added by Luke B; and (3) passages expressing Luke C's sense that the Christian future lay only with the Gentiles. I end by noting that the reconstruction meets the test of plausibility: it makes expository sense as a consecutive document.

Criteria for Luke B

Characteristics foreign to Luke A but appearing in Luke B include: (1) universality; (2) kingship: Matthew likes power, and in his Scripture fulfillment passages, he gives Scripture the function of foretelling Christ. Matthew adds a disruptive king to a Luke A parable, and Luke B adds a nonfunctional king to a parable *derived* from Matthew;[2] (3) comfort with large amounts of money; and (4) harshness. Examples include:

Universality. Some material already present in Luke A was relocated in Luke B, in some cases to further emphasize the theme of universality:

- **Lk 13:20-21**, the Leaven Parable < Mt 13:33. In the preceding Mustard Seed parable, Luke agrees with Matthew against Mark (and against nature) in making the mustard bush into a more impressive tree. Luke then *relocates* that parable from the end of Mark's Kingdom parables, which feature growth of the small. Matthew's Leaven illustrates the power of the small to transform the large.

The relocated Mustard Seed and the new Leaven have the same meaning: the taking over of the larger by the smaller. Here is Matthew's supersessionism in miniature.

Kingship. Several Mt/Lk passages speak of Jesus as not only powerful, but as *uniquely* powerful. These fit the Matthean / Luke B Kingship emphasis:

- **Lk 10:22**. "All things are delivered to me" < Mt 11:27
- **Lk 11:23**. "He who does not gather with me, scatters" < Mt 12:30. This again follows a unit (the Beelzebub accusation) which has been *relocated* in Luke.

Note the tendency for Luke B passages to be associated with relocated material.

---

[1]Continuing Brooks **Acts-Luke** and Brooks **Steward**.

[2]For the bidirectionality argument, see Brooks **Acts-Luke** 152. Matthew's kingship interest begins to permeate Luke at the Luke B stage, when Luke is adding material from Matthew.

Alpha v1 (2017)

Money. Luke's Minae parable clumsily imitates Matthew's Talents parable, but it does represent a more accepting attitude toward money than that of Luke A. So also:

• **Lk 16:10-12**. This, the second of three attempts to explain the Canny Steward parable (Lk 16:1-13),[3] borrows terms ("faithful in little") from the Luke B Minae parable (Lk 19:17), and thus is probably not itself earlier than Luke B.

• **Lk 19:1-10** (Zacchaeus) is a rich man redeemed by restoring to those he had defrauded, and giving alms of half his goods. In contrast to the Lazarus story (Luke A), *crimes of money are now redeemable*. Jesus' remark "forasmuch as he also is a son of Abraham" is probably an evocation – and a mitigation – of the unforgiving Abraham in the Luke A Lazarus story (Lk 16:25).

Whether by Luke or borrowed from Matthew, these are probably Luke B passages.

Harshness in passages probably taken from Matthew will be noticed as it occurs.

Criteria for Luke C

Acts II depicts the severance between Judaism and Christianity. Paul recognizes the Jews' rejection of Christ, and turns to the Gentiles (Ac 28:23f). Passages which contain that message, or add it to Luke, have previously been identified. They are:

• **The Nazareth Addition**, Lk 4:25-30. Jesus cites Scripture showing the favor of God *to Gentiles rather than to Jews;* the Nazareth mob try to kill Jesus.

• **The Seventy**, Lk 10: 1-12, symbolizing the Mission to the Gentiles.

• **The Feast Addition**, Lk 14:24. The Feast parable, Lk 14:15-24, derived from Mt 22:1-10, ends with the servants filling the hall (Mt 22:10, Lk 14:23]. A further line, Lk 14:24. with no parallel in Matthew, rules, *"For I say unto you, that none of those men that were bidden shall taste of my supper."* The exclusion of the first-called (the Jews) marks this as the more drastic Luke C.

• **The Lazarus Addition**, Lk 16:27-31. The basic Lazarus story (Lk 16:19-26) condemns the rich man to hell, just because he is rich. This is basic Luke A poverty doctrine. In the addition, the rich man asks to return from the dead to warn his brothers. This Abraham denies; *"If they hear not Moses and the prophets, neither will they be persuaded, if one rise from the dead,"* that is, not even the resurrected Jesus, himself risen from the dead, will persuade them. This turns from the Jews just as decisively as does Paul in Ac 28:2 (in Acts II, and thus contemporary with Luke C).

• **The Good Samaritan**, Lk 10:29-37, shows a priest and a Levite refusing to render aid to the wounded man; *only a Samaritan* [Gentile] does so.

• **The Ten Lepers**, Lk 17:11-19, shows ten healed, but only one, a Samaritan, returning to give thanks. Jesus notes that *"only this foreigner"* thanks him.

The point of the Samaritan stories is not that merit is shown by Samaritans (Gentiles) but that merit is shown *only* by Samaritans, and not by the Jews in those same stories. Samaritans are a code word for Gentiles throughout Acts. The entry of the Gentiles coincides with, and is contrasted with, the moral exit of the Jewish leadership.

---

[3]For the separation of the several explanations of this parable, see Fitzmyer 2/1104f. For the difficulty of the parable itself, see Snodgrass 401f. For a suggestion as to what this baffling parable means, and why it expresses that meaning so confusingly, see Brooks **Steward**.

Continuity Criteria

The directionality between two passages can sometimes be determined. Separately, an original sequence will tend to make more sense than a derived sequence.

The Sermon on the Way: Lk 9:51-18:14

The portion of the Sermon still to be examined in detail is Lk 11:29-14:35, its middle segment. The format of the previous studies will be followed: first identifying possible later material, and then assessing what remains when it is removed.

For the sake of continuity, I begin by repeating the Sermon sections identified in my Acts-Luke paper. Those sections were:

[1. Total Dedication to the Way]
┌9:57-62. A man is warned of the hardships of following Jesus
│9:59-60. A man is chided for hesitation in following Jesus
└9:61-62. A man is chided for hesitation in following Jesus
10:38-42. Mary and Martha
[2. Prayer as a Companion on the Way]
┌11:1-4. The Lord's Prayer
│11:5-8. Illustration suggesting that prayer will be answered
└11:9-13. Assurance that prayer will be answered appropriately
11:27-28. Jesus rebukes veneration of his earthly mother

We may now take up the next stretch of canonical Luke. As before, I mark previously identified passages as Luke [A], [B], or [C]. Non-A passages are indented. Harsh details are *italicized*; Matthean parallels and implied directionalities are given at right.

Lk	Mt
11:29-30. An *evil* generation	< 12:38-40
11:31-32. Queen of the South and Noah will *condemn* it	< 12:42, 41
11:33. Let your light shine	> 5:15
11:34-35. The eye is the lamp of the body	< 6:22-23
11:36. If your whole body is full of light	
11:37-38. [Introduction to dinner with Pharisees]	
11:39-43. *Woe* to Pharisees	< 23:25, 23:23, 23:6
11:44. Pharisees like unseen *graves*	< 23:37
11:45-46. Bind *heavy burdens*	< 23:4
11:47-48. Build the *tombs* of the prophets	< 23:29
11:49-51. Wisdom of God sends prophets	< 23:24
11:52. They have *taken away* the key	< 23:13
11:53. [Narrative conclusion]	
12:1. *Beware* the leaven of the Pharisees	< 16:6, 16:11b
12:2-3. Nothing can be covered up	> 10:26-27
12:4-5. Fear only him who can kill the soul	> 10:28
12:6-7. You are worth many sparrows	> 10:29-31

The 11:37-38 Introduction precedes the First Pharisee dinner, which is more hostile than the Lk 14 one. No story needs two Dinners with Pharisees, so probably one of Luke's is secondary. Of them, the harsher Lk 11:39-12:1 is the better candidate for influence from censorious Matthew. So also the harsh 11:29-32.

Lk 11:33 ("Let your light shine") has a keyword link with 11:34f ("The eye is the lamp of the body"), but no organic connection.[4] 11:33, seemingly an order for open advocacy of the Gospel, is not thematically resumed until 12:2f (all will be revealed) and 12:4f, on the dangers of advocacy; 12:6-7 reads like a concluding encouragement. These considerations lead to the elimination of most of Lk 11, and we have left:

[3. Fearless Witnessing]

┌11:33. Let your light shine
 12:2-3. Nothing can be covered up
└12:4-5. Fear only him who can kill the soul
 12:6-7. Encouragement: You are worth many sparrows

We may now consider the rest of Lk 12:

Lk	Mt
12:8-9. Who acknowledges me, I will acknowledge	> 10:32-33
12:10. Who blasphemes against the Holy Spirit	> 12:32t
12:11-12. The Holy Spirit will teach what to say	> 10:19-20
12:13-15. Jesus refuses to divide an inheritance	
12:16-21. Parable of the Rich Fool	
12:22-28. Do not be anxious	> 6:25-34
12:29-32. Do not be concerned for daily things	> 6:19-20
12:33-34. Sell what you have; gain treasure in Heaven	> 6:21
12:35-46. Be like watchful servants	> 25:1-13
12:47-48. Ignorance will receive lighter punishment	
12:49-50. Would the end were near	
12:51-53. I come not to bring peace, but division	> 10:34-36

There are no previously identified B or C passages, and nothing suggests a thematic intrusion. The material easily fits the previous pattern of triplet-based sections, thus:

[4. Warning Against Apostasy]

┌12:8-9. Who acknowledges me, I will acknowledge
 12:10. Who denies the Holy Spirit will not be forgiven
└12:11-12. Warning: You will be put on trial before the authorities

[5. The Dangers of Worldliness]

 12:13-15. Introduction: Jesus refuses to adjudicate an inheritance
┌12:16-21. **The Rich Fool**
 12:22-28. Do not be anxious
└12:29-31. Do not be concerned for daily things
 12:32. Encouragement: "Your Father will give you the Kingdom"

[6. Watchful Waiting]

┌12:33-34. Sell what you have; gain treasure in Heaven
 12:35-46. Be like watchful servants
└12:47-48. Ignorance will receive lighter punishment
 12:49-53. Warning: I come not to bring peace, but division

Notice that the ends of successive sections alternate warnings with encouragements.

---

[4]Easton 188, "somewhat strained;" Fitzmyer 2/940, "The function of 'lamp' has changed here;" Johnson 186 "muddled."

The next part of the Sermon has a few previously identified [**B**] or [**C**] passages. There are also some pairs where the Matthean member seems to be primary:

Lk	Mt
12:54-56. Signs of the End	16:2-3
12:57-59. Agree with your accuser	> 5:25-26
13:1-5. Repent or perish	
13:6-9. Time will be allowed to repent	
13:10-17. Healing an infirm woman on the Sabbath	< 12:11
13:18-19. Mustard Seed (*relocated*) [**B**]	
13:20-21. Parable of the Leaven [**B**]	< 13:33
13:22. Introduction: Journeying toward Jerusalem	
13:23-24. Few will find the Way	> 7:13-14
13:25. The householder will deny them entry	> 25:10-12
13:26-27. Their protests of earlier support will be in vain	> 7:22-23
13:28-30. Many will come and take your places	< 8:11-12
13:31-33. Pharisees warn about Herod	
13:34-35. Lament over Jerusalem	< 23:37-39
14:1. Introduction: Dinner with a Pharisee	

Lk 13:22, which introduces what follows, cannot be an integral part of what precedes. Of what precedes, eliminating known B passages leaves four passages about the dangers of exclusion at the End, plus an extraneous Sabbath healing.[5] After the 13:22 introduction come three passages about the difficulty of finding the Way. Two are in Matthew's agglomerative Sermon on the Mount,[6] and are presumably from Luke A. Like Jesus' self-descriptions in Lk 17:22-37,[7] Jesus' Jerusalem lament is extraneous. Luke's Sermon is not about Jesus, it is about his followers.

These considerations lead to the following reconstruction:

[7. Preparation For the End]
  ⌈12:54-56. Signs of the End
   12:57-59. Agree with your accuser
  ⌊13:1-5. Repent or perish
  13:6-9. Encouragement: Time will be allowed to repent

[8. Danger of Being Excluded]
  13:22. Introduction: Journeying toward Jerusalem[8]
  ⌈13:23-24. Few will find the Way
   13:25. The householder will deny them entry
  ⌊13:26-27. Warning: Their protests of earlier support will be in vain

Again the triplet-based sections and alternating final warnings and encouragements.

[5]Lk 13:10-17 is ill-placed in context, combines elements of healing and exorcism stories, and is a female counterpart ("a daughter of Abraham") to Zacchaeus [**B**], a "son of Abraham." See Creed 283, Marshall 556-559, Fitzmyer 2/1010-1014, and Nolland 2/7220-725.

[6]The term is Streeter's; **Four** 167, 250, 264. He expresses horror at Luke strewing gobbets of Matthew's Sermon on the Mount over his own Gospel. It is far more plausible that Matthew stole Luke A's Sermon on the Plain, and bulked it out with tidbits from elsewhere in Luke.

[7]See Brooks **Steward** 164-165.

[8]This resumption of the Travel Motif occurs exactly halfway through the Sermon.

We now return to Lk 14:1, and the second, and milder, of Luke's two Dinner with Pharisees scenes (the first was the notably hostile one in Lk 11).

Lk	Mt
14:1. Dinner with a Pharisee	
14:2-6. Sabbath healing of man with dropsy; Pharisees accept	
14:7-11. Take the lowest place	
14:12:14. Invite the poor, who cannot repay you.	
14:15-23. **The Feast [A]**	> 22:2-10
14:24. None invited shall taste my feast [C]	
14:25-27. Must renounce all	> 10:37-38
14:28-33. Count cost before beginning	
14:34-35. If the salt has lost its taste	> 5:13

The Dinner with Pharisees continues to the end of the Parable of the Feast, which seems to be its climax; at 14:25 Jesus instead addresses the crowds. The Feast Parable may not be encouraging to the Pharisees (who are admonished), but it does encourage the nobodies – Luke's audience – who will replace them at the Final Feast.

The words to the crowd make what seems to be a standard Lukan Triplet, and this time it is the Christians who are admonished, to weigh the need of total renunciation, not to embark on the Way if they cannot see it through, and not to be complacent about their membership. As in Lk 13:26-27 above, membership can be lost.

The priority of the Sermon on the Plain has been noted above, and will include the directionality Lk 14:34-35 > Mt 5:13. As for Mt 10:37-38, it is part of Matthew's Second Discourse, which like Matthew's First Discourse (the Sermon on the Mount) is suspect as an agglomerative production. Here is the Matthean context:

Mt	Lk
10:34-36. I do not come to bring peace	> 12:51-53
10:37-39. Who loves father or mother more than me	< 14:26-27
10:40-11:1. [End of the Discourse]	

Strife *within* families (Mt 10:34-36) is not the same as the need to *abandon* family (10:37-39). It is easy to see how they might have been put together, but this does not contradict the possibility of an agglomerative gathering in Matthew based on separate sayings which are themselves coherent in Lukan context. We then have, in Luke:

[9. The Need for Humility]
14:1. Introduction: Dinner with a Pharisee
⌐14:2-6. Healing of man with dropsy; Pharisees *accept* Sabbath healing
 14:7-11. Take the lowest place, and you will be exalted
└14:12:14. Invite those who cannot repay you; you will feast in the next life
14:15-23. Encouragement: **The Feast**. "That my house may be filled"

[10. The Cost of Discipleship]
⌐14:25-27. Must renounce all
 14:28-33. Count cost before beginning
└14:34-35. Warning: If salt has lost its taste, it will be discarded

The pattern of alternate encouragements and warnings continues here. It will be even more conspicuous when we assemble the whole, and find that the feast in 15:15-23 recurs in the feast which concludes the Lost Son parable, two sections away.

The Sermon on the Way (Luke 9:51-18:14)

The above arguments do not suffice to show that the Lukan Sermon on the Way is coherent as a whole. I here repeat the above analyses, as a test of that requirement, for both the thematic and the formal aspects of the Sermon. Focal pieces, in sections that have them, are **emphasized**.

[§1. Total Dedication to the Way]

9:51a. Introduction: Departing for Jerusalem
⌐9:57-58. A man offers to follow; Jesus dissuades him
  9:59-60. A man asks to bury his father; Jesus refuses
└9:61-62. A man asks to say farewell; Jesus refuses
  10:38-42. **Mary and Martha** [against domestic distraction]

[§2. Prayer as Companion Along the Way]

⌐11:1-4. **The Lord's Prayer**
  11:5-8. The Friend at Midnight: Repeated prayer will be answered
└11:9-13. Ask and the Father will give you good gifts
  11:27-28. Praise of Jesus' mother rebuked [against sentimental distraction]

[§3. Fearless Witnessing]

11:33. Theme: Let your light shine
⌐12:2-3. Nothing can be covered up
  12:4-5. Fear only him who can kill the soul
└12:6-7. Encouragement: You are worth many sparrows

[§4. Warning Against Apostasy]

⌐12:8-9. Who acknowledges me, I will acknowledge
  12:10. Who denies the Holy Spirit will not be forgiven
└12:11-12. Warning: On trial, the Holy Spirit will teach you what to say

[§5. The Dangers of Worldliness]

12:13-15. Introduction: Jesus refuses to adjudicate an inheritance
⌐12:16-21. **The Rich Fool**
  12:22-28. Do not be anxious
└12:29-31. Do not be concerned for daily things
  12:32. Encouragement: Your Father will give you the Kingdom

[§6. Watchful Waiting]

⌐12:33-34. Sell what you have; gain treasure in Heaven
  12:35-46. Be like watchful servants
└12:47-48. Ignorance will receive lighter punishment
  12:49-53. Warning: I came not to bring peace, but division

[§7. Preparation For the End]

⌐12:54-56. Signs of the End
  12:57-59. Agree with your accuser
└13:1-5. Repent or perish
  13:6-9. Encouragement: Time will be allowed to repent

[§8. Danger of Being Excluded]

13:22. Introduction: Journeying toward Jerusalem
⌐13:23-24. Few will find the Way
  13:25. The householder will deny them entry
└13:26-27. Warning: Their protests of earlier support will be in vain

[§9. The Need for Humility]

14:1. Introduction: Dinner with a Pharisee

⌐14:2-6. Healing of man with dropsy; Pharisees *accept* argument for Sabbath healing

 14:7-11. Take the lowest place, and you will be exalted

└14:12:14. Invite the poor, who cannot repay you, and you will feast in the next life

 14:15-23. Encouragement: **The Feast**. "That my house may be filled"

[§10. The Cost of Discipleship]

⌐14:25-27. Must renounce all

 14:28-33. Count cost before beginning

└14:34-35. Warning: If salt has lost its taste, it will be discarded

[§11. Joy in Heaven Over The Saved]

 15:1-2. Introduction: Pharisees criticize Jesus' eating with sinners

⌐15:3-7. The Lost Sheep

 15:8-10. The Lost Coin

└15:11-32. Encouragement: **The Lost Son** [note the final feast]

[§12. The Dangers of Wealth]

⌐16:1-9. **The Canny Steward**, with Luke A's explanation

 16:14-15. Wealth-loving Pharisees rebuked

└16:19-26. Warning: **The Rich Man and Lazarus**

[§13. Sin and Forgiveness]

⌐17:1-2. Woe to those by whom temptations come

 17:3-4. Need for repeated forgiveness of a brother

└17:7-10. Servant must do more than is required

 17:20-21. Encouragement: The Kingdom is in the midst of you

[§14-15. Exit Portal: Two Concluding Parables in Aesopic Form]

⌐18:1-5. **The Unjust Judge**

└18:6-8. Moral: God listens to prayer (echoing §2)

⌐8:9-13. **Pharisee and Publican**

└8:14. Moral: The humble, who have renounced all, will be exalted (echoing §1)

Reflections on the Reconstruction

The Sermon typically presents its arguments in triplicate, sometimes with an extra piece preceding or following. Introductions maintain contact with the journey motif.

The first two segments have the same message (the dangers of distraction); both end with an illustration in the feminine sphere. After that dual warning at the outset, successive sections end by alternating encouragement and warning (#3-13). The exit segments reinforce the encouragement of #13. The pace is quickened by abandoning the triplet expository feature, and the tone is lightened by use of the Aesopic form, complete with promythium and epimythium as in the recent Latin version of Phaedrus. This concluding rhetorical lightness is itself encouraging: the final mood is not dark.

Lk 17:20-21 "The Kingdom is in the midst of you" does not envision a Present Kingdom;[9] it is merely a momentary encouragement, echoing the one at 12:32.

_____

[9]So Creed 210, Nolland 3/853, and others. But the idea of an immanent, not an imminent, Kingdom *was* in the air at the time; see Gospel of Thomas #3 (= 51, 113) and #30 (= 77).

The Logic of Luke's Additions

Why did Luke put the borrowed passages where he did? Though they are certainly less comfortable in Luke, we can usually find some logic in their present placement.[10] In the following suggestions, the original Luke A material is **highlighted**:

Mt	Layer	Lk	Pericope
	A	**9:51a**	**Setting out for Jerusalem**
	B	9:51b-56	Samaritan Rejection
	A	**9:57-62**	**Gathering Followers**
	B	10:1-10	Sending of the Seventy
	⌐B	10:17-20	Return of the Seventy
11:25-27	⌊B	10:21-22	"I Thank Thee, Father"
13:16-17	B	10:23-24	"Blessed Are Your Eyes"

Luke B's Jesus winnows his followers before sending seventy of them off; his praises of them on return (with material taken from Matthew) are appropriate to the reported success of their mission. There is a link between 10:17-20 and 10:21-22f.

	⌐C	10:25-28	The Lawyer's Question [relocated]
	⌊C	10:29-37	The Good Samaritan
	⌊A	**10:38-42**	**Mary and Martha**

The Lawyer's Question was moved to this place to introduce the Good Samaritan, which Luke may have thought of as a male counterpart to Mary and Martha.[11]

Mt	Layer	Lk	Pericope
	A	**11:1-4**	**The Lord's Prayer**
	A	**11:5-8**	**The Friend at Midnight**
	⌐A	**11:9-13**	**Answer to Prayer**
12:22-30	⌊B	11:14-23	The Beelzebub Controversy
12:43-45	B	11:24-26	Return of the Evil Spirit
	⌐A	**11:27-28**	**Enthusiasm for Jesus' Mother**
12:38-42	⌊B	11:29-32	Seeking a Sign
	⌐A	**11:33-36**	**Let Your Light Shine**
23:1-36	⌊B	11:37-12:1	Against the Pharisees
	A	**12:2-12**	**Fearless Confession**

Prayer is part of exorcism, and the Luke B challenge to Jesus' exorcisms (as involving traffic with Satan) logically follows the Luke A sequence on prayer. The Return of the Evil Spirit, taken from a nearby passage in Matthew, relates thematically to the subject of evil spirits. The Luke A woman who is focused on Jesus' mother is looking for something in the wrong place, as are those who in Luke B's addition seek a sign from Jesus himself. The last link juxtaposes the Pharisees, who follow wrong principles, with the disciples, who are told to let their light (that is, their right principles) shine, in the adjacent Luke A passage.

---

[10]The usual view is that Luke's placements have "no special appropriateness. A theory which would make an author capable of such a proceeding would only be tenable if, on other grounds, we had reason to believe he was a crank" (Streeter **Four** 183). For Goulder's rejoinder to Streeter, see Goulder **Crank**.

[11]So Goulder **Luke** 2/493.

Mt	Layer	Lk	Pericope
	A	**12:13-21**	**The Rich Fool**
	A	**12:22-34**	**Cares for Earthly Things**
	A	**12:35-46**	**Watchfulness**
	A	**12:47-48**	**The Servant's Wages**
	A	**12:49-56**	**The Present Time**
	A	**12:57-59**	**Agree With Your Accuser**
	⌐A	**13:1-9**	**Repentance**
	└B	13:10-17	Healing an Infirm Woman
13:31-32	⌐B	13:18-19	The Mustard Seed [relocated]
13:33	⌐B	13:20-21	The Leaven
	└A	**13:22-27**	**Exclusion From the Kingdom**

The word "eighteen" links the Luke A Repentance passage and Luke B's Healing story (the woman had been infirm for eighteen years). The Mustard Seed parable was moved from its probable original position (at the end of Mark's Parables of the Kingdom) in connection with including Matthew's Parable of the Leaven. This inclusive piece may have been placed where it is to offset the forbidding tone of the following A passage, which emphasizes that few will enter the Kingdom.

Mt	Layer	Lk	Pericope
	⌐A	**13:22-27**	**Exclusion From the Kingdom**
8:11-12	└B	13:28-29	Gnashing of Teeth
20:16	B	13:30	The Last Will Be First
	⌐B	13:31-33	Warning from Friendly Pharisees
	└B	13:34-35	Lament Over Jerusalem
	A	**14:1-24**	**Dining With Pharisees**

Luke A's Exclusion is enhanced by warning passages from Matthew. The travel motif in 13:31-33 introduces Matthew's Lament Over Jerusalem, developing the idea of danger in 13:22-27, though here it is danger to Jesus rather than to his followers.

Mt	Layer	Lk	Pericope
	A	**14:1-24**	**Dining With Pharisees**
	A	**14:25-35**	**Cost of Discipleship**
	A	**15:1-32**	**Parables of Losing and Finding**
	A	**16:1-9**	**Parable of the Canny Steward**
Lk B 19:11f	B	16:10-12	Second explanation of parable
6:24	B	16:13	Third explanation of parable
	A	**16:14-15**	**Wealth-loving Pharisees Rebuked**
11:12	B	16:16	The Law was until John
5:18	B	16:17	Not a jot will pass from the Law
5:32	B	16:18	Against divorcing a wife
	A	**16:19-26**	**The Rich Man and Lazarus**
	C	16:27-31	Not even Moses

The borrowed further explanations of the Steward Parable naturally follow that norotiously difficult Parable. The three legal items are not inappropriately associated with the Pharisees, whose expertise is the Law. The Luke C extension of the Lazarus story is authorial, and naturally follow the story which it extends, adding a dimension not in the original, but very much part of the Luke C agenda.

Mt	Layer	Lk	Pericope
	A	**17:1-2**	**Woe to those by whom temptations come**
	A	**17:3-4**	**Need for repeated forgiveness of a brother**
17:20	B	17:5-6	If you had faith
	A	**17:7-10**	**Servant must do more than is required**
	C	17:11-19	The Ten Lepers
	A	**17:20-21**	**Encouragement: The Kingdom is within**
	B	17:22-37	Apocalyptic miscellany
	A	**18:1-5**	**The Unjust Judge**
	A	**18:6-8**	**Moral: God listens to prayer**
	A	**18:9-13**	**Pharisee and Publican**
	A	**18:14**	**Moral: The humble will be exalted**

As noted earlier,[12] 17:5-6 comes in abruptly; the "sea" in which tempters are drowned in 17:1 gave a hook for the "sea" of the sycamine tree in 17:6. "Doing more than others" may have linked the servant of 17:7f with the single grateful leper of 17:11f. The "kingdom" of 17:21 perhaps legitimizes the apocalyptic miscellany of 17:22-37. All in all, the intrusions, though indeed intrusive, cannot be said to be entirely random.

Dating the Synoptics

The argument in this and the preceding papers assumes only *relative* dates, namely:

Luke A > Matthew > Luke B and Acts I > Luke C and Acts II

but there are also some implications for absolute dates, which I explore here.

First, neither Matthew nor Luke is likely to have been written before the deaths of Paul (c60) and Peter (c64) ended the Apostolic Age and created a crisis of continuity, which required new teaching material and new administrative structures. That both Matthew and Luke are parasitic on Mark merely shows that Mark at that time was the authoritative account of Jesus, which had to be respected as well as surpassed.

Second, it has been well argued that Matthew was earlier than the destruction of the Temple in 70.[13] Certain passages in Luke, probably to be ascribed to Luke B, clearly describe the destruction of the Temple,[14] so Luke B must be post-70.

Third, the editing of Paul's letters for wider circulation (and to fill the authority vacuum in a different way than that pursued by the Second Tier Gospels) included interpolations. In one of them, 1 Thess 2:13-16, Paul alludes to the destruction of the Temple in 70. Then the Pauline editing process must have extended into at least 71. Luke B is of the same date as Acts I, and as several over the years have recognized, Acts is aware of Paul's letters.[15] This gives an earliest date of c72 for Acts I.

[12]Brooks **Steward** 164, citing Fitzmyer and others.

[13]The argument of Gundry **Matthew** 599-609 for a pre-70 Matthew is not, in my opinion, refuted by the partial counter-argument in Davies and Allison 1/127-138.

[14]Luke 21:20 (B) is an absolutely unambiguous reference to the siege of Jerusalem in 70. To Luke B also belongs the unique, interruptive, and almost equally clear 19:39-44.

[15]See Elbert **Possible**, with references to earlier work.

Fourth, Acts II may be one response to the issuance of the Birkat ha-Minim in c85.[16] For the whole Luke-Acts formation process, we might then have:[17]

c64 Peter dies, ending the Apostolic Age
c66 Luke A written, as a first response to the need for a new Gospel
c68 Matthew written, drawing on and competing with Luke A
 70 Destruction of the Jerusalem Temple
c71 Paul's letters edited, as another response to the need for authority texts
c72 Luke B and Acts I written, in response to the popularity of Matthew
c80 Gamaliel II at Jamnia; hardening of Judaism toward the Jesus sect
c85 Birkat ha-Minim prayer effectively excludes Christians from synagogues
c88 Acts II (Antioch) responds with a symmetrical turning to the Gentiles
c90 John 9:22, 12:42, 16:2 (Ephesus) speaks of expulsion from synagogues
c91 First persecutions of expelled Christians in distant Pontus (Pliny)
c91 1 Peter B responds to persecutions in Pontus and Bithynia
c94 "Sudden misfortunes" (1 Clement 1:1) reflect persecutions in Rome
c96 1 Clement written from Rome after a delay; asserts church unity

Authorship Questions

Given three stages in the formation of Luke-Acts, there may have been as many as three "Lukes." Are they the same person? In favor of identity is the consistency of style in Luke-Acts, including a Septuagintal tone in moments of high seriousness. Against it is the shift in affinity from Luke A (oblivious to Gentiles) to Luke B (concern for amity between Jewish and Gentile Christians), to Luke C (who takes the Gentile side against a newly hostile Judaism). The differences can be explained by outer events; the similarities argue for one person. The span here suggested (from 66 to 87, 21 years) is compatible with a single person.

What is a sermon? Probably, something delivered on one occasion. The "Sermon" here identified may be too long for that, but it could at any rate serve as a repertoire of sermon material; a pastor'ssourcebook. What it does *not* suggest is material with which to preach to the unconverted.

There is disagreement about Luke's racial identity. The deutero-Pauline witness Colossians 4:11-14 groups him outside "those of the circumcision," whereas Syrian tradition is that he was a Jew. Perhaps the division into Luke A, B, and C can clarify. Luke A shows no sympathy for, or even awareness of, Gentiles. This may tilt the uncertainty in favor of a Jewish Luke, who over time responded to, and came to accept, the Gentile tendency which grew increasingly strong in the first century. Confronted with a choice between Jewishness and Christianity, he chose the latter.

---

[16]Once excluded from the synagogues, Jesus followers were exposed to the requirement of Emperor worship. For 1 Peter B (1:1-2 and 4:12-end; so Perdelwitz), see Beare. For the c91 date of the first persecutions in Pontus, see Brooks **Pliny** 214. 1 Clement 1:1 refers to recent "sudden calamities" as a reason for not writing earlier. The Birkat ha-Minim probably spread gradually from Palestine, and need not have been uniformly observed in the places it reached. But the many reflections of something out of the ordinary in c85-c94 seem to point to a reality.

[17]With an eye on the conclusions reached in Brooks **Pliny** 214.

Implications

However the authorship questions may turn out, one thing seems certain. During its entire formation process, the Luke-Acts text was under one *proprietorship*, if only that of a sponsoring church. The third author (or the only author, in his final revision) could not only compose new material (Acts II), *he could insert harmonizing passages into the previous material*, both in Acts I and in the Gospel. Theories which separate Acts and Luke would seem to be ruled out by this consideration.

That the Q theory is challenged by the Luke A/B/C model, which accounts otherwise for the bidirectionality of the Luke/Matthew common material not in Mark, has been noted in an earlier study.[18]

Let it not pass without mention that this Sermon, if correctly reconstructed, is of immense interest to students of early Christianity. For one thing, even after removing what there is reason to believe are later additions, and even if it be regarded as a repertoire for preaching rather than a sample of preaching, it is the longest known piece of early Christian paraenesis. Its systematic alternation between warning and encouragement gives us a tour of the subject as at least one early church saw it.

Works Cited

Francis Wright Beare. The First Epistle of Peter. 1947; 3ed Blackwell 1970

E Bruce Brooks. Acts-Luke. Alpha v1 (2017) 143-157

E Bruce Brooks. The Epistle of Jacob. Alpha v1 (2017) 58-70

E Bruce Brooks. Luke's Parable of the Canny Steward. Alpha v1 (2017) 158-166

E Bruce Brooks. Jerusalem and Paul. Alpha v1 (2017) 104-109

E Bruce Brooks. Pliny at Pontus. Alpha v1 (2017) 209-214

John Martin Creed. The Gospel According to St Luke. Macmillan 1930

W D Davies and Dale C Allison Jr. The Gospel According to Matthew. 3v Clark 1988, 1991, 1997

B S Easton. The Gospel According to St Luke. Scribners 1926

Paul Elbert. Possible Literary Links between Luke-Acts and Pauline Letters Regarding Spirit-Language; in Brodie, Intertextuality of the Epistles, Sheffield (2006) 226-254

Joseph A Fitzmyer. The Gospel According to Luke. 2v Doubleday 1970, 1985

Michael D Goulder. Luke: A New Paradigm. 2v Sheffield 1989

Michael D Goulder. The Method of a Crank; in Tuckett (ed) Synoptic Studies, Sheffield (1984) 111-130

Robert H Gundry. Matthew. Eerdmans 1982

Luke Timothy Johnson. The Gospel of Luke. Liturgical 1991

Helmut Koester. Ancient Christian Gospels. Trinity 1990

I Howard Marshall. The Gospel of Luke. Eerdmans 1978

John Nolland. Luke. 3v Word 1989, 1993, 1993

Klyne R Snodgrass. Stories with Intent. Eerdmans 2008

Burnett Hillman Streeter. The Four Gospels. Macmillan 1924

---

[18]See Brooks **Acts-Luke** 152, whose conclusion is annexed herewith.

Questions About Luke A/B/C

Paul Foster
University of Edinburgh
(4 March 2014)

EDITORS' NOTE: These questions on Brooks **Acts-Luke** ("Luke A/B/C") were predistributed, with responses from the A/B/C side, for the Alpha Christianity Seminar at the Eastern Great Lakes Biblical Society meeting on 28 Mar 2014. With the respondent's permission, that exchange is revised for this volume of *Alpha.*

PF. How different is Luke A from what I would term Q?

ABC. Luke A is the entire original text of Luke; Q is a conjectural text including only a small set of passages common to Matthew and Luke.

PF. Or does it look like "Proto-Luke" postulated by Streeter, Taylor, and others?

ABC. No. Streeter and Taylor envisioned an early Luke based on Q, to which Markan passages were later added. The only similarity is that Taylor's Proto-Luke begins with Lk 3:1, and thus, like Luke A, lacks a Birth Narrative.

Luke A/B/C is not a rehash of Taylor or any other previous proposal. For what it may be worth, it is something new on the Synoptic scene.

PF. Where does Mark fit into this? Is it integrated at the Luke A, B, or C stage?

ABC. Mark precedes all; this is the only Synoptic model that fully acknowledges Markan Priority (many Q supporters regard Q as earlier than Mark). The picture is:

Mark > Luke A original > Matthew > Luke B and Acts I > Luke C and Acts II

PF. How were these various stages of Luke and Matthew in circulation?

ABC. A text compiled, or known, at one church can have had a penumbra of acquaintance in nearby churches, through overlapping membership or personal contact, previous to systematic publication for the Empire audience.

Individual Passages

PF. Mt 16:13-20 [The Confession at Caesarea Philippi]. Triple tradition passage. Why does Luke not know Matthew's addition in Mt 16:16-19?

ABC. The ecclesiastical extension in Mt 16:17-19, making Peter the head of the future church, is probably a later addition, meant to identify Matthew more strongly with Peter and thus secure canonical approval for Matthew as a fully Apostolic text.[1] Then it was not present for Luke B, and the question of his ignoring it does not arise.

---

[1] Matthew otherwise merges Peter with the Twelve (Mt 19:28 > Luke B as Lk 22:28-30). Similar Petrine appendages are Jn 21 ("feed my sheep"), in an otherwise anti-Petrine Gospel, and (with Perdelwitz) 1 Pet 1:12 and 4:12-5:14. Paul was the other acceptably Apostolic figure, and Heb 13:22-25, following a similar strategy of canonical qualification, turns the otherwise anonymous Hebrews into a specifically Pauline epistle. See Brooks **Apostolic**.

Cases where Luke ignores something in Matthew refute the image of Luke as a passive copyist; he is an author with his own agenda and theology. He makes his own choices. This recognition affects considerations of what Luke is likely to do or not do (omit, repeat, vary, expand, condense, relocate) at any given place in his text.

There are places at which Luke B *does* take note of Matthew's additions to Mark. To the description of John (Mk 1:2-6 ‖ Mt 3:1-6 ‖ Lk A 3:1-6, all virtually identical), Matthew added the Preaching of John (Mt 3:7-10, a denunciation of the Pharisees). This Luke B copied with only slight changes, at Lk 3:7-9. But Luke, gentle as always, added a further extension, in which John *preaches salvation to the multitude:*

> **Lk 3:10**. And the multitudes asked him, saying, What then must we do? [11] And he answered and said unto them, He that hath two coats, let him impart to him that hath none, and he that hath food, let him to likewise. [12] And there came also publicans to be baptized, and they said unto him, Teacher, what must we do? [13] And he said unto them, Extort no more than that which is appointed you. [14] And soldiers also asked him, saying, And we, what must we do? And he said unto them, Extort from no man by violence, neither accuse wrongfully, and be content with your wages.

That comes straight out of Luke A's core theology, as laid out in the Sermon on the Plain. It does not denounce (as Matthew loves to do). It guides. It saves. It shows the way to justice and compassion in this world, and to eternal life in the next. Does John here sound like Jesus elsewhere in Luke? Yes, he does; the two are close in Luke ("Wisdom is justified by *all* her children," Lk 7:35). It is a trait of that Gospel.

PF. Mt 5:3-12 ‖ Lk 6:20b-23. Why are Luke's Beatitudes so much shorter?

ABC. It has been suggested that the First Beatitude is primary in Luke ("the poor") and altered by addition in Matthew ("poor *in spirit*"), so we might instead ask, Why are Matthew's Beatitudes so much more numerous? A general answer is that Matthew often enough expands Mark, and we need not be surprised if he sometimes expands Luke A. Specifically, we may note that though the Lukan Four Beatitudes echo Isaiah, the Matthean Extras are largely based on the Psalms. Here is the detail:

	Matthew	OT	Luke
5:3	poor *in spirit*	Isa 61:1 >	6:20b poor
5:4	that mourn	Isa 61:2 >	6:21b weep
5:5	meek	< Ps 37:11	
5:6	hunger and thirst *after righteousness*	Isa 55:1-3 >	6:21a hunger
5:7	merciful	< Ps 18:26	
5:8	pure in heart	< Ps 24:3-5	
5:9	peacemakers	< Ps 34:14	
5:10	persecuted	< Ps 24:3-4	
5:11	reproach	Isa 51:71	6:22 reproach

Doesn't everybody find the Matthean extensions somewhat repetitious? What new information about conduct do "merciful" and "peacemakers" add to "meek?" For that matter, isn't the nub of Matthew's "persecuted" already implicit in Luke's "reproach?" It thus seems possible to see Matthew's Beatitudes as an economic upgrade of Luke's (attenuating genuine poverty into suburban angst), plus some repetitive extensions which are not well distinguished from each other. This tactic of soft upgrade is one origin of the Nice Jesus picture which Matthew and Luke B together present.

PF. Mt 23:15-36 ‖ Lk 20:45-47 [Beware the scribes]. Same problem as above. Both are double tradition passages.

ABC. Yes and no. We need to consider the larger context. Mk 12:37-40 is a warning of Jesus ("Beware of the scribes"); Luke A, in 20:45-47, includes all of it. Then Matthew, in Mt 23:1-36, enormously expands it. *From that expansion*, Luke B has taken a few passages, which he locates in Lk 11 (again, in the Travel Narrative). The two processes are separate in time; thus:

Mark	Luke A	Matthew	Luke B adopts
12:37f He said	20:45 he said	23:1 Then said	
		23:2f Moses' seat	
		23:4 heavy burdens	11:46 burdens
12:38b robes	20:46 robes	23:5f phylacteries	
		23:13 shut	11:52 key
12:30 widows	20:47 widows	[23:14 widows][2]	
		23:15 proselyte	
		23:16f swears	
		23:23f tithe mint	11:42 tithe mint
		23:25f outside	11:39 outside
		23:27f tombs	11:44 graves
		23:29f prophets	
		23:32f will kill	11:49 will kill
		23:35f generation	11:50f generation

In other words, Luke A 20:45-47 counterparts virtually all of Mk 12:37-40. From Matthew's long vituperative ("child of hell") extension of the Mark passage, Luke B takes some of the least offensive paragraphs, and rearranges them in a Pharisee story of his own, which may be read consecutively in Lk 11:37-12:1. There, a Pharisee invites Jesus to dine with him, and the accusations ("woes") of Jesus then follow.

But Luke also has a quite separate Pharisee story, in Lk 14:1-24. It begins, "One Sabbath when he went to dine at the house of a ruler who belonged to the Pharisees." In *this* dinner scene, Jesus meets the usual objections to Sabbath healing (not in fact spoken by anyone), and heals a man with dropsy. "And they could not reply to him." His rebuke to those who "chose the places of honor" is again received silently. Jesus proceeds to state a theory of gift and repayment which exactly mirrors the core idea of Luke's Sermon on the Plain. It is received with enthusiasm, "When one of those who sat at table with him heard this, he said to him, Blessed is he who shall eat bread in the Kingdom of God!" Jesus follows with a warning against confidence in the Kingdom: the Parable of the Feast. This has a Matthean counterpart. and it is easily shown that the Lukan version is prior.[3] The directionality is Lk > Mt, and we must assign the Lk 14 dinner to Luke A. And what author in his right mind really needs two Dinners with Pharisees stories? The local directionalities and the literary probabilities together suggest that Luke A has followed Mk 12:37-40, and that Luke B (in 11:37f) later added material from Matthew's extensions to Mark.

[2]Mt 23:14 is missing in the best texts.

[3]See Brooks **Acts-Luke** 152.

But why? What is sensitive Luke doing with this hell-and-damnation stuff from Matthew? Perhaps it is a matter of market share. Matthew's Gospel followed Luke's (that is, Luke A) at a very short interval, and quickly gained widespread acceptance.[4] Luke's adjustments, most conspicuously his addition of a Birth Narrative in Lk 1-2,[5] seem to have been meant to make his own Gospel more appealing to an audience which had proved receptive to the stronger medicine that Matthew was offering them.

PF. Mt 20:1-16. [The Wages of the Laborers in the Vineyard]. Single tradition. Why has Luke the lover of parables not used this congenial Matthean parable?

ABC. The Matthean parable asks: Why do they who converted late get the same reward (eternal life) as we who came early? The mathematical answer is that you cannot divide infinity. Luke A had treated that problem (the rejoicing over latecomers) in his Parables of Lost Things (Lk 15:3-7, 8-10, 11:32). Luke B, coming on Matthew's monetized and thus not at all congenial parable, feels no need to be taught by Matthew on this already-covered subject, and passes it by.

Was Matthew instead instructed by Luke? Gundry has shown[6] that Matthew's Parable of the Two Sons is a Matthean transform of Luke's Parable of the Lost Son (minus the abject poverty of Luke's original, which probably offended his high-budget sensibilities). Matthew more directly counterparts another of Luke A's three "Lost" parables: Mt 18:12-14 ‖ Lk 15:3-7. He seems to omit the other "Lost" parable, the Woman with the Lost Coin (Lk 15:8-10), perhaps because he has less interest in women characters than egalitarian Luke. But is it not possible that the woman's coin and the laborer's denarius may have something to do with each other? And that work on a great estate (the scene of his Vineyard and Two Sons parables) may be Matthew's preferred setting for transferred lessons of this kind? If so, then Matthew has made use of all three of Luke A's "Lost" parables.

However that may be, we end by suggesting that if the Luke A/B/C model is correct, it will no longer be enough to ask why "Luke" did or didn't do something. We must say, of the three now available, which "Luke" we mean. We have here tried to suggest that making that distinction can help clarify some otherwise puzzling questions – questions which any reader of Luke must somehow solve.

Works Cited

E Bruce Brooks. Acts-Luke. Alpha v1 (2017) 143-157
E Bruce Brooks. Apostolic Alignments. Alpha v1 (2017) 204-205.
Robert H Gundry. Matthew. Eerdmans 1982
Robert H Gundry. Matthew's Parable of the Two Sons. Alpha v1 (2017) 133-135
Édouard Massaux. The Influence of the Gospel of Matthew on Christian Literature before Saint Irenaeus. 1950; 3v Mercer 1990-1993

[4]For the date of Matthew, see the extended discussion in Gundry **Matthew** 599-609; for its popularity, see Massaux **Influence**.

[5]For the secondarity of Lk 1-2, see Brooks **Acts-Luke** 130, citing Fitzmyer.

[6]Gundry **Matthew** 421-424 or Gundry **Sons**.

Objections to Luke A/B/C

Joseph Verheyden

Katholieke Universiteit Leuven

(9 March 2014)

EDITORS' NOTE: These comments on Brooks **Acts-Luke** ("Luke A/B/C") were predistributed for the Alpha Christianity Seminar at the Eastern Great Lakes Biblical Society meeting on 28 Mar 2014. With the respondent's permission, that exchange has been revised for this volume of *Alpha.*

JV. In the Parable of the Talents and the Parable of the Feast, it is shown that each in turn has a more complicated version, which is regarded as the result of messing up an original simpler and more straightforward one. For the material that falls under Luke A > Matt [the Feast Parable], it is not proven that the latter had stood in Luke A.

ABC. Q proponents would presumably say that Luke has more accurately copied the original Q parable, and Matthew has copied it less accurately. The Luke A/B/C theory would say that Luke's is the more original form of the parable, which Matthew spoiled in the process of later adapting it. *These statements are formally equivalent.* The only difference is in whether there was a Q, which is precisely the point at issue.

JV. Luke A/B/C does not envision the possibility that Matthew/Luke may have been cleaning up an original messy text. If an author can mess up things in rewriting a "good" original, he must be "capable" of also composing messy stuff of his own (which others have to clean up).

ABC. That copying or adaptation can produce inconcinnity is the oldest principle in the book. If we run it backwards, the basis on which directionality decisions are made (including those lying behind IQP) simply vanishes. Luke, operating on his own, produces coherent text. That he wrote the incoherent Parable of the Minae, hoping that a future Matthew would fix it up, is not, in our view, a literarily plausible position.

Specifically, that Parable also contains a clear indication of secondarity in the change from Matthew's three servants to ten, a change which is abandoned later when Luke after all *reverts to three servants.* This is a perfect example of what Goodacre has called "editorial fatigue." It establishes the direction Mt > Lk, and shows that in this case the simpler story (Mt) is also the original story. Left to himself, Luke is fine. It is only *when taking over material from Matthew* that his judgement is liable to falter.

JV. The Beatitudes may prove that Matthew has expanded on a text like Luke 6:20b-22, not that it *was* Luke 6:20b-22.

ABC. Same point as above. We have functionally equivalent statements: Q > Mt or Lk > Mt. Note that this and the previous example together establish bidirectionality in the common Mt/Lk material. This bidirectionality refutes the Farrer-Goulder hypothesis (FGH), which allows only Mt > Lk. The only models which acknowledge that bidirectionality are Q and Luke A/B/C. The choice between them must rest on other evidence than bidirectionality as such. We may now proceed to that evidence.

JV. If it were Luke's intention to "outdo" Matthew, how explain that he writes up a messy text on the basis of a "clean" one in Luke 19?

ABC. Again the Parable of the Minae, Lk 19:11-27. We have seen that Luke may write problematic text when he is borrowing from Matthew, and this remains a fine example. Does it conflict with Luke's Birth Narrative, a prime example of Luke trying to *outdo* Matthew? Only if Luke's Birth Narrative, as a Luke B addition, creates inconsistencies with the rest of Luke. Which it does: (1) In the Birth Narrative John is Jesus' cousin; in Luke proper, at the Baptism scene, they meet instead as strangers. (2) In the Birth Narrative, John is said to be himself the herald of God's return to Israel. But in the Gospel proper (Luke A) John instead appears as *the herald of Jesus*.[1] The presence of intrusive material thus correlates with inconcinnities in the text.

JV. Matthew and Luke B are said to share an interest in "kingship," but they do not seem to share it always at the same moment, for when Luke B finds it in the Parable of the Feast (it is assumed that Luke B not only checked Matthew for material he did not yet have, but also for such material of which he could find a different version in Matthew), he hastens to do away with it.

ABC. Luke does not like Matthew's authority focus. He takes no special pleasure in listening to the screams of the damned (Mt 8:12, 13:42, 13:50, 22:13, 24:51, 25:30).[2] As Beare has noticed, it is pre-eminently in Matthew that we meet King Jesus, the all-powerful Christus Pantocrator. Why then does Luke B sometimes adopt Matthew's king theme? Presumably for the same reason that he sometimes adopted Matthew's miracle theme (not alone in the Birth Narrative): because it was popular. Massaux has shown how quickly Matthew became the Gospel of choice in Christian leadership circles. Is it not reasonable that Luke should wish to get a bit of what was working for Matthew, to secure for his own Gospel at least a share of the future?

Luke introduces a Kingship detail when he adapts Matthew's Talents Parable, with disastrous results which have been hilariouly chronicled by Goulder. Perhaps Luke thought that the image of a Returning King would evoke Jesus' return at the Last Days, or perhaps he wanted to allude to the journey of Archelaus to Rome to claim his father Herod the Great's kingdom as heir, a claim opposed by a delegation of 50 sent to Rome (Josephus Ant 17/9:1-3). Perhaps he thought both. This would merely be an example of the confusion likely to result from handling somebody else's material.

The uses of the word "king" in Luke outside the Birth Narrative and the Trial scene are exactly two:

- Lk 14:31. Example of a king going to war unprepared.
- Lk 19:38. The disciples hail "the King who comes in the name of the Lord."

Both are Luke A. Lk 14:31 makes fun of a heedless king; it does not attest a Lukan interest in Kingship. In Lk 19:38, Luke has dropped Mark's "the kingdom of our father David that is coming" (retained in Mt 21:9), presumably to avoid a conflict with Jesus' admission (Mk 12:35-37a = Lk 20:41-44) that he is *not* a descendant of David.

---

[1] It has been plausibly suggested that Luke's Birth Narrative here draws on Baptist tradition.

[2] The only Lukan instance, Luke 13:28, is a Luke B borrowing from Mt 8:12.

Neither passage can be said to show a Lukan inclination toward a King motif. What Luke does show is a concern to clean up Mark's sometimes careless narrative. So Luke A, consistent with his emphasis on lowliness, has nothing going in the King department, and when Luke B, playing catch-up with Matthew, adds that detail, he royally louses up. So much for the idea that Luke A or B had "an interest in kingship." What Luke B had that Luke A did not was an interest in retaining market share.

JV. And when, apparently under the benign influence of Matthew, he finally redeems his earlier position of staunchly rejecting the possibility that the wealthy can be saved and now goes for "a more accepting attitude" (assuming there really is a contradiction here in Luke), he seems to have forgotten that he once with equal enthusiasm had argued for the opposite. A few strokes of the pen would have spared him this embarrassment.

ABC. No doubt the Lazarus story (the rich man is condemned to eternal torment) and the Zacchaeus story (the rich man may be saved if he restores ill-gotten gains and gives alms), differ importantly. The question is, why did not Luke B delete Lazarus to avoid that inconsistency? The answer is that authority texts can add, but they cannot delete and *still retain acceptance among those to whom they are already familiar*. The whole premise of an authority text is that it is a reliable resource for the reader. If part of it is later acknowledged as no longer operative, the text reduces its own credibility. Authority texts are not read once and then discarded; in their nature, they are repeated. Their audience knows them. Their familiarity is part of their authority.[3]

Comment
The Editors

The above queries did not touch on the proposed restoration of the Luke A version of the so-called Travel Narrative, Lk 9:51-8:14. This however is one of the chief points at which the two theories can be judged. It is required by the Q hypothesis (as by the FG hypothesis) that Luke, whatever his sources, was written *on one occasion*. Any inconsistencies in the text are thus inexplicable on the assumption of a rational author. The Luke A/B/C model provides for multiple stages of composition, and sees internal inconsistencies as changes in the strategy of the author, or as unintended artifacts of the author updating his own previous text. Luke A's "Travel Narrative" appears, on the A/B/C theory, as a heretofore unsuspected specimen of early Christian paraenesis. The convincing character of that reconstruction may perhaps be counted as evidence for the explanatory power of the Luke A/B/C model.

Works Cited

E Bruce Brooks. Acts-Luke. Alpha v1 (2017) 143-157
E Bruce Brooks. Luke's Sermon on the Way. Alpha v1 (2017) 167-179
E Bruce Brooks. The Reader in the Text. Alpha v1 (2017) 23-27
Mark Goodacre. Fatigue in the Synoptics. NTS v44 (1998) 45-58
Michael D Goulder. Luke: A New Paradigm. 2v Sheffield 1989

[3]For one device employed by texts in dealing with their earlier states, see Brooks **Reader**.

Later Texts and Tendencies

Judas Armed and Dangerous

Keith L Yoder

University of Massachusetts at Amherst

GPG (8 Apr 2010)

The portrayal of Judas in the arrest scene in the Gospel of John (Jn 18:3) is surprisingly different from that in the Synoptics. One difference turns on the Greek word λαβών. I find that John presents a negatively enhanced version of that in Luke, which already moves away from Mark and Matthew.

John 18:3. Here is the RSV translation, with my parenthesized annotations:

> So Judas, procuring (λαβών "having taken") a band of soldiers (σπεῖραν "cohort") and some officers from the chief priests and the Pharisees, went (ἔρχεται "he comes") there with lanterns and torches and weapons.

And here is the parallel passage in Mark 14:43:

> And immediately, while he was still speaking, Judas came, one of the Twelve, and with him (μετ' αὐτοῦ) a crowd with sword and clubs, from the chief priests and the scribes and the elders.

Matthew 26:47 has only minor changes from Mark 14:43. But Luke 22:47 begins to move away from his predecessors, in the direction that John took in Jn 18:3:

> While he was still speaking, there came a crowd, and the man called Judas, one of the Twelve, was leading (προήρχετο "going before") them. He drew near to Jesus to kiss him.

Note the progression from accompanying (Mk) to leading (Lk) the arrest band.

Beyond the Synoptics. I observe the following three features in John 18:3:

1. Judas procured or "took" the arrest band, rather than coming "with" them or "leading" them. What does "take" (dictionary form λαμβάνω) mean? Commentators harmonize it with the Synoptics in two ways: (a) Carson, following Bruce, reads "guiding,"[1] which harmonizes John with Luke, but "guide" is not listed for λαμβάνω in Danker, nor does Carson cite Greek parallels, so the case seems weak. (b) Others read λαβών as "with" in the sense of accompanying, thus harmonizing John with Mark. Danker 583b: "The ptc can here be rendered by the prep 'with' . . . 'he came with a detachment.'" Danker cites five passages in support of this reading:

> • Sophocles Trachiniae line 259. "When he [Heracles] had been purified, he gathered λαβών a mercenary army and went ἔρχεται against the city of Eurytus." This is the closest parallel to Jn 18:3. It uses the same verbs in the same order, but it does not support Danker's reading of λαβών as "with" or "accompanying" this army: rather, Heracles procured it and is in charge of it.

---

[1] Carson **John** 577: "It is mere pedantry that understands the participle labōn to mean that Judas was 'taking' the troops to Jesus, as if he had the authority to command them."

• Greek Apocalypse of Ezra 6:17. "For the Lord, having taken λαβών a numerous army of many angels, said λέγει to the prophet . . . " Same verb, and once again the Lord "takes" and is obviously in charge of this angelic army; he is not simply "with" them.[2]

• Hebrews 9:19. "He took λαβών the blood of calves and goats, with water and scarlet wool and hyssop, and sprinkled ἐρράντισε both the book itself and all the people." Danker translates "with the blood he sprinkled the people." But this is "with" in an instrumental sense, not as simple accompaniment. So far, reading λαβών in Jn 18:3 as "taking and being in charge of" is preferable.

(Danker's last two references have the same instrumental sense as Hb 9:19, and thus also fail to establish the simple accompaniment meaning).

Danker's suggestion of λαβών as "with" may hold for *instrumental* "with," but not if we take "with" as meaning simple accompaniment. Danker does not make that distinction explicit, and so encourages a Mk-harmonistic interpretation of the passage. Interpretation (a), λαβών as "guiding," is more nearly in the right direction, but that specific sense seems not to be attested. Danker's citations actually support the stronger sense "take, procure," as in Sophocles.

2. A Roman "cohort" σπεῖρα was part of the group, and the group is an organized arrest force of soldiers and temple police, not a simple "crowd." Many take from the word "cohort" the inference that John was not pro-Roman (or anti-Semitic) after all; John implicates the Romans from the start in the death of Jesus. Whether "cohort" here indicates a full 600 men or something less, I suggest John may have a different motive: rather than saying something about the Romans, "cohort" is really saying something about Judas. Judas is so important (and evil) that he was in charge not only of the Jewish officers sent to arrest Jesus, he was even in charge of a Roman cohort.

Possibly John simply transposed the σπεῖρα from the mocking scene at Mk 15:16, which scene John completely omits, to Jesus' arrest here in Jn 18:3. As to John's intent to magnify the role of Judas, consider the next paragraph.

3. Judas himself, and not the band/crowd, "comes (singular verb ἔρχεται) with torches and lamps and weapons." Mark's word order (in Mk 14:43) is " . . . Judas approaches, one of the Twelve, and with him a crowd with swords and clubs from the high priests and the scribes and the elders . . ." John 18:3 transposes the word order, so that not only does Judas "take" the arrest band in his charge, but it is now Judas, not the crowd, who "comes with" the torches and weapons.

So John paints Judas with his arms full of torches and weapons. Even if we envision them as carried by the soldiers and officers, the writers's word order suggests that Judas is in charge of the weapons, no matter who is carrying them. Luke took the weapons out of his description to concentrate on Judas, but John brings them back, putting them in Judas' possession and/or control. Luke moves away from Mk/Mt with a negatively enhanced picture of Judas advancing *at the head* of the arresting band; John goes further in putting him *in charge* of the band and their weapons.

[2]Charlesworth 1/578; Greek text from Tischendorf **Apocalypses** 31.

But John is also concerned to magnify the power of Jesus. First, he gives Jesus foreknowledge of the arrest (Jn 18:4, Jesus "knew all that was coming on upon him"). Once contact is made, Jesus is in charge; Judas is merely one of the crowd (Jn 18:5, "Judas the betrayer was standing with them"). His identification of Jesus with a kiss (Mk 14:45, Mt 26:49, already resisted in Lk 22:47 "*drew near* to Jesus to kiss him") is given instead to Jesus, who says "I am he" Ἐγώ εἰμι. At this, in acknowledgment of Jesus' power, the soldiers and Judas "draw back and fall to the ground" (Jn 18:6).

Appendix: Formal Emphasis

Judas in John. In his passion narrative, John makes Judas the first in a list of the six parties responsible for Jesus' crucifixion. The literary device he uses for each of the six, plus one repeat for a total of seven, is ὁ "the" + οὖν "then" + [subject]:

Jn 18:3	ὁ οὖν Ἰούδας	"then [the] Judas"
Jn 18:12	Ἡ οὖν σπεῖρα	"then the cohort"
Jn 18:19	ὁ οὖν ἀρχιερεύς	"then the high-priest"
Jn 19:13	ὁ οὖν Πιλᾶτος	"then [the] Pilate"
Jn 19:23	οἱ οὖν σρατιῶται	"then the soldiers"
Jn 19:24	οἱ μὲν οὖν σρατιῶται	"so then the soldiers"
Jn 19:31	οἱ οὖν Ἰουδαῖοι	"then the Jews"

This sequence is used only these seven times in John's passion narrative, including all, and only, those responsible for Jesus' death. There may be an intentional echo between the first and last, Judas, the first enemy, being connected by his name with the last enemy, the Jews: Ἰούδας ~ Ἰουδαῖοι.

Comment
E Bruce Brooks (GPG, 8 Apr 2010)

Keith has convincingly shown that the awfulness of Judas's action is progressively emphasized in the sequence Mk/Mt > Lk > Jn. I suggest that similar heightening can be seen between Mark and Matthew. Here are some corresponding passages:

Mk 14:10 . . . went to the chief priests in order to betray him to them
Mt 26:14f . . . went to the chief priests and said, What will you give me if I deliver him to you? [Mt is more vivid, and emphasizes Judas' initiative]

Mk 14:11a. And when they heard it they were glad . . .
Mt   [No direct parallel in Mt; the initiative is more exclusively with Judas]

Mk 14:11b . . . and promised to give him money
Mt 26:15b. And they paid him thirty pieces of silver [Mt is again more vivid].

Mk 14:17-21. [The disciples ask, one by one, if they are the betrayer; Jesus promises woe to the betrayer, whoever he is]
Mt 26:24. [Essentially parallel; no significant changes]

Mk   [no parallel in Mk at this point]
Mt 26:25. "Judas, who betrayed him, said, Is it I, Master? He said to him, You have said so" [The suspense is not dissipated, as in Mk, but is here brought to its climax in a direct identification]

And in the scene of the arrest, we have:

Mk 14:43 . . . and with him a crowd with swords and clubs . . .
Mt 26:47 . . . and with him a great crowd with swords and clubs . . . [the size
of the arresting force has been increased]

Mk 14:45 . . . and said, "Master!" And he kissed him.
Mt 26:49 . . . and said, "Hail, Master!" And he kissed him [Judas' greeting is
more friendly, and thus more false, than the one in Mk]

Mk   [no parallel text]
Mt 26:50. Jesus said to him, "Friend, why are you here?" [The irony of the
salutation "Friend" continues the previous note; the betrayal is emphasized]

In this comparison, Matthew comes across as a consistent if subtle intensification of
Mark's story: the greed of Judas, his leading role in the betrayal (gained by slightly
muting the initiative of the chief priests), and the more vivid and sinister detail, from
"thirty pieces of silver" (Zechariah 11:12-14; so like Matthew to let Scripture drive his
story) to the treacherous salutation "Hail." In this way the initiative and the falseness
of Judas are more apparent to the hearer than was the case in Mark. The writer of John
was surely a dramatist, but Matthew, it seems to me, here operates in a dramatic way
on his Markan source.

If so, then we have, through all four Gospels, a Judas Trajectory development, in
which each stage in turn magnifies and intensifies the perfidy of Judas, in the order

Mk > Mt > Lk > Jn

The Trajectory is evidence for that order of the Gospels, or at any rate of their final
compositional states. Similar trajectories can be demonstrated for the divinization of
Jesus and the respect and sympathy shown to Mary, for the decreasing prominence of
Jesus' baptism, and for the increasing prominence of Jerusalem in the story of Jesus.[3]
Except for the last, which is probably a reflection of the transfer of the center of the
Jesus movement from Galilee to Jerusalem, and is thus merely circumstantial, none of
these developments is very likely to have run in the opposite direction. Taken together,
they would appear to put the priority of Mark beyond serious doubt.

Works Cited

E Bruce Brooks. Four Gospel Trajectories. Alpha v1 (2017) 15-16
F F Bruce. The Gospel of John. Eerdmans 1983
D A Carson. The Gospel According to John. Eerdmans 1991
James H Charlesworth. The Old Testament Pseudepigrapha. 2v Doubleday 1983, 1985
Frederick William Danker. Greek-English Lexicon of the New Testament [BDAG].
   3ed Chicago 2000
Konstantin von Tischendorf (ed). Apocalypses Apocryphae . . . 1866; Olms 1966

[3]See Brooks **Four**. To the developmental sequences there mentioned, there may now be
added a fifth: a Judas Trajectory.

Gematria and John 21

Keith L Yoder
University of Massachusetts at Amherst
GPG (28 Dec 2013)

Richard Bauckham notes the use of gematria in John 21,[1] and given other passages where that feature exists, concludes that the whole Gospel, including John 21, is integral. I find, on the contrary, that gematria links Jn 21 with passages which for other reasons are late in the formation history of John, and is thus consistent with the von Wahlde three-stage formation model.

Bauckham's Argument for the integrity of Jn 21 may be summarized as follows:

1. Jn 21 is not a "second ending: to the book, but rather an "epilogue." There are already seven "signs" in Jn 2-20, including the Resurrection, which is called a "sign" in 2:18-19, so the catch of 153 fish is not one of the "signs" of Jn.

2. The Prologue (Jn 1:1-18) consists of 496 syllables. 496 is both a "triangular" number (496 = the triangle of 31 = the sum of digits 1 through 31) and a "perfect" number (the sum of its divisors). 496 is also the number of the word "only-begotten" (μονογενής) in Greek gematria.[2] He proceeds to show that chapter 21 consists of 496 words, after excluding 8 words that the NA27 critical text marked as doubtful, making a numerical match for the 496 syllables of the Prologue.

3. He notes that each of the two "endings," 20:30-31 and 21:24-25, contains 43 words. He concludes from that match that these are not separate endings, but rather two "stages" of a single unified ending, the first stage (20:31) references many other "signs" Jesus did, while the second stage (21:24-25) cites many other "things" Jesus did, there being no additional "signs" in Jn 21.

4. He notes that the "epilogue" part of Jn 21 falls into two sections, 21:1-14 and 21:25-23, and each section contains exactly 276 words. Like 496, 276 is also a "triangular" number, the triangle of 23.

5. While there is no gematria in Jn 21 equivalent to μονογενής in the Prologue, the number of 153 fish stands out in 21:11. 153 is the triangle of 17.

6. The key words of the "first stage ending" 20:30-31 are "sign," "believe," "Christ," and "life." Jn 20:30-31 represents the last occurrence in Jn of each of these four key words. Their usage counts in Jn are as follows:

"sign" σημεῖον	= 17
"believe" πιστεύω	= 98
"Christ" Χριστός	= 19
"life" ζωή	= 36

---

[1]Bauckham **153.**

[2]To this point, Bauckham relies on Menken **Numerical.**

Alpha v1 (2017)

7. The sum of the last three numbers (98 + 19 + 36) = 153, which is the "triangle" of the first number, 17. Thus, the catch of 153 big fish in Jn 21 is encoded in the counts of the key words of the first ending 20:30-31; counts that encompass the entire Jn. The number relationship 17 => 98 + 19 + 36 also matches the thematic relationship presented in 20:30-31. That is, as a result of the (17) signs, many people (the 153 "fish") will be brought to "believe" in "Christ" and have "life." Bauckham's conclusion (p282) is, "This phenomenon is surely attributable only to an author who meticulously designed the whole Gospel, including chapter 21, and intended the explicit appearance of the number 153 in chapter 21 as an integral feature of his Gospel."

I have checked all of Bauckham's word and syllable counts and his gematria calculations, and can confirm their accuracy. And I agree with him (and with Menken) that at least the final author/editor of Jn had an interest in word/syllable counts and gematria. But his conclusion, that this requires Jn 21 to be part of the original design of Jn, is flawed. Fortna and von Wahlde envision a final editor of Jn who not only (re)designed the Prologue and the Jn 21 epilogue, but also rewrote the rest of the Gospel in between. Bauckham's argument would carry weight only if the final editor of Jn simply tacked a new Prologue to the beginning and a new Epilogue to the ending of a pre-existing codex. But that is not what Fortna and von Wahlde envision. They both propose a final author/editor who rewrote the entire pre-existing Jn document, and could move text around and/or tinker with various key word counts at will. Making the counts of the key words in 20:30-31 come out to the 17:153 match between the "signs" and the "fish" would have been a trivial matter.

Bauckham notes the "disciple" word count of 77 as the only other key word in Jn that seems to have "significance" (p281 n32). With all his attention to numerical detail, he has missed the fact that Ἰουδαῖος "Jew" occurs 71 times (Dunn **Jews** p182), which I find "significant," as 71 is the traditional number of members of the "Great Sanhedrin" of the "Jews," the Johannine Jesus' first and last enemy.[3]

In sum, I think Bauckham, and Menken before him, are to be commended for pointing out these numerological features of Jn. But his numerological argument for the integrity of Jn 21 is after all compatible with the theory that the final writer/editor of Jn was responsible for these features. The proposal of text development from earlier edition(s) or pre-Johannine source(s) would seem to be left standing.

The Problem of 153 Fish (John 21:11)

Bauckham cites J A Emerton's proposal that the source of the 153 is the catch of "many large fish" in Ezekiel 47:10. The gematria of the place names in that vision (Gedi גדי and Eglayim עגלים) are 17 and 153 respectively. He further notes that the gematria of בני אלהים, the Hebrew equivalent of "children of God" (τέκνα Θεοῦ) from Jn 1:12 is also 153. He cites in support the allusions to Ezekiel 47 in Jn 7:38 and 19:34. He emphasizes that the 153 fish symbolize the many "children of God" who will come to believe in Jesus as the result of Apostolic preaching.

---

[3]Thus m.Sanhedrin; see Neusner **Mishnah** p584.

More recently, Brooke has found a connection between these two numbers in the contemporary scripture exegesis of the Commentary on Genesis in 4Q252. This document has Noah's ark coming to rest on Mt Ararat on the 153rd day after the start of the Flood, also stated to be the 17th day of the 7th month, the Sabbath eve in the octave of Sukkoth.[4] So, if the Hebrew place name gematria of Ezekiel 47:10 connects 153 with "many big fish," the exegesis of 4Q252 also connects 153 (and 17) with the Noahic tradition elsewhere associated with Simon Peter, the man pulling the fish ashore all by himself in Jn 21:11.

Comment
E Bruce Brooks

The 153 fish have long been a problem for scholarship. Brown 2/1074f gives a detailed summary of major suggestions. The most plausible, it seems to me, is that the miraculous catch of fish in Jn 21 has the same meaning as the miraculous catch of fish in Lk 5:9-10: the future success of the missionary effort. It was Jerome who first suggested that the number 153 was the number of fish known to the Greek zoologists, and thus is a metaphor for "all kinds of men," emphasizing the variety of people called to Christ (compare Mt 13:47, "fish of every kind"). Jerome cites Oppian of Cilicia (c180) as "the most learned poet among the Greek zoologists." It has been objected that Oppian actually mentions, not 153, but rather 157, kinds of fish. In the light of the above, which establishes the fact that triangular numbers were of formative interest to the final author of Jn, may it not suffice to say that to this meaningless number 157, the final author preferred the nearby triangular number 153?

As to the deep meaning of 17, there may be none. We may as well ask, of the seemingly intentional and identical syllable counts of the Prologue and the Epilogue (496, the triangle of 31), why 31? The triangularity of 496 may be magic enough.

Not that any reader would have made that count, but it is useful to know that the final author of Jn liked to amuse himself in this way, and that his amusement may sometimes have affected the construction of the Gospel as we have it.

Works Cited

Richard Bauckham. The 153 Fish and the Unity of the Fourth Gospel; in Bauckham, The Testimony of the Beloved Disciple, Baker 2007

George J Brooke. 4Q252 and the 153 Fish of John 21.11; in The Dead Sea Scrolls and the New Testament, Fortress (2005) 287-297

Raymond E Brown. The Gospel According to John. 2v Doubleday 1966, 1970

James D G Dunn (ed). Jews and Christians. Mohr 1992

J A Emerton. Hundred and Fifty-Three Fishes in John xxi.11. JTS v9 (1958) 86-89

J A Emerton. Some New Testament Notes. JTS v11 (1960) 335-356

M J J Menken. Numerical Literary Techniques in John. Brill 1985

Jacob Neusner. The Mishnah: A New Translation. Yale 1988.

Urban C von Wahlde. The Gospel and Letters of John. 3v Eerdmans 2010

---

[4]Brooke **4Q252** 289.

Apostolic Alignments

E Bruce Brooks

University of Massachusetts at Amherst

(14 March 2016)

The New Testament canon was still fluid in the 4c, as witness the presence of Barnabas and Hermas in Codex Sinaiticus. But already in the late 1c we see an interest in the authority claims of texts. Papias, defending Mark in the early 2c, is a later voice in that discussion. Additions made to many texts identify those texts with an Apostle. The names at the top of the list of acceptable Apostles were Paul and Peter.

Paul

Paul's letters (plus the editorial Colossians) were the first Christian canon. Then:

• **2 Timothy** (probably by Timothy), by including an invented farewell address by Paul, sought to increase the prominence of Timothy in the Paul movement by making him, and not Onesimus or another, **Paul's** designated heir.

• **Acts II** (from 15:36 onward) shifts its narrative emphasis entirely to **Paul**, and in its "we" passages, claims companion status for Luke, the author of Acts.

• **Hebrews** (by Apollos; see 1 Cor 1:12), at first without indication of author, was converted to a **Pauline** Epistle by adding the Heb 13:22-25 personalia.

Peter

No writing can be credibly attributed to Peter, but his importance was great.

• **Matthew** downplays Peter in favor of more equal treatment of all the Twelve, but the later Mt 16:18-19 identifies **Peter** as the Rock of the future Church.

• **John** makes the "Beloved Disciple" (John Zebedee) constantly upstage Peter (Jn 13:21f, 18:15f, 19:26f, 20:3f). The added Jn 21[1] instead assigns the future care of the flock to **Peter** (Jn 21:14, 16, 17).

• **1 Peter**, originally an anonymous baptismal homily (1 Pet 1:3–4:11), received additions which encouraged those suffering exclusion from the synagogues, and added **Peter** as the writer of that text, now transformed into an Epistle.

• **2 Peter**, referring to 1 Peter (2 Pet 3:1) but in a very different style, swallows Judas (which had aligned itself with Jacob the Brother of Jesus, then thought to be the author of the Epistle of Jacob) and converts it into a **Petrine** text. It counters 2 Timothy by seeming to contain *Peter's* last testament (2 Pet 1:13-15, compare the prediction of Peter's death in Jn 21:18-19).

• Papias (early 2c) defended Mark as deriving from the preaching of **Peter**.

Paul and Peter were becoming the two poles of the Alpha/Beta theological argument.

---

[1]Perhaps based on an early version of the Gospel of Peter. I regard it as John E, Jn 16-17 as John D, Jn 15 (with 16-17, also queried by Wellhausen) as John C, and the rest as John A/B.

Ecumenical

There is also a tendency to reconcile Peter and Paul, in both directions:

- **Gal 2:7-8**, an editorial interpolation, calls **Peter**, but not Paul, an apostle.[2]
- **Acts I** (to 15:35) symmetrizes the two: **Peter** is the first to convert a Gentile.
- **1 Peter 5:12** uses **Paul's** associate "Silvanus" as an amanuensis.
- **2 Peter 3:15-16** refers to "our beloved brother **Paul**," while acknowledging some difficulties with the Pauline writings.

Other Shifting Affiliations

A Gospel connection was desirable for at least one previously unaffiliated text:

- **Didache**, a circular liturgical advisory text, in its final layer absorbs material from Matthew (and some from Luke), and adds an End Days section based on Matthew, which in another place is called "the Gospel of our Lord" (Did 8:2).[3]

Some texts affiliated with Jacob the Lord's Brother later shifted to a member of the recognized Twelve. For Judas, see above. Another shift from Jacob the Brother is:

- **The Gospel of Thomas**, whose probable core (gTh 1-12, note gTh 12) had aligned itself with Jacob the Lord's Brother, later (Introduction and gTh 13) claimed an association instead with Thomas, who was neither Peter nor Paul, but was at least an officially recognized member of the Jesus Twelve.[4]

The Judas > 2 Peter rewrite abandons Judas' reference to Enoch (Judas 14, compare Heb 11:5), a contemporary Jewish text. Enoch may have been experiencing disesteem among the Rabbinic authorities, who at that time (post-70) were presumably in charge of defining the Hebrew Scriptures, on which the Christians and their texts also relied.

All this implies a late 1c shakeout in the list of accepted authority figures, and a scramble of texts to be associated with the top names. Behind the scramble, in the Pastorals (after 70) and the rulings of Jamnia (also after 70), as the Post-Apostolic Age got itself gradually underway, we seem to sense the presence of new decision makers, scrutinizing authority claims and making authority choices.

Works Cited

E Bruce Brooks. The Didache. Alpha v1 (2017) 48-57

E Bruce Brooks. The Epistle of Jacob. Alpha v1 (2017) 58-70

E Bruce Brooks. Acts-Luke. Alpha v1 (2017) 143-157

E Bruce Brooks. Paul's Editors. Alpha v1 (2017) 121-126

E Bruce Brooks. Thomas A. Alpha v1 (2017) 198-201

William O Walker Jr. Galatians 2:8 and the Question of Paul's Apostleship; in Paul and His Legacy (Polebridge 2015) 29-35

Julius Wellhausen. Erweiterungen und Änderungen im vierten Evangelium. Reimer 1907

---

[2]See Walker **Question**, and for further detail on the editorial process, Brooks **Editors**.

[3]There follows the Matthean version of the Lord's Prayer (Mt 6:9-13). See also Did 15:3 (compare Mt 18:15-18) and Did 15:4 (Mt 6:1-4, 5-15), and for further detail, Brooks **Didache**.

[4]He was also the *twin*, not merely the *brother*, of Jesus, a more convincing kind of intimacy. For Jacob and Thomas as later Gnostic authority figures, see further Brooks **Thomas A**.

Thomas A

E Bruce Brooks

University of Massachusetts at Amherst

(21 March 2016)

Formation models have been suggested for the Gospel of Thomas.[1] I here propose a core comprising sayings §1-12 (my "Thomas A"), which *do not mention* Thomas, but have instead Jacob, the Brother of Jesus, as their authority figure.

Inventory. DeConick divides the 12 sayings into 20 passages; I subdivide further. I here give most of her Gospel parallels, and recognize a few others (in *italics*):

1 (§1)	Who finds the meaning of these will not die.				Jn
2 (§2:1)	Who seeks should seek until he finds.				
(§2:2-4)	When he finds, he will be amazed, be king, rest.				
3 (§3:1-2)	The Kingdom is not in heaven or in the sea.			Lk	
(§3:3)	The Kingdom is inside you and outside you			Lk	
4 (§3:4)	Who knows himself will find it.				
5 (§3:5)	You will know you are children of the Father.				
6 (§4:1)	Ask a little child about the place of life.				
7 (§4:2-3)	Many who are last will be first.	Mk	Mt	Lk	
8 (§4:4)	And they will become single people.				
9 (§5:1)	Understand what is in front of you.				
(§5:2)	Nothing hidden will not be manifested	Mk	Mt	Lk	
10 (§6:1)	How to fast or pray or give alms.	*Mk*	*Mt*	*Lk*	
11 (§6:2)	Do not tell lies.				
12 (§6:3)	And what you hate, do not do.		Mt	*Lk*	
13 (§6:4)	Everything faced with truth is brought to light.			*Lk*	
14 (§6:5)	Nothing hidden will not be manifested.	Mk	Mt	Lk	
15 (§7:1-2)	Blessed is the lion that the man will eat.				
16 (§8:1-3)	The wise fisherman keeps the large fish.		Mt		
17 (§8:4)	Who has ears to hear should listen.	Mk	Mt	Lk	
18 (§9:1-5)	Parable of the sower.	Mk	Mt	Lk	
19 (§10)	I have cast fire upon the world.			Lk	
20 (§11:1)	Heaven will pass away.	Mk	Mt	Lk	
21 (§11:2)	The dead are not alive; the living will not die.				
(§11:3-4)	When you were one, you became two.				
22 (§12:1)	We know you are going to leave us.				*Jn*
23 (§12:2)	Go to Jacob the Righteous One.				

Whatever may be the directionality between Thomas and these Gospel counterparts, we may get a better idea of the text's own ideology by first considering those sayings which are *without* obvious Gospel counterparts.

---

[1] For a review of stratification proposals, see Plisch 15-26, Pokorný 20-25, Skinner 240-28. For DeConick's own idea of the Thomas core ("kernel"), see **Original** 25-31.

Thomas A Sayings Without Gospel Counterparts[2]

The text looks a little different for those familiar with eastern meditation tradition. Some of these non-Gospel sayings have parallels with Chinese meditation sayings in the Dàu/Dv́ Jīng (DDJ), Gwǎndž 49, the Nèi Yè (NY) or "Inner Working," and the Mencius (MC), all from the late 04c and early 03c:

2 (§2:2-4). "And when he finds, [he will be amazed. And] when he is [amazed], he will be a king. And [once he is a king], he will rest."[3] For kingship, we have NY 9:6 能君萬物 "will be able to master all things." The final goal of Chinese (and Indian) meditation is repose (níng 寧, NY 3:9) or tranquility (jìng 靜, NY 5:13).

4 (§3:4). Self-knowledge as the key to higher knowledge. Chinese meditation begins with the self (Nèi Yè 內業 means "The Inner Enterprise") and ends with the universe. For the latter, see NY 19:2 萬物備存 "all things [the pleroma] will abide," and MC 7A4 萬物皆備於我矣 "all things are complete in me." For the former, see §5:1 below.

5 (§3:5). "Children of the Father" has no *Gospel* counterpart, but compare 1 Jn 3:2, "Beloved, we are God's children now." Exclude from consideration here.

6 (§4:1). "Ask a little child." In Mk 10:14, Jesus implies that even children can understand (salvation is not a monopoly of the learned scribes), but children as *sources* of wisdom are different. For the infant as complete in virtue, and thus as a model of understanding, see DDJ 10 and DDJ 55 含德之厚，比於赤子 "He who holds virtue in its fulness, I would compare to an infant." The infant is near to the moment of birth, and therefore is also nearer to the soul's higher origin, and recalls it.

8 (§4:4). "They will become single people." That the higher beings are ungendered is clear in Mk 12:25 ("as the angels in Heaven"), but this merging of genders is different. One way to avoid sexual *desire* is to get rid of sexual *distinctions*.

11 (§6:2). DeConick notes parallels in Jacob 3:14, Col 3:9, Eph 4:25. These are not Gospel sayings, but are indebted to other Christian literature. Exclude.

15 (§7:1-2). The lion and the human are the animal and higher aspects of man. Which will eliminate ("eat") the other? For the danger of sexual desire to meditation, see NY 12:5, 不以官亂心 "Don't disturb your mind with sensory input."

21a (§11:2). "The dead are not alive, and the living will not die." Those who have Life will keep it. Compare the warning in NY 6:6-7 人之所失以死，所得以生也 "when people lose it, they die; when they get it, they live," referring to the secret Way, the path to the true self which begins with meditation.

21b (§11:3-4). "When you were one, you became two. When you are two, what will you do?" As in §4:4 above, the theme is the obliteration of gender distinctions, and ultimately, the elimination of the ground of sexual desire. The saying concludes with a challenge to the reader, to renounce desire and follow the Way of Life.

For analytical purposes, it turns out that the category of "Gospel saying" needs to be expanded to encompass "Christian saying."

[2]Translations of Thomas (sometimes slightly adapted) are from DeConick **Original**.
[3]From the Greek of POxy 654:5-9. The presumably later Coptic text differs.

The Non-Christian Sayings as the Thomas A Core

Which came first, the Gospel echoes, or the others? Is this text a Christianization of something older, or is it a heretical departure from an originally Christian position? If, as an experiment, we list only the non-Christian sayings, we get the following:

[Finding Rest]
2. Seek persistently, and you will find rest.

[The Secret]
4. The secret is within you.
6. Your child self remembers it.

[The Dangers of Sexual Desire]
8.Eliminate the dangers of attraction between the sexes.
15. Beware of carnal distractions ("the lion"), or they will consume you.

[Challenge]
21a. Those who have life will live.
21b. What will you do, since you now dwell in the realm of sexual desire?

[Conclusion].
23. Recommendation of the text patron, Jacob.

It seems that these form a reasonable progression; a small but coherent treatise on how to escape – individually, not, as with the Last Days expectation, simultaneously – from the troubles of the world. The heart of the message, avoidance of sexual desire, is now interspersed by Christian echoes which teach other things. The implication is that the non-Christian sayings are primary, and the Christian echoes are secondary.

Escaping from worldly troubles is characteristically Buddhist, as is the warning about sexual desire. It suffices to note the Eastern parallels (albeit in Chinese form), in terms of which the later identification of this text with Thomas, who was himself associated with India, the home of the meditation art, seems to make sense.

The ascent of Jesus to his divine origin in the Philippi Hymn (Php 2:6-11) may have been suggestive to the early Christians. What it may have suggested to them was that they too, if they knew how, might imitate Jesus by returning to *their* divine origin. This they would accomplish, not by following purity rules, but by self-knowledge. Philippi was the capital of Macedonia, from which Alexander had marched forth to conquer the world as far as the Indus.[4] Later information from the world beyond the Indus is not unlikely to have reached Alexander's capital in the years after Alexander. The location of that hymn, in that particular town, may thus not be accidental.

---

[4]After Alexander came the Maurya Empire. Megasthenes, the Seleucid ambassador to the court of the first Maurya ruler Chandragupta (Gk "Sandrakottos," r c0321-c0297), mentions (perhaps without understanding them very thoroughly) a group of prophets at the top of Indian society (Arrian Indica 11:1-8). By the time of Chandragupta's grandson Asoka (r c0268-0232), full resident Buddhist monasticism existed. Asoka sought to reform some of its abuses, and also to spread Buddhism beyond his own kingdom. For 05c Chinese knowledge of Buddhism and its meditation tradition, including familiarity with the Mahâ-Parinibbâna Sutta (describing the death and ascent of the Buddha), see Brooks **Reader** 27. Ideas about meditation seem to have reached the Mediterranean world from both of these sources. Early Christianity may not be fully intelligible except from what may be called a continental perspective.

Thomas A as the Thomas Core

There are reasons to see gThos 1-12 as a coherent text. First, the only authority mentioned is Jacob the Lord's Brother. Second, it is framed by echoes with the Gospel of John: §1 "who finds the meaning of these words will not die" ~ Jn 8:51 "Verily, verily, I say unto you, If a man keep my word, he shall never see death;" and §12:1"We know you are going to leave us" ~ Jn 14:19 "Yet a little while, and the world beholdeth me no more." This looks like a conscious literary device.

Jacob himself is plausible as the text authority; he is associated with several Gnostic texts at Nag Hammadi.[5] A close verbal link: §2:3-4 ("rise, reign, rest") occurs in one of those texts, the 2nd Apocalypse of Jacob.[6] And Jacob's incessant praying ("he used to enter alone into the Temple, and be found kneeling and praying . . . so that his knees grew hard like a camel's because of his constant worship of God"),[7] is compatible with the meditational character of the non-Synoptic passages.

The transition to Thomas' proprietorship in §13:1-8 rejects descriptions of Jesus by Peter ("righteous angel") and Matthew ("wise philosopher), for that of Thomas: Jesus is indescribable. Thomas is told "three words;" he refuses to divulge them lest he be stoned. The "three words" motif recurs in Acts of Thomas 47. Stoning is the penalty for blasphemy, and DeConick 85 suggests a claim that Jesus is God. Jesus in the Gospel of John claimed unique *access* to God; in §13, we have *identity* with God, a claim which surely amounts to blasphemy.

Affiliation shifts occur in several texts at this time, such as the Gospels of Matthew (aligning itself with Peter in Mt 16:18-19) and of John (the same, in Jn 21).[8] The shift from Jacob to Thomas here may also be in part a shift from the *brother* (Jacob) to the *twin* brother (Didymus Thomas) of Jesus – clearly, a more authoritative informant.

Works Cited

Harold W Attridge. The Acts of Thomas. Polebridge 2010

E Bruce Brooks. Apostolic Alignments. Alpha v1 (2017) 196-197

E Bruce Brooks. The Epistle of Jacob. Alpha v1 (2017) 58-70

E Bruce Brooks. Luke's Parable of the Canny Steward. Alpha v1 (2017) 158-166

E Bruce Brooks. Pliny at Pontus. Alpha v1 (2017) 209-214

E Bruce Brooks. The Reader in the Text. Alpha v1 (2017) 25-29

April D DeConick. The Original Gospel of Thomas in Translation. T & T Clark 2007

John Painter. Just James. T & T Clark 1999

Uwe-Karsten Plisch. The Gospel of Thomas. Deutsche Bibelgesellschaft 2008

Petr Pokorný. A Commentary on the Gospel of Thomas. Clark 2009

Harold D Roth. Original Tao [translation of Nèi Yè]. Columbia 1999

Christopher W Skinner. What Are They Saying About the Gospel of Thomas? Paulist 2012

[5]DeConick 50. For discussion of all the Jacob texts, see Painter **James** 159-181.

[6]A faint variant ("rest and reign") also occurs in a Thomas text (Acts of Thomas 136).

[7]Eusebius **History** 2/23:6, quoting Hegesippus (2c; see Painter **James** 119).

[8]See Brooks **Alignments**.

Yoḥanan ben Zakkai

E Bruce Brooks

University of Massachusetts at Amherst

(5 July 2016)

The usual view is that Yoḥanan ben Zakkai was the key figure in the transition from the Temple, after its destruction in 70, to a reinvented Rabbinic Judaism with its center at Yabneh (Jamnia) near the sea in Judaea. The earliest evidence is the mentions of Yoḥanan in the Mishnah, which according to Neusner[1] was closed in c200. These roughly confirm the usual view, along with some adulatory and hostile passages, and some which implausibly make Yoḥanan a teacher of Torah with five disciples. I here give the 30 Yoḥanan passages by group, numbered consecutively for later reference.

Seemingly Reportive (16)

2/1. Shabbat

[01] 16:7. [On the Sabbath] they cover a lamp with a dish, so that it will not scorch a rafter, and the excrement of a child,[2] and a scorpion, so that it will not bite. Said R Judah, A case came before Rabban Yoḥanan ben Zakkai in Arab,[3] and he said, I suspect [he is liable] for a sin offering.

[02] 22:3. [On the Sabbath] someone breaks a jar to eat dried figs from it . . . Said R Judah, A case came before Rabban Yoḥanan ben Zakkai in Arab, and he said, I fear on his account that he should bring a sin offering [for violating the Sabbath].[4]

2/4. Sheqalim

[03] 1:4. Said R Judah, Testified Ben Bukhri in Yabneh, Any priest who pays the sheqel does not sin. Said to him Rabban Yoḥanan ben Zakkai, Not so.[5] But any priest who does not pay the sheqel sins.

2/6. Sukkah

[04] 2:5. They brought Rabban Yoḥanan ben Zakkai some cooked food to taste, and to Rabban Gamaliel two dates and a dipper of water. And they said, Bring them up to the sukkah. And when they gave to R Zadoq food less than an egg's bulk, he took it in a cloth and ate it outside of the sukkah and said no blessing after it.[6]

---

[1]Neusner **Mishnah** xvi. For his comments on the Yoḥanan passages see **Legend** 41-64.

[2]So the text. For another interpretation, interpreting all three actions as undertaken to prevent future injury, see Danby 114 n12.

[3]A Galilean town (Gk Garaba; Gabara); it supplied priests for the Temple rotation. Yoḥanan's cases concern Sabbath observance. Later tradition invents a curse on Galilee by Yoḥanan (y.Shabbat 16:8, **Legend** 133).

[4]Here and above, Yoḥanan takes a strict view of what can be done on the Sabbath.

[5]Evidently there were several opinions, and Yoḥanan's word was not law in Yabneh.

[6]No blessing was said since the portion was too small to constitute a meal.

2/6. Sukkah

[05] 3:12. [Formerly], the lulab [bundle of palm, willow, or myrtle branches] was carried in the Temple for seven days, and in the provinces, for one day. When the Temple was destroyed, Rabban Yoḥanan ben Zakkai ordained that the lulab should be carried in the provinces seven days, as a memorial to the Temple; and that the whole of the day on which the omer is waved [16th Nisan] should be forbidden [for the use of new produce, which may be used only from the waving of the omer and thereafter; this had formerly been at noon].

2/8. Rosh Hasshanah

[06] 4:1. The festival day of the New Year which coincided with the Sabbath: in the Temple they would sound the shofar, but not in the provinces. When the Temple was destroyed, Rabban Yoḥanan ben Zakkai made the rule that they should sound the shofar in every locale in which there was a court.[7] Said R Eleazar, Rabban Yoḥanan ben Zakkai made that rule only in the case of Yabneh alone. They said to him, All the same are Yabneh and every locale in which there is a court.

[07] 4:3. [Formerly], the lulab was taken up in the Temple for seven days, and in the provinces, for one day. When the Temple was destroyed, Rabban Yoḥanan ben Zakkai made the rule that in the provinces the lulab should be taken up for seven days, as a memorial to the Temple; and that the day on which the omer is waved [16th Nisan] should be wholly prohibited [in regard to the eating of new produce].[8]

[08] 4:4. At first they would receive testimony about the new moon all day long. One time witnesses came late, and the Levites . . . made the rule that they should receive testimony only up to the afternoon offering . . . When the Temple was destroyed, Rabban Yoḥanan ben Zakkai made the rule that they should [once more] receive testimony about the new moon all day long.[9]

[09] Said R Joshua ben Qorha, This rule too did Rabban Yoḥanan ben Zakkai make: Even if the head of the court is located somewhere else, the witnesses should come only to the location of the council [to give testimony, and not to the location of the head of the court].

3/2. Ketubot

[10] 13:1. He who went overseas, and his wife [left at home] claims maintenance: Hanan says, Let her take an oath at the end, but let her not take an oath at the outset [that is, she takes an oath when she claims her marriage contract after her husband's death, or after he returns, that she has not held back any property of her husband]. Sons of high priests disputed with him,[10] and ruled, Let her take an oath at the outset and at the end. Ruled R Dosa ben Harkinas in accord with their opinion. Said R Yoḥanan ben Zakkai, Well did Hanan rule. She should take an oath only at the end.

[11] 13:2. He who went overseas, and someone went and supported his wife: Hanan says, He [who did so] has lost his money. Said R Yoḥanan ben Zakkai, Well did Hanan rule. He has put his money on the horn of a gazelle.[11]

---

[7]The court here functions as a ritual successor to the Temple.

[8]This same ruling appears at Sukkah 3:12 and again at Menahot 10:5; see below.

[9]The absence of the Temple makes the provision unnecessary.

[10]"Sons of the priests" implies a post-Temple priestly party. Yoḥanan here opposes them, and supports the view of Hanan ben Abishalom (who appears nowhere else in the Mishnah).

[11]His action is speculative, and not a contract on which to base a claim for reimbursement.

3/5. Sotah

[For Sotah 5:2 and 5:5, see under Hostile, below]

[12] 9:9. When adulterers became many, the ordeal of the bitter water[12] was canceled. And Rabban Yoḥanan ben Zakkai canceled it, since it is said, I will not punish your daughters when they commit whoredom, nor your daughters-in-law when they commit adultery, for they themselves go apart with whores [Hosea 4:14].[13]

[For Sotah 9:15, see under Adulatory, below]

[4/4. Sanhedrin: For Sanhedrin 5:2, see under Adulatory, below]

[4/7. Eduyyot. For Eduyyot 8:3 and 8:7, see under Hostile and Adulatory, below]

[4/9. Abot. For Abot 2:8-12, see under Yoḥanan's Five Disciples, below]

5/2. Menahot

[13] 10:5. After the Temple was destroyed, Rabban Yoḥanan ben Zakkai ordained that the day of waving [of the omer, the second day of Passover] should be wholly prohibited [in respect to new produce].

6/1. Kelim

[14] 2:2. Rabban Yoḥanan ben Zakkai says, [As to] large store jars, the measure is two logs.[14] [As to] Galilean cruses and little jars, the measure [of liquid to be held for uncleanness to persist is], for their bottoms, any quantity whatsoever. And they do not have sides [to be susceptible to uncleanness when broken].[15]

[15] 17:16. [Anything, including a beggar's staff, which has a receptacle is susceptible to uncleanness]. And concerning them all did Rabbi Yoḥanan ben Zakkai say, Woe is me if I speak; woe is me if I do not speak.[16]

6/11. Yadayim

[16] 4:6. Say Sadducees, We complain against you, Pharisees, for you say, Holy Scriptures impart uncleanness to hands, but the books of Homer do not impart uncleanness to hands.[17] Said Rabban Yoḥanan ben Zakkai, And do we have against the Pharisees only this matter alone? Lo, they say, The bones of an ass are clean, but the bones of Yoḥanan the high priest are unclean.[18] They said to him, According to their preciousness is their uncleanness, so that a man should not make the bones of his father and mother into spoons. He said to them, So too Holy Scriptures. According to their preciousness is their uncleanness. But the books of Homer, which are not precious, do not impart uncleanness.

---

[12]Undergone by women accused of uncleanness.

[13]Here, Yoḥanan appears to advantage as having Scriptural sanction for his ruling.

[14]This follows a series of rulings by the later R Aqiba on the uncleanness of vessels. Presumably, of the earlier rulings by Yoḥanan, only these were thought to retain their validity.

[15]A surface has no inside. Only things that can hold liquid are vessels, and come under the usual rule as to what is susceptible to uncleanness.

[16]The extension of rules for vessels to other items with cavities is intrinsically uncertain. The dilemma may be clarified in the revised remark by Yoḥanan in t.Kelim Baba Mesia 7:9.

[17]Sacred texts impart uncleanness; secular texts do not. For Christian texts kept in synagogues, see t.Yadayim 2:13 (no counterpart passage in m.Yadayim).

[18]There may be confusion in this passage with Yoḥanan the High Priest (John Hyrcanus); see Neusner **Pharisees** 1/160-176 for the later association of this figure with the Sadducees. Given this doubt, I do not conclude that Yoḥanan ben Zakkai was, or became, a Sadducee.

Adulatory (2) and Apologetic (2)

3/5. Sotah

[17] 9:15. When Rabban Yoḥanan ben Zakkai died, the splendor of wisdom came to an end.[19]

4/4. Sanhedrin

[18] 5:2. The more a judge tests the evidence, the more is he deserving of praise. Ben Zakkai[20] once tested the evidence even to the inquiring about the stalks of figs [under which the incident took place].[21]

4/7. Eduyyot

[19] 8:7. Said R Joshua, I have a tradition from Rabban Yoḥanan ben Zakkai, who heard it from his master, and his master from his master, as a law revealed to Moses at Sinai, that Elijah is not going to come to declare clean or unclean, to put out or draw near.[22]

6/11. Yadayim

[20] 4:3 . . . They voted and decided: Ammon and Moab give a poor man's tithe in the Sabbatical year. And when R Yose the son of the Damascene came to R Eliezer at Lydda, he said to him, What new things have you in the bet hammidrash today? He said to him, they voted and decided, Ammon and Moab give poor man's tithe in the Sabbatical year. R Eliezer wept, saying, [q of Ps 25:14]. Go and tell them, Do not be anxious about your vote. I have received a tradition from Rabban Yoḥanan ben Zakkai, who heard it from his teacher, and his teacher from his teacher, a law given to Moses at Sinai, that Ammon and Moab give poor man's tithe in the Sabbatical year.[23]

Hostile (3)

3/5. Sotah

[21] 5:2. Said R Joshua [ben Hurqanos], Who will remove the dust from your eyes, Rabban Yoḥanan ben Zakkai? For you used to say, Another generation is going to come to declare clean a loaf of bread in the third remove [from the original source of uncleanness], for there is no Scripture in the Torah which indicates that it is unclean. But now has not Aqiba, your disciple, brought Scriptural proof from the Torah that it is indeed unclean? [quote from Lev 11:33].[24]

[22] 5:5. Said R Joshua, Who will remove the [dust] from your eyes, Rabban Yoḥanan ben Zakkai? For you used to expound for your entire life that Job served the Omnipresent only out of awe [quote from Job 1:8] . . . And now has not Joshua, the disciple of your disciple, taught that he did what he did out of love?[25]

---

[19]From a list of rabbis noted for some particular quality; that list concludes the Sotah.

[20]This, the sole reference to Yoḥanan by his patronymic, has been thought to be hostile, but the passage as a whole is positive. It shows Yoḥanan in his role as a sitting judge.

[21]Presumably to see if the witness is correct about the season of the year.

[22]No teacher is named, but Yoḥanan's rulings are vaguely claimed to go back to Moses.

[23]This too is apologetic rather than adulatory. A Yoḥanan follower notes that Yoḥanan's rulings are forgotten *as his*, but are still affirmed by the sense of the current ruling majority.

[24]Yoḥanan's prediction of future laxity is ridiculed as having been proved false.

[25]Another criticism of Yoḥanan as lacking in Scriptural learning.

4/7. Eduyyot

[23] 8:3. Testified R Joshua and R Judah ben Beterah concerning a widow of an Israelite family suspected of contamination with unfit genealogical stock, that she is valid for marriage into the priesthood. For a woman deriving from an Israelite family suspect of contamination with unfit genealogical stock is herself valid for being declared unclean or clean, being put out and being brought near. Said Rabban [Simeon ben] Gamaliel, We should accept your testimony. But what shall we do? For Rabban Yohanan ben Zakkai decreed against calling courts into session for such a matter.

Yohanan's Five Disciples (7)[26]

4/9 Abot

[24] 2:8. Rabban Yohanan ben Zakkai received [teaching] from Hillel and Shammai.[27] He would say, If you have learned much Torah, do not puff yourself up on that account, for it was for that purpose that you were created.

He had five disciples, and these are they: R Eliezer ben Hyrcanus, R Joshua ben Hananiah, R Yose the priest, R Simeon ben Netanel, and R Eleazar ben Arakh.

He would list their good qualities: R Eliezer ben Hyrcanus: A plastered [cistern], which does not lose a drop of water. R Joshua: Happy is the one who gave birth to him. R Yose: A pious man. R Simeon ben Netanel: A man who fears sin. And R Eleazar ben Arakh: A surging spring

He would say, If all the sages of Israel were on one side of the scale, and R Eliezer b Hyrcanus were on the other, he would outweigh all of them.

Abba Saul says in his name, If all the sages of Israel were on one side of the scale, and R Eleazar [b Arakh] were on the other side, he would outweigh all of them.[28]

[25] 2:9. He said to them, Go and see what is the straight path to which someone should stick.

R Eliezer says, A generous spirit. R Joshua says, A good friend. R Yose says, A good neighbor.[29] R Simeon says, Foresight. R Eleazar says, Good will.

He said to them, I prefer the opinion of R Eleazar ben Arakh, because in what he says is included everything you say.

He said to them, Go out and see what is the bad road, which someone should avoid. R Eliezer says, Envy. R Joshua says, A bad friend. R Yose says, A bad neighbor. R Simeon says, Defaulting on a loan. All the same is a loan owed to a human being and a loan owed to the Omnipresent, blessed be he, as it is said, The wicked borrows and does not pay back, the righteous person deals graciously and hands over [what he owes; Ps 37:21].[30] R Eleazar says, Bad will.

He says to them, I prefer the opinion of Eleazar ben Arakh, because in what he says is included everything you say.

[26]Perhaps modeled on Jesus with his five disciples, a grouping of which the Rabbis were aware; see b.Sanhedrin 43a.

[27]Vague and implausible; "Hillel" and Shammai are emblematic opposites in the Mishnah.

[28]For the meaning of this reversal of Yohanan's estimate of Eliezer, see below.

[29]Compare Lk 19:29-37 (the Good Samaritan), used to redefine the concept "neighbor."

[30]An echo of the distinctive Alpha Christian commandment against fraud (Mk 10:19).

[4/9 Abot]

[26] 2:10. They said three things. R Eliezer says, (1) Let the respect owing to your fellow be as precious to you as the respect owing to you yourself.[31] (2) And don't be easy to anger, (3) And repent one day before you die. And (1) Warm yourself by the fire of the sages, but be careful of their coals, so you don't get burned. (2) For their bite is the bite of a fox, and their sting is the sting of a scorpion, and their hiss is like the hiss of a a snake. (3) And everything they say is like fiery coals.[32]

[27] 2:11. R Joshua says, (1) Envy, (2) desire of bad things, and (3) hatred for people push a person out of the world.[33]

[28] 2:12. R Yose says, (1) Let your fellow's money be as precious to you as your own.[34] And (2) get yourself ready to learn Torah, for it does not come as an inheritance to you. And (3) may everything you do be for the sake of Heaven.[35]

[29] 2:13. R Simeon says, (1) Be meticulous in the recitation of the Shema and the Prayer. And (2) when you pray, don't treat your praying as a matter of routine. But let it be [a plea for] mercy and supplication before the Omnipresent, blessed be he, as it is said, For he is gracious and full of compassion, slow to anger and full of mercy, and repents of the evil (Joel 2:13). (3) And never be evil in your own eyes.[36]

[30] 2:14. R Eleazar says, (1) Be constant in learning of Torah. (2) And know what to reply to an Epicurean.[37] (3) And know before whom you work, for your employer can be depended upon to pay your wages for what you can do.[38]

————··•·•——————

[31] An echo of what is easily the most popular of all Christian precepts, the Golden Rule, first articulated at Lk 6:31 as part of his Sermon on the Plain. In its Matthean form (Mt 7:12) it was later attributed to Hillel, but of that development there seems to be no trace in the Mishnah.

[32] This astonishing critique of the sages (the learned tradition of the Torah) has no parallel in the Mishnah. It finds a more extreme form in the Christianity of Saul of Tarsus. For the general situation, see the summary appreciation at the end of this essay.

[33] "Pushing someone out of the world" may imply interest in the next world, which is absent in other Yohanan passages but held by the Pharisees, to whom Yohanan is here assimilated. Yohanan was a sufficiently prominent figure to be annexed by various persuasions within Rabbinic tradition: the Christianizers as well as their opponents, the Pharisees.

[34] As in n33 above, again Yose and a concern for other people's money, perhaps held on deposit for another and requiring to be paid back scrupulously. A promise of future payment, whether to laborer or friend, is sacred. This is the only economic aspect of Jesus' teachings; it is embodied in Jesus' new (non-Mosaic) commandment against fraud (Mk 10:19)..

[35] As in n36 above, again a possible interest in the world to come.

[36] Note the seeming appearance of the factor of conscience, not simply lawfulness.

[37] Or "unbeliever;" see Danby p397 n4 (ap m.Sanhedrin 10:1, the only other Mishnah mention of Epicureans, in a long list of those who "have no share in the world to come").

[38] If this is another instance of seeming Christianization, the employer may be God, and paying wages may imply the two options for the afterlife. That wages are to be paid, one way or the other, in the afterlife is the point of Luke's Parable of Lazarus (Lk 16:19-26), illustrating a point made more theoretically in Luke's Sermon on the Plain (Lk 6:20-49).

Summary: The Mishnah Evidence for Yoḥanan

Reasonable inferences are the following. (1) **Teacher**. He had no famous teacher [**19-20**], and was probably taught by his father Zacchaeus. (2) **Galilee**. In his early years, he ruled on Sabbath and domestic propriety in Gabara [**01- 02**, cf **14-15**], a town which provided priests for the Temple. His rulings were strict, compatible with reports of the Galilean Shammai. (3) **Temple**. There is no direct evidence for a Jerusalem phase: his approval of Hanan [in **10-11**] is ambiguous, and his one ruling about priests [**10**] was given in Yabneh. He is not a "son of the high priests" [**10**]. Implication that he was of the priestly Sadducee party [**16**] is insecure, though he never mentions the afterlife, agreeing with Sadducees. (4) **Transition**. His judiciousness [**17**] would make him valuable in the transition from the Temple to the courts. He makes rulings for that period. [**05-08, 13**, cf **12**], but was not unopposed at Yabneh [**10**]. (5) **Courts**. His rulings often concern courts and evidence [**06, 09**, cf **17-18**]. His rule on what may be heard in courts, though disliked by some, held firm [**23**]. (6) **Succession**. One passage [**04**] implies that Gamaliel II was his junior; this is plausible if, as is widely thought, Gamaliel later succeeded him at Yabneh.

Inconsistent and implausible: (7) **Students**. Aqiba (died c135) and Joshua, who ridicule Yoḥanan's Scripture interpretations [**21-22**], are not a plausible lineage; still less the Abot portrait of Yoḥanan [**24-30**]. The slightly Christianized sayings of the five disciples [**25-30**] probably reflect a special, and temporary, development.

It is a something of a relief to report that of the story of Yoḥanan being smuggled out of Jerusalem in a coffin, and being granted Yabneh by the Roman general in charge of the siege, a doublet of a story told by Josephus about himself, does not appear in this investigation. The legendary side of Yoḥanan thus continued to grow after the period or periods to which the Mishnah is our primary witness.

Judaism at this time faced the challenge of the loss of the Temple in 70. With the Temple went (1) the sacrifices, and (2) the judicial function of the Sanhedrin. For the solution of these problems, Yoḥanan seems to have been, as traditions says, the central figure. He continued some observances connected with the sacrifices, but now diffused to the local synagogues; and at Yabneh, he founded a new judicial center.

Why the traces of Christianization? The end of the Temple in 70 threatened the survival of Judaism, while the Jesus sect was winning converts among the Gentiles, whom Scripture saw as coming eventually into the fold. The appeal was ethical. It derived from those Prophets (Isaiah 1:10-17, Amos 5:21-24, Micah 6:6-8) who had rejected the Temple cult in favor of an ethical definition of the duty of man. Mainline Judaism in the end remained with ritual, but some may have favored the other option, and tried to adjust the image of Yoḥanan in order to countenance it.

Works Cited

Herbert Danby. The Mishnah. Oxford 1933
Jacob Neusner. Development of a Legend. Brill 1970
Jacob Neusner et al. The Mishnah. Yale 1988
Jacob Neusner. The Rabbinic Traditions About the Pharisees. 3v Brill 1971

Pliny at Pontus

E Bruce Brooks

University of Massachusetts at Amherst

GPG (7 July 2013)

The Pliny/Trajan correspondence gives us one of the few firm dates in the history of Christianity. It also documents the Christian communities in Sinope, the Black Sea port in the Roman province of Pontus. These these turn out to be Alpha in character. I consider that evidence and note implications for the Birkat ha-Minim, the synagogue prayer said to have been introduced by Gamaliel II at Yabneh (Gk Jamnia).

Pliny

Pliny was a seasoned fiscal administrator. In 98-100 he was head of the Temple of Saturn, the main Roman treasury, and later was appointed Curator of the Tibur, a responsible post involving flood control; in 104-107 he was a member of Trajan's cabinet. His most notable law cases involved officials accused of fiscal wrongdoing. Despite a seemingly serious illness not long before, he was the obvious choice for the Governorship of Bithynia/Pontus, where irregularities in the expenditure of public funds had occurred. The date of his appointment is uncertain. Pliny died in his third year there; the official Pliny/Trajan correspondence (now Book 10, letters 15-121) was probably edited by Suetonius, Pliny's protégé and companion in Bithynia.

The Bithynia Chronology. The original letter dates (and opening formulae) were removed by the editor. The *relative* chronology is easily derived from the letters. Taking 110 as the start date,[1] we would have the following:

- 10:15, Aug 110. Reports reaching Ephesus by sea
- 10:17, Sept 110. Reaches Bithynia, celebrates Emperor's birthday [18 Sept]
- 10:35, Jan 111. New Year felicitations to Trajan [1 Jan]
- 10:52, Jan 111. Felicitations on anniversary of Trajan's accession [28 Jan]
- 10:88, Sept 111. Birthday felicitations to Trajan [18 Sept]
- 10:90, 111. At Sinope, the major Black Sea port of Pontus
- 10:92, 111. At Amisus, at the east end of Pontus, and thus *east* of Sinope
- 10:94, 111. Asks a favor for his protégé Suetonius
- 10:96, 111. Asks for advice about the handling of accused Christians
- 10:98, 111. At Amastris, a major city *west* of Sinope
- 10:100, Jan 112. New Year felicitations to Trajan [1 Jan]
- 10:102, Jan 112. Felicitations on anniversary of Trajan's accession [28 Jan]
- 10:120, 112. Pliny requests an official travel pass for his wife
- 10:121, 112. Trajan replies, granting the request [end of the correspondence]

---

[1] Following Williams and Walsh. Other options are 109 (Sherwin-White), 111 (Mommsen).

It may be that Pliny's earlier illness was not fully cured. At any rate, we find him, as he reports on his progress, keeping an eye on his health:

> **Letter 10:17A**. Although I had a very healthy voyage, Sir [domine], as far as Ephesus, yet thereafter, when I had begun to pursue my journey by carriage, I was troubled by the most oppressive heat and also by slight attacks of fever, and I halted at Pergamum. Subsequently, when I had shifted to coastal vessels, I was held back by opposing winds, and I entered Bithynia later than I had hoped, on September 17th. I cannot however complain about this delay, since it was my good fortune to celebrate your birthday in the province, which was a very good omen. At the moment I am examining the expenditures, revenues, and debtors of the state of Prusa; from the very process of investigation I am learning more and more that this is necessary. For many sums of money are being kept in their possession by private persons under different pretexts; moreover some sums are being paid out on wholly unlawful outlays. I have written to you about this, Sir, at the very moment of my arrival.[2]

Pliny's experience as an advocate came into play in Bithynia:

> **Letter 10:94**. Suetonius Tranquillus, that most upright, honorable, and learned man, having admired both his character and his learning, I have included, Sir, among my friends, and have begun to love him all the more now that I have had a closer insight into his character. Two reasons make it necessary for him to be awarded the rights of a parent of three children: he both earns the good opinion of his friends and has had an unfortunate experience of marriage, and he must obtain from your kindness through our agency that which the hostility of fortune has denied him.[3] I know, Sir, how great is the favor for which I apply, but I am applying to you, and I have experience of your generosity in all my requests. For you can infer how greatly I want this from the fact that I should not be asking for it in my absence if I only wanted it in a moderate degree.

By this time, late in 111, having begun in the western part of his territory, Pliny has reached the easternmost city of Amisus, at the boundary with the Parthians, and is retracing his route westward. He is yet to reach the previously visited city of Amastris, whose affairs will occupy him in Letter 98, and thus is in the vicinity of Sinope, when a case arises for which he feels his previous legal experience has not prepared him.

> **Letter 10:96**. It is my custom, Sir, to bring before you everything about which I am in doubt. For who can better guide my uncertainty or inform my ignorance? I have never been present at trials of Christians; for that reason, I do not know what the charge usually is and to what extent it is usually punished. I have been in no little uncertainty about whether a distinction should be made between different ages, or whether, however young they may be, they should be treated no differently from the more mature ones; whether pardon should be granted for repentance or whether it is of no help to the man who has been a Christian to have given it up; whether it is the name itself, if it is free from crimes, or the crimes associated with the name which are being punished.

---

[2] tr adjusted from Williams; so below.

[3] A favored status established by Augustus to encourage more children among the elite; those with fewer children could be granted that status by special dispensation.

Meanwhile, in the case of those who were prosecuted before me on the charge of being Christians, I followed this procedure. I asked the people themselves whether they were Christians. Those who admitted that they were, I asked a second and a third time, warning them of the punishment. Those who persisted I ordered to be executed. For I was in no doubt that, whatever it might be that they were admitting to, their stubbornness and unyielding obstinacy certainly ought to be punished. There were others of a similar madness whom I have listed as due to be sent on to the city, because they were Roman citizens.

Subsequently, in the course of dealing with the matter, as usually happens, the charge spread widely and more forms of it turned up. An anonymous pamphlet containing the names of many persons was posted. Those who denied that they were or had been Christians, after they had called upon the gods when I dictated the formula, and after they had made offerings of incense and wine to your statue which I had ordered to be brought in with the images of the gods for this purpose, and had also cursed Christ, none of which acts, it is said, those who are truly Christians can be compelled to perform, I decided should be discharged. Others, named by an informer, said that they were Christians and then denied it; they said that they had in fact been Christians but had given it up, some three years before, some longer ago than that, and a few as much as twenty (non nemo etiam ante viginti). All these also both paid homage to your statue and to the images of the gods and cursed Christ. Moreover, they maintained that this had been the sum of their guilt or error, that they had been in the habit of gathering together before dawn on a fixed day, and of singing antiphonally a hymn to Christ as if to a god, and of binding themselves by oath not to some wickedness but not to commit acts of theft or robbery or adultery, not to break faith, and not to refuse to return money placed in their keeping when called upon to do so. When these ceremonies had been completed, they said it had been their custom to disperse and to meet again to take food, but food that was ordinary and harmless; they said that they had given up doing even this after my edict in which, in accordance with your instructions, I banned secret societies.

So I believed it to be all the more necessary to ascertain what the truth was from two slave women who were called deaconesses (ex duabus ancillis, quae ministrae dicebantur), and under torture. I found nothing other than a depraved and extravagant superstition.

And so I postponed the hearing and hastened to consult you. For the matter seemed to me worthy of your consideration, especially on account of the number who are endangered. For many persons of every age, of every rank, of both sexes, are and will be brought into danger. The infection of this superstition has spread, not only through the towns, but also through the villages and the countryside; it seems possible for it to be checked and put right. At any rate, it is established that temples which just now were almost abandoned have begun to be thronged, and customary rites which had long been suspended to be renewed, and the flesh of sacrificial victims, for which until recently very few buyers were to be found, to be sold far and wide. From this it is easy to conjecture what a host of people could be reformed, if room were given for repentance.

Thus far Pliny, ending with an appeal for clemency for those who repent.

Pliny's concern for the traditional sacrifices is more intelligible once we know that, at his request, he had earlier been granted priestly status. Also evident is discomfort with anonymous denunciation, and a wish to drop charges against Christians who renounce their membership; his report is a sort of advocacy on their behalf.

To clarify the legal issue as it appeared to the Emperor, here is Trajan's reply:

> **Letter 10:97.** You followed the procedure which you ought to have followed, my dear Secundus, in examining the cases of those who were being prosecuted before you as Christians. For no rule with a universal application, such as would have, as it were, a fixed form, can be laid down. They should not be sought out; if they are prosecuted and proved to be guilty, they should be punished, provided, however, that the man who denies that he is a Christian and makes this evident by his action, that is, by offering prayers to our gods, shall obtain pardon for his repentance, however suspect he may be with regard to the past. However, pamphlets posted without an author's name ought to have no place in any criminal charge. For they both set the worst precedent and are not in keeping with the spirit of our age.

Trajan agrees that membership in the Christian sect is to be punished. The crime is refusal to worship the state gods, and will be canceled for those accused who forswear membership and worship the state gods, including but not limited to the Emperor. That required Emperor worship was the whole point of the Caligula threat of 40. No Jew, and no Christian with his inherited One Jewish God, could accept that requirement.

The Alpha Christians of Pontus

So Pliny is definitely dealing with Christians, but what kind? It turns out that everything in his report matches the characteristics of Alpha Christianity:

> • The "commandments" are not just from the Decalogue, they are from the part of the Decalogue that was recognized by Jesus in Mk 10:19.
> • The signature Jesus commandment against fraud (Mk 10:19) is also visible.
> • Women as leaders, long after the deutero-Paulines (2 Tim 2:12) had dropped them.
> • Simple observances, including a communal meal (as in Didache 9).

The hymn to "Christ as God," looks like a late trait, but that motif occurs already in the Philippians 2:4-9 hymn quoted by Paul in the 50's, more than half a century earlier.

Establishing the Churches. These then look like Alpha churches,[4] preserved from an earlier century. What was their origin? The largely fantastical list of first bishops in the 4c Apostolic Constitutions, at 7:46, does not even mention Bithynia or Pontus.[5]

We now come to a curious passage. In Acts 16:7, Paul and company "attempted to go into Bithynia, and the Spirit *of Jesus* suffered them not." This is the only place in Acts where Jesus, not God, gives direction. Did Luke know Bithynia (the first "we" passage follows, at Acts 16:10) as an early Alpha zone, one not reached by Paul?

---

[4]For the term Alpha" see Brooks **Two** 39; for details, see further below.

[5]For Rome, it gives Linus "ordained by Paul" and Clemens "ordained by me, Peter," but the Roman Mass preserves *three* names: Linus, Anacletus, and Clemens. For Caesarea, fictional Zacchaeus (Lk 19:1-10) followed by fictional Cornelius (Ac 10:1-48), an obvious absurdity.

The Birkat ha-Minim and the Dating of Texts

If the first denunciations in Pontus went back 20 years before 111, that is, to c91, we have confirmation of the 80's date which has been suggested for the composition of the Nineteenth Benediction, as issued from Yabneh under Gamaliel II:[6]

> • For the apostates let there be no hope, and let the arrogant government be speedily uprooted in our days. Let the Nazarenes and the Minim [heretics] be destroyed in a moment and let them be blotted out of the Book of Life and not be inscribed together with the righteous.[7]

and thus a clue about the dates of the NT texts which respond to it. One is the second layer of 1 Peter, which frames the original core.[8] That later material is here indented:

> • **1 Pet 1:1**. Peter . . . to the elect who are sojourners of the Dispersion in Pontus, Galatia, Cappadocia, Asia, and Bithynia, [2] according to the foreknowledge of God the Father, in sanctification of the Spirit, unto obedience and sprinkling of the blood of Jesus Christ . . .
>
> • **1 Pet 1:3**. Blessed be the God and Father of our Lord Jesus Christ, who according to his great mercy, begat us again unto a living hope by the resurrection of Jesus Christ . . .[4:11] . . . that in all things God may be glorified through Jesus Christ, whose is the glory and dominion for ever and ever. Amen.
>
> > • **1 Pet 4:12**. Beloved, think it not strange concerning the fiery trial among you, which cometh upon you to prove you, as though a strange thing happened unto you; [13] but inasmuch as ye are partakers of Christ's sufferings, rejoice, that at the revelation of his glory also ye may rejoice with exceeding joy. [14] If ye are reproached for the name of Christ, blessed are ye, because the Spirit of glory and the Spirit of God resteth upon you. [15] For let none of you suffer as a murderer, or a thief, or an evil-doer, or as a meddler in other men's matters, [16] but if a man suffer as a Christian, let him not be ashamed, but let him glorify God, and if it begin first at us, what shall be the end of them that obey not the Gospel of God? . . .

Suffering death "for the name," and dying "as a Christian" are precisely what the Christians of Pontus were facing, as early as somewhere around the year 91.

Three passages in the Gospel of John refer to expulsion from synagogues:

> • **Jn 9:22**. . . . they feared the Jews, for the Jews had agreed already, that if any man should confess him to be Christ, he **should be put out of the synagogue**.
>
> • **Jn 12:42**. . . . many believed on him, but because of the Pharisees they did not confess it, lest they **should be put out of the synagogue**.
>
> • **Jn 16:1**. These things I have spoken unto you, that ye should not be caused to stumble. [2] They shall **put you out of the synagogues**; yea, the hour cometh that whosoever killeth you shall think that he offereth service unto God.

These probably reflect persecutions at Ephesus, the locale often assigned to John.

---

[6]Now the 12th Benediction. Its composition by Samuel the Small at the request of Rabbi Gamaliel II is recorded at b.Berakoth 28a; see Martyn **History** 59f. For the earlier toleration of Christian writings in synagogues, see Torrey **Documents** 98, quoting Tosephta Yadaim 2:13.

[7]tr Martyn **History** 62 (modern versions, like that quoted in Lohmeyer **Prayer** 303, have been sanitized; Martyn's version is based on the better text of the Cairo Genizah).

[8]See Beare **Peter**. The analysis is due to Perdelwitz.

There is also the opening of 1 Clement, a Roman text commonly dated to c96:

> • **1 Clem 1:1**. Owing to the sudden and repeated misfortunes and calamities which have befallen us, we consider that our attention has been somewhat delayed in turning to the questions disputed among you, beloved . . .

Acts II, with its threefold theme of separation from Judaism (*13:46, 18:6, 28:29), is another seeming reaction to this event, this one probably in Antioch.

Chronology

The new prayer probably made its way gradually outward from Yabneh, and need not have been universally adopted in the places it reached; the Rabbis had no power of enforcement. But they were the only authority left in Judaism, and their sense of what was proper in the daily prayers will have been influential. Allowing for a roughly constant rate of diffusion, and noting the location of major roads, we get something like this sequence of places affected, and any literary responses (most dates circa):

70. Destruction of Temple at Jerusalem
71. Yoḥanan ben Zakkai at Yabneh; toleration of Jesus sect in synagogues
80. Accession of less tolerant Gamaliel at Yabneh
85. Birkat ha-Minim (12th Benediction) framed at Yabneh (Judaea)
86. Birkat effect in Judaea
87. Birkat effect reaches Syria
88. Acts II responds to Birkat-induced separation from Judaism
89. Birkat effect reaches Iconium
90. Birkat effect reaches Ankyra and Ephesus (John 16, c91)
91. Birkat effect reaches Pontus (1 Peter B, c92) and Nicomedia
92. Birkat effect reaches Philippi
93. Birkat effect reaches Illyria and Corinth
94. Birkat effect reaches Rome (later recalled in 1 Clement, c96)
108. Renewed denunciations of Christians at Pontus
111. Pliny presides over further trials of Christians at Pontus

There is obviously a certain amount of give in the system. But this chronology is compatible with dates previously suggested for several texts and their modifications, and incorporates all relevant data from Rabbinic sources. It may thus perhaps serve as a working hypothesis for subsequent discussion of the dates and intertextual relations of other texts in the late 1st century.

Works Cited

F W Beare. The First Epistle of Peter. 3ed Oxford 1970

E Bruce Brooks. The Two Ways. Alpha v1 (2017) 39-47

Ernst Lohmeyer. The Lord's Prayer. 1952; tr Collins 1965

J Louis Martyn. History and Theology in the Fourth Gospel. 3ed Westminster 2003

Betty Radice. Pliny: Letters. 2v Harvard 1969

A N Sherwin-White. The Letters of Pliny. Oxford 1966

Charles Cutler Torrey. Documents of the Primitive Church. Harper 1941

P G Walsh. Pliny the Younger: Complete Letters. Oxford 2006

Wynne Williams. Pliny: Correspondence with Trajan from Bithynia. Oxbow 1990

End Matter

Working Chronology 2017

An editorial compilation of selected results, to test consistency. Will be regularly updated
Many dates circa. **Emperors.** *Texts.* *Interpolated passages

28	[**Tiberius**]. John the Baptist preaches at the Jordan; baptism of Jesus
29	John the Baptist executed. Jesus teaches in Galilee; arouses opposition
30	Crucifixion of Jesus. *Mark* begun. Saul of Tarsus persecutes Jesus converts
31	Jacob of Alphaeus replaces Levi at Capernaum
32	Shift to Jerusalem; Matthew replaces Levi at Jerusalem. Resurrection doctrine
33	Conversion of Saul > Paul; he visits Jerusalem to confer with Cephas [Peter]
34	Paul preaches under the direction of Antioch
35	
36	
37	**Caligula.**
38	
39	*Didache* core?
40	Caligula threat to desecrate the Temple is reflected at Mk 13:14
41	Caligula assassinated; desecration threat vanishes. **Claudius**
42	Abandonment of prediction of Signs of the End (Mk 13:32-37)
43	Atonement doctrine appears; is added to *Mark* (Mk 10:45, 11:24)
44	Paul visits Jerusalem; receives liberal ruling on Gentiles. Herod kills Jacob Zebedee Peter flees; Matthew is briefly in charge at Jerusalem
45	*Mark* completed by adjustments for Gentiles. John Mark leaves for Antioch Jacob the Lord's Brother succeeds Matthew; counters previous ruling. *Didache* 6:3?
46	Confrontation of Peter and Paul over Gentile commensality at Antioch John Mark accompanies Paul; is unsuccessful in preaching to Gentiles at Perga
47	John Mark goes to Alexandria, where he becomes a leading figure
48	
49	
50	
51	*1 Thessalonians*
52	
53	*Philippians* conflation includes a letter from Paul's imprisonment at Ephesus *Galatians. Philemon.* Onesimus becomes Paul's manager at Ephesus
54	**Nero**
55	*Didache* 12:2-14:3, authorizing longer Apostolic visits such as those of Paul?
56	*1 and 2 Corinthians.* Paul proposes a second collection for Jerusalem Factions at Corinth: Paul, Apollos, Cephas [Peter], "Christ" [Alpha Christians]
57	*Romans.* Faith/works dispute between Paul and *Jacob* [of Alphaeus]
58	Paul delivers collection to Jerusalem; is arrested there and detained at Caesarea
59	Paul transported to Rome
60	Paul executed at Rome
61	*Didache* 1-5 (Two Ways tract) added?
62	Jacob the Lord's Brother killed by Jewish authorities at Jerusalem
63	
64	Nero persecutions at Rome. Peter killed. Post-Apostolic period begins
65	Linus becomes first post-Apostolic leader at Rome
66	*Luke A* written to fill post-Apostolic gap in Christian literature. Jewish War begins
67	Josephus surrenders to Vespasian at Jerusalem
68	**Galba.** *Matthew* written as conservative counter to *Luke A*

69   **Otho. Vitellius. Vespasian**.
70   Jerusalem Temple destroyed by Titus
      Rabbinic center established by Yohanan ben Zakkai at Yabneh (Jamnia) in Judaea
71   Paul's letters edited by Onesimus, Timothy, Titus, Silvanus, Sosthenes
      Paul's editors know *Luke A* and *Matthew*
      Colossians written as preface to the Pauline collection. Collection published
72   *Luke B* written to counter *Matthew*. Lk 21:20 updates Mk 13:14
      Acts I (Ac 1:1-15:34) knows Paul's letters. Equates Peter and Paul; stresses amity
      Post-70 detail added at Mt 22:7 to imitate *Luke B*'s post-70 update at Lk 21:20
73   Jewish War ends
74
75   Josephus *Jewish War* (lost Aramaic original)
76   Did 15:1-3 (on local church governance) added?
77   Anacletus becomes second leader at Rome
78
79   **Titus**.
      Josephus *Jewish War*, Greek translation (Books 1-6)
80   Gamaliel II becomes leader at Yabneh. *1 Peter A*, a baptismal homily
81   **Domitian**. Onesimus becomes Bishop at Ephesus. *Ephesians*
82   *Didache* 16 (Matthean-style Apocalypse) added?
83
84
85   Birkat ha-Minim composed at Yabneh.
86   Birkat effect in Judaea; no literary reflection
87   Birkat effect in Syria
88   *Acts II* (Antioch) responds to Birkat separation by "turning to the Gentiles"
89   Birkat effect in Iconium; no literary reflection
      Clement becomes third leader at Rome
90   *John D* (*9:2, *12:42, 16:2; Ephesus) speaks of exclusion from synagogues
91   Birkat effect in Pontus and Nicomedia
      1 Peter B (1:1-2, 4:12–5:14) reflects the Birkat crisis in Pontus
      1 Peter B, with added Petrine personalia, bids for recognition as Petrine
      Matthew, with added *16:18-20, bids for recognition as Petrine
92   *John E*, with added *Jn 21, bids for recognition as Petrine
93   *Hebrews*, with added Pauline personalia *13:22-25, bids for recognition as Pauline
      Josephus *Antiquities*, apologetic defense of Judaism as a philosophy
94   Birkat effect in Rome; later recalled by Clement in *1 Clement*
95
96   **Nerva**. *1 Clement* moves to assert domination of other churches by Rome
      1 Clement begins by recalling the previous (c94) Birkat crisis in Rome
97
98   **Trajan**.
99
100   Death of Clement, said to have been martyred under Trajan
105
106
107
108   Renewed trials of denounced Christians at Pontus
109
110   Statement of Papias about *Mark* and *Matthew*, quoted by Eusebius
111   Pliny, after consulting with Trajan, executes unrepentant Christians at Pontus

Journal Abbreviations

BAR. Biblical Archaeology Review
CBQ. Catholic Biblical Quarterly
EChr. Early Christianity
ETL. Ephemerides Theologicae Lovanienses
HTR. Harvard Theological Review
JBL. Journal of Biblical Literature
JECS. Journal of Early Christian Studies
JHC. Journal of Higher Criticism
JJMJS. Journal of the Jesus Movement in its Jewish Setting
JQR. Jewish Quarterly Review
JRel. Journal of Religion
JSNT. Journal for the Study of the New Testament
JSOT. Journal for the Study of the Old Testament
JSPL. Journal for the Study of Paul and His Letters
JTS. Journal of Theological Studies
Neot. Neotestamentica
NovT. Novum Testamentum
NTS. New Testament Studies
VC. Vigiliae Christianae
WSP. Warring States Papers
ZNW. Zeitschrift für Neutestamentliche Wissenschaft

Works Frequently Cited

These need not be included in Works Cited lists at the ends of individual articles

ABD. Anchor Bible Dictionary. 6v Doubleday 1992
Barrington Atlas of the Greek and Roman World. Princeton 2000
BDAG: Frederick William Danker. A Greek-English Lexicon. 1957; 3ed Chicago 2000
Raymond Brown. Introduction to the New Testament. Doubleday 1997
J K Elliott. The Apocryphal New Testament. Oxford 1993
IB. Interpreter's Bible. 12v Abingdon 1951-1957
IQP. James M Robinson et al (ed). The Critical Edition of Q. Fortress 2000
Josephus. Jewish War. tr Thackeray et al, 3v Harvard 1927-1928
Josephus. Jewish Antiquities. tr Thackeray et al, 8v Harvard 1930-1965
Werner Georg Kümmel. Introduction to the New Testament. 17ed 1973; tr Abingdon 1975
LSJ. H G Liddell, R Scott, and H S Jones. A Greek-English Lexicon. 9ed Oxford 1996
Bruce M Metzger. A Textual Commentary on the Greek New Testament. 2ed UBS 1994
James Moffatt. Introduction to the Literature of the New Testament. Scribner 1911
NA. [The cited edition of the Nestle-Aland critical text of the NT]. NA 28 = UBS 5
OCD. Oxford Classical Dictionary. 2ed Oxford 1970 [3ed, 1996; 4ed, 2012]
Robert H Pfeiffer. Introduction to the Old Testament. Harper 1941
Udo Schnelle. The History and Theology of the New Testament Writings. 1994; Fortress 1998
Strack/Billerbeck. H L Strack and P Billerbeck. Kommentar zum Neuen Testament aus Talmud
    und Midrasch. 6v in 7 Beck 1922-1961
Reuben Swanson. [The appropriate volume of Swanson's New Testament Greek Manuscripts]
UBS. [The cited edition of the United Bible Societies critical text of the NT]. UBS 5 = NA 28
James P Ware. Synopsis of the Pauline Letters in Greek and English. Baker 2010
William O Walker Jr. Interpolations in the Pauline Letters. Sheffield 2001
Theodor Zahn. Introduction to the New Testament. 2ed 1900; tr 3v T & T Clark 1977

Passages Discussed

Major entries only; discussion may extend beyond the pages here given

Subject Index

Major entries only. Discussion may extend beyond the pages here given